LESBIAN AND GAY VOICES

LESBIAN AND GAY VOICES

*An Annotated Bibliography
and Guide to Literature
for Children and Young Adults*

FRANCES ANN DAY
Foreword by Nancy Garden

GREENWOOD PRESS
Westport, Connecticut • London

Library of Congress Cataloging-in-Publication Data

Day, Frances Ann.
   Lesbian and gay voices : an annotated bibliography and guide to literature for children and young adults / by Frances Ann Day ; foreword by Nancy Garden.
      p. cm.
   Includes bibliographical references and index.
   ISBN 0–313–31162–5 (alk. paper)
   1. Children's literature, American—Bibliography.   2. Homosexuality and literature—United States—Bibliography.   3. Young adult literature, American—Bibliography.
   4. Lesbians in literature—Bibliography.   5. Gay men in literature—Bibliography.
   6. Gays in literature—Bibliography.   I. Title.
   Z1037.D24   2000
   [PS169.H65]
   016.8108'09282—dc21   00–021047

British Library Cataloguing in Publication Data is available.

Library of Congress Catalog Card Number: 00–021047
ISBN: 0–313–31162–5

First published in 2000

Greenwood Press, 88 Post Road West, Westport, CT 06881
An imprint of Greenwood Publishing Group, Inc.
www.greenwood.com

Printed in the United States of America

The paper used in this book complies with the Permanent Paper Standard issued by the National Information Standards Organization (Z39.48–1984).

10 9 8 7 6 5 4 3 2 1

Dedicated to Roxanna, my lifetime companion

Contents

Foreword

This is a book whose time has come.

Way back in the 50s when I was around 16, I fell in love. It happened on a warm evening in the soft glow of a light at the end of a driveway where I was standing with a girl I'd met on our school playground a few years earlier. Sandy was my age but in the class ahead of me, and now we were both rehearsing for a group of one-act plays to be given at a neighboring school. That night, while waiting for my mother to pick us up after rehearsal, we talked as we'd never talked before—and I knew I'd found my soul mate.

I can still see her standing there, bathed in the light's radiance, and I can still feel myself there, too, with that flutter of wonder and excitement that comes when love first visits one. It was a rare moment, and it remains a beautiful, precious memory.

But what followed was not so beautiful.

What followed was similar to what followed for most gay and lesbian kids in that era and still does for many today. When Sandy's mother found a letter I'd written, she told Sandy not to see me any more. Of course we disobeyed, and of course we got caught—several times, in fact. We knew we loved each other, but when we turned to encyclopedias to find out what that meant and what it meant to be lesbians, we read that we were psychopaths, perhaps paranoid, and likely to be addicted to alcohol or drugs. Religious works told us we were morally deficient. And the cheap paperback novels with lurid covers that I found in the local bus station indicated that we were doomed to suicide, incarceration in mental institutions, or subject to arrest unless we were swept off our feet by wonderfully strong and forgiving men who were willing to marry us and turn us into "real" women.

Because of the climate of the times and the lack of accurate information in books, our real selves were forced into an invisibility that lasted for many, many years; in fact, we spent a long time denying that we were gay. Like most gay people of our generation, we were so hungry to see ourselves and our people in books that we sought out stories about same-gender friendships, and identified with their characters. As time went on and we began acknowledging our true sexuality, we assumed— again, as did many of our peers—that some close friendships described in books were, in fact, gay love relationships. In some cases, perhaps many, this was true; many gay and lesbian authors in those days and earlier disguised the "love that dare not speak its name" by *not* speaking its name and by hedging on details.

Now Sandy and I are comfortable with ourselves and each other. In fact, we've been together for more than 30 years, after several separations during the first part of our lives. But back when we were kids, *Lesbian and Gay Voices*, this wonderfully complete and helpful book, could have spared us a great deal of pain and anxiety.

Of course back in the fifties, *Lesbian and Gay Voices* couldn't have existed because back then there were no books for kids about homosexuals and very few for adults. There were even very few of those oh-so-discreet ones in which love was disguised as deep and perfect and, sometimes, tragically doomed friendship. I did find Radclyffe Hall's *The Well of Loneliness* when I was in high school, and despite its melodrama and sad ending, it did help me. But looking for it and a handful of others in my local public libraries—including a large city one—taught me that gay books are often supressed. Even when the books I wanted were listed in the card catalog, they were not on the shelves, and they remained off them long past the time when, if they had been borrowed, they would have been returned. Sadly, this is a trick also used by today's amateur censors. Although I suspect that the books I sought in the 50s had been removed by fearful librarians, today they're more apt to be removed or endlessly charged out by indignant patrons, like the woman in Brevard County, Florida, who with her friends took turns borrowing Michael Willhoite's picture book *Daddy's Roommate* over and over again for more than a year. (Indeed, as you'll see in the following pages, several of the books listed in *Lesbian and Gay Voices* have been victims of censorship and censorship attempts.)

It wasn't until 1969, when Harper & Row courageously published John Donovan's *I'll Get There: It Better Be Worth the Trip*, that the subject of homosexuality was finally broached in a young adult (YA) novel. After a two-year hiatus, it was followed in 1972 by *Sticks and Stones* by Lynn Hall (Follet); *The Man Without a Face* by Isabelle Holland (Lippincott); and a book written as a young adult novel but published as an adult one, *Patience and Sarah* by Isabelle Miller (McGraw-Hill). There were four more gay-themed YA novels in the 70s: *Trying Hard to Hear You* by Sandra Scoppetone (Harper & Row) in 1974, *Ruby* by Rosa Guy (Viking) in 1976, *Hey Dollface* by Deborah Hautzig (Greenwillow) and *Happy Endings Are All Alike* by Sandra Scoppetone (Harper & Row) in 1978. By the 80s, homosexuality in books for the young, though still controversial, had emerged firmly from its own closet and in the 80s and 90s there was a steady stream of YA (and a few middle-grade) novels dealing positively with the gay experience. In increasing numbers they've been joined, as you'll see in *Lesbian and Gay Voices*, by picture books, short story collections, nonfiction titles, and biography/autobiography.

Yes, *Lesbian and Gay Voices* is a book whose time has come, especially because, despite the virtual explosion of gay books for youngsters in the 90s (for example, more than 50 gay-themed YA novels appeared in that decade alone), they are not always easy to find. I've been asked many times to recommend books that might help gay kids and their straight peers understand homosexuality, and I'm sure that other writers, and of course librarians and teachers, have been in the same position. Out of necessity, most of us have developed personal lists, gleaned from our own discoveries, from journal articles and reviews, and from conversations with colleagues and friends, but until *Lesbian and Gay Voices* there has been no single authoritative source, critically annotated, that can lead teachers, librarians, parents, and youngsters to honest, accurate, gay-themed and gay friendly works for young people. And as if that weren't gift enough, *Lesbian and Gay Voices* also includes author profiles, a list of important dates, and a list of resources.

And make no mistake: this is a book that can save lives. The (Massachusetts) Governor's Commission of Gay and Lesbian Youth has found that a third of all teen suicides are of homosexual kids. The *Journal of Pediatrics* in 1998 reported that gay students are four times more likely than straight ones to be threatened by weapons in school; the Governor's Commission says 45 percent of gay students and 20 percent of lesbian students have had some experience of violence in school. According to the National Network of Runaway and Youth Services, somewhere between a quarter and half a million lesbian, gay, and bisexual kids run away from home or are thrown out of their homes every year. Twenty-eight percent of them drop out of school annually. A Massachusetts Youth Risk Behavior survey reports that around 50 percent of gay and lesbian kids are involved in a fight or hurt or threatened with a weapon in school. Many (one out of six in a 1998 study in Seattle, for example) are so badly beaten in school they need medical attention; many stay home from school because they're afraid to go, and most hear anti-gay taunts and jokes every day.

There are many causes of homophobia. One of them is ignorance; honest, accurate books can help counter this. Homophobia is made possible when some people believe that gays and lesbians, or people perceived as being gay or lesbian, are subhuman and/or evil, expendable, and worthy only of contempt; honest, accurate books can help counter this. One result of unrelenting homophobic harrassment can be a loss of self-respect and confidence on the part of the victim; honest, accurate books can help counter this.

Not every suicidal kid, it's true, can be deterred because of a book. Yet, I know of at least one who was, and I know of many who, after reading a book that shows gay people in an honest, positive way, have said, "This book made me feel good about myself for the first time in my life."

Gay and lesbian kids need to read about people like themselves, just as kids in other minorities do. They need to read about ordinary people who are gay and lesbian, and, also like kids from other minorities, they need to read about the artists, athletes, performers, educators, political figures, and other notables who have come from our community. *Lesbian and Gay Voices* can lead them to their own special heroes and role models, fictional and real, famous and not famous, young and old, historical and contemporary. *Lesbian and Gay Voices* can also show straight kids that many of the people who have made important contributions to society at large are or were gay or lesbian.

This is a book whose time has come, and its very existence is evidence that there is already a respectable body of gay-positive literature for young people. I'm sorry that the late John Donovan isn't alive to see the changes he wrought with *I'll Get There: It Better Be Worth the Trip* just over thirty years ago!

It's my hope that *Lesbian and Gay Voices* will encourage publishers and authors to produce more works like those it now lists, for the need for positive gay-themed books for kids is both ongoing and changing. Youngsters are coming out and facing homophobia at earlier ages than ever before, more and more straight kids are growing up in families headed by gay or lesbian parents, scholars are "discovering" that increasing numbers of famous people are or were or might have been gay or lesbian—or bisexual or transgendered; in fact, more and more young people are openly identifying themselves not only as gay or lesbian, but also as bisexual or transgendered; it is to be hoped that these kids will soon emerge from invisibility in books as well. Future gay-themed books (and I'm using the term "gay" in its broadest, most inclusive sense) for both kids and adults will, I trust, address and reflect all these developments.

The greatest contribution the books on this list make, along with those of the future that I hope will necessitate further editions of *Lesbian and Gay Voices*, is that they help bring the gay community out of invisibility into the light of understanding and acceptance. That light in turn helps our young people to grow up to be strong, healthy members of society, and helps society realize that those same young people matter and deserve to be recognized, included, and accepted for who they truly are.

This is indeed a book whose time has come! I welcome it and applaud it, and I hope that you will, too.

Nancy Garden

Acknowledgments

First and foremost, I want to honor Roxanna, my companion of almost twenty years, who has celebrated and suffered with me through the many ups and downs of this compelling project. She was always there, solid, listening to inspirations, struggles, rages, joys, and sorrows, and always believing in me. Without her presence, patience, fortitude, humor, love, and support, this book could not have been written.

Next, I pay tribute to the memory of Amelia and Isis, two of the best friends I have ever had. They taught me profound lessons about life, love, and loss. Indeed, grieving the loss of these magnificent comrades has been an integral part of my writing process. Like many others, I have discovered that loss, change, and memory are central to my creativity.

Heartfelt thanks to Lynn Malloy, my editor, whose understanding, support, and expertise helped me a great deal. Special gratitude is also due to Ray Coutu, who recognized the significance of this project early on and generously offered ideas, support, and encouragement.

I am genuinely thankful to the courageous authors profiled in this book. I honor each of them for the contributions they are making to the field of lesbian and gay literature for young readers. Their words provide desperately needed validation and hope for young lesbian and gay people.

Many thanks go to Carolina Clare at Northlight Books in Cotati, California; Anat at A Different Light Bookstore in San Francisco, California;

and Carol Wilson and Alice Malloy at Mama Bears Bookstore in Oakland, California.

I thank the knowledgeable librarians and staff at the Sonoma County Libraries, who answered numerous questions and guided me to sources of information. I acknowledge the crucial role librarians have played and will continue to play in defending the rights of young lesbian and gay people to get important information about their lives.

Special appreciation to Kevin Jennings, Matthew Lavine, and the other inspiring folks at the Gay, Lesbian and Straight Education Network (GLSEN), who work tirelessly to teach respect for young lesbian and gay people in our schools. Acknowledgment is also due to all of the people involved in Parents, Families, and Friends of Lesbians and Gays (PFLAG), Project 10, and other organizations who are working to improve the lives of lesbian and gay people.

To my students at Sonoma State University, I appreciate your heartening words, thoughtful messages, strong ideals, and kind encouragement.

I also acknowledge Pat Staten, Carolyn Gage, Debra Goodman, Sandy Tate, Daisy Blincoe, Kay Hones, Judith Dehnert, Ardy Tibby, Edith King, and Yoko Kawashima Watkins for help, reassurance, and inspiration.

And finally, I would like to recognize and honor young lesbian and gay people everywhere. This book is for you.

Introduction

Where did I turn for comfort and support? There was no type of support for someone in my situation. I had nowhere to turn, but within myself and to the library. . . . It probably saved my life. . . . I spent many, many hours in that library reading, anything and everything I could find on the topic of homosexuality. Since I didn't have anyone to talk to, these books reaffirmed that I was not mentally ill, a freak of nature, or a pervert. I was not evil or any of the other things my classmates called me at school.

> Dan, a teenager quoted in *Being Different*
> by Larry Dane Brimner, pp. 75–76

Noted author M. E. Kerr remembers reading *The Well of Loneliness*, the classic by Radclyffe Hall, when she was twelve years old, with "my hands shaking and my heart beating, knowing that I had stumbled upon myself" (*Children's Book Council Features*, Fall–Winter 1995, unpaginated). Because she did not dare to check the book out, she read it quickly one afternoon and then went back day after day and read each page carefully. Although she found the book to be depressing, it reassured her that she was not alone. Reading this book was her first step toward self-acceptance.

Nancy Garden, another highly acclaimed author of books for young readers, recalls searching for positive images of lesbians, but almost all of the books she found ended in mental illness, suicide, or with the lesbian(s) becoming heterosexual. After reading *The Well of Loneliness*, which ends sadly but with an impassioned plea for justice, Garden vowed that she would someday write a book about young lesbians that ended happily.

Many other lesbian and gay adults remember their early years, when they took refuge in books where they found their first images of people like themselves. In her preface to *Borderlands/La Frontera*, Gloria Anzaldúa writes, "Books saved my sanity, knowledge opened the locked places in me and taught me first how to survive and then how to soar." Michael Nava spent his youth "buried in books looking for a way to make sense of life" ("Abuelo" in *A Member of the Family*, p. 19).

Indeed, books have the power to touch the hearts and minds of readers of all ages and backgrounds. Marion Dane Bauer writes, "Stories help us make sense of our world. They teach us what is possible. They let us know that others before us have struggled as we do" (*What's Your Story?* p. ix).

As these writers and others so eloquently point out, books can play an important role in helping young lesbian and gay people survive the life-threatening circumstances in which they find themselves. The statistics have been well documented: because they live in a culture that is homophobic and heterosexist, young gay and lesbian people suffer alarming levels of emotional isolation, physical and verbal abuse, parental rejection, depression, homelessness, dropout risk, and suicide. One way to provide hope to these isolated youngsters is to share compassionate books that deal honestly with the very issues with which they are grappling. By making affirming books available to them, we help them find the self-acceptance and self-respect to live joyous, full lives.

Michael Cart, a nationally recognized expert in children's and young adult literature, writes,

[B]ooks are important . . . because they offer engagement and enlightenment— first for the mind by stimulating thought but then for the spirit, too, since by giving readers the opportunity to eavesdrop on the hearts of others, books stimulate empathy and sympathy. In short, books are important because they have the power to enlarge and change both minds and lives. This is why it is so important to have books for and about gay and lesbian young adults. Not only so that homosexual youth can see themselves positively represented in literature (there were no gay role models in books when I was growing up in the 1950s) but also so that heterosexual teenagers can read about the homosexual experience and, accordingly educate and expand their own hearts and minds. (*Gay and Lesbian Literature: Volume 2*, p. 77)

Books can make a difference. No one knows this better than librarians, many of whom have a proud history of guiding young readers toward quality literature. They care deeply about youngsters and their positive growth and development, and have demonstrated an unwavering commitment to acquiring good books and making them available to young people. Many educators are also working hard to make a difference in their students' lives. In *Loving Someone Gay* Don Clark writes, "From nursery school through college the teacher and the librarian are the two professionals who are certain to have contact with each developing gay person. . . . Teachers and librarians have thousands of opportunities to teach youngsters to appreciate their unique selves and to appreciate differences among people in general" (p. 351).

In *Queer Kids*, Robert E. Owens estimates that there are 3 million lesbian and gay youth in the United States. Libraries often become safe havens for these young people who are trying to understand who they are. As they find books featuring characters with feelings and experiences similar to their own, they will hopefully find the strength to listen to their own hearts, believe in themselves, and embrace all the parts of themselves. In addition, April Martin in *Love Makes a Family* estimates that there are between 3 million and 8 million children who have lesbian or gay parents and many more who have lesbian or gay relatives. It is critical that books portraying these nontraditional family constellations be made available to youngsters of all ages.

SCOPE OF THIS BIBLIOGRAPHY

This bibliography of more than 275 titles includes only recommended books. Many additional books were considered, and even though most of them have some strengths, they were rejected because they promote negative stereotypes or do not meet the criteria set forth in the "Suggested Guidelines for Evaluating Books with Lesbian and Gay Content" (following the Introduction).

Most of the books in this bibliography are in print. A few out-of-print titles, such as *Ruby* by Rosa Guy and *I'll Get There, It Better Be Worth the Trip* by John Donovan, are included because of their historical significance.

All books in this bibliography have been published in English. Most are set in the United States but a few take place in Australia, Canada, China, England, New Zealand, and the West Indies. Every effort has been made to include books that represent lesbian and gay people from diverse cultures. However, there is a need for more books featuring lesbian and gay people of color, especially in the young adult fiction category.

The books in this bibliography feature both major and minor lesbian and gay characters. Only books appropriate for young readers are included, although a few titles have been marketed primarily to an adult audience. Recommended age levels are indicated along with notes regarding the inclusion of strong language and/or explicit sex. The annotations include an analysis of the strengths and weaknesses of each book, often accompanied by a summary of the praise and/or criticism the book received from other reviewers. Topic heading, and awards won by the book are also included.

In addition to the annotations of picture books and young adult fiction, chapters featuring short stories, nonfiction, and biography are included. The titles in the biography chapter are included to help young lesbian and gay people find the role models often denied them. Martin Duberman, editor of the highly acclaimed biography series published by Chelsea House, wrote,

This series is designed, above all, to fill that huge, painful cultural gap. It is designed to instill not only pride in antecedents but encouragement, the kind of encouragement that literature and biography have always provided: proof that someone else out there has felt what we have felt, experienced what we have experienced, been where we have been—and has endured, achieved, and flourished. (*k. d. lang*, p. 9)

This bibliography also includes a chapter featuring books written for librarians, educators, parents, and other interested adults. There are many new and exciting resources available to help adults in their quest to support gay and lesbian youth.

Profiles of sixteen courageous authors who have written books about lesbian and gay themes for young readers are also provided. (Several additional authors did not respond to invitations to be included in this book.) The authors profiled here are to be commended for the important work they are doing. Marion Dane Bauer notes, "As a lesbian writer, I have wanted for a long time to do something for gay and lesbian young people. There was nothing when I was growing up, at least nothing positive, and I felt a responsibility to help young people understand that they are not alone" ("Gay Books for Young Readers: When Caution Calls the Shots" by Michael Thomas Ford, *Publishers Weekly* 241 [February 21, 1994], p. 25).

MY HOPE

Lesbian and Gay Voices: An Annotated Bibliography and Guide to Literature for Children and Young Adults celebrates a significant body of work that has the potential to make a difference in the lives of young people. The guide was written to support librarians, educators, parents, and other adults in their efforts to find positive images in lesbian/gay-themed literature for young readers.

I wrote *Lesbian and Gay Voices* with a love for good books, respect for the diversity of all peoples, and hope for the future of young lesbian and gay people. While celebrating the power of stories to heal and transform, I hope to stir the consciousness of a nation of adults and awaken empathy for young lesbian and gay people everywhere. This has been one of the most compelling and rewarding projects I have undertaken in my many years as an educator and writer.

My wish is that young lesbian and gay people will never again have to hide who they are or apologize for being themselves, that they will find the strength to love themselves and embrace their identities, and that their lives will be filled with happiness, dignity, love, and hope.

We owe young people and ourselves nothing less than the best possible world we can imagine. Let us take energetic action to get these wise and compassionate books into the hands of young people everywhere.

Suggested Guidelines for Evaluating Books with Lesbian and Gay Content

The following guidelines were formulated by the author to help in the evaluation of lesbian/gay-themed books for young readers. Although the complexities involved in appraising the intangibles in the literary arts cannot be encompassed in a checklist, these suggestions are offered as a starting point for examining individual titles and entire collections.

General Selection Criteria: The same criteria regarding literary quality, strong social values, and authenticity used in the selection of any book apply to evaluating lesbian/gay-themed books. These include analyzing books for racism, anti-Semitism, sexism, classism, ageism, ableism, size oppression, and looksism.

Self-Esteem: Will this book bolster or diminish self-esteem? All children need to find positive images of themselves and members of their families and communities in the books they read. Because young lesbian and gay people are often subjected to misinformation, ridicule, ostracism, hostility, and violence, they especially need to know that they are not alone. It is imperative that a strong collection of good books be made available to this population of over 3 million teenagers. These books should combine honesty and realism with a life-affirming sense of hope. Good books should also be available that portray children with lesbian and gay parents and other relatives.

Homophobia and Heterosexism: Homophobia is the irrational fear or intolerance of lesbian and gay people. Heterosexism is the assumption that all people are heterosexual or that heterosexuality is the superior sexual identity. In *Strong Women, Deep Closets*, Pat Griffen writes,

Heterosexism is a system of dominance in which heterosexuality is privileged as the only normal and acceptable form of sexual expression. In this system of dominance, heterosexual identity is valued and rewarded, while homosexual and bisexual identity are stigmatized and punished. Heterosexism operates on multiple levels (individual, institutional, and cultural). (p. xv)

Books should be examined carefully for blatant or subtle homophobic and heterosexist messages.

Omission: Does the collection include many of the titles annotated in this guide? Even though more books with lesbian and gay themes are finally being written and published, omission continues to be one of the biggest problems in the field. Exclusion is one of the most insidious and painful forms of bias—lesbian and gay titles are often excluded from an entire collection. The absence of representation in literature is a form of symbolic annihilation. Indeed, Michael Cart, a nationally recognized expert in children's and young adult literature, cautions, "Silence equals death—not only of the body but of the spirit" (*Gay and Lesbian Literature: Volume 2*, p. 77).

Characterization: Are lesbian and gay characters portrayed as complex, multidimensional individuals? Do they each have unique interests, personalities, and lifestyles? Is their lesbian or gay identity portrayed as only one of a number of significant social groups with which they identify? Young lesbian and gay people should be shown coping adequately with the homophobia they will realistically encounter. They should grow and change as a person as the story develops. Lesbian and gay individuals should also appear as secondary characters in a wide range of roles, including friends, relatives, librarians, educators, neighbors, community members, and national and international figures.

Language: Does the book use language that is respectful of lesbian and gay people? Examples of offensive terms are: *lifestyle, preference, choice,* and *mannish*. In *Setting Them Straight*, therapist and activist Betty Berzon writes, "There are many lifestyles among gay and lesbian people, just as there are many lifestyles among heterosexual people. Refer to my sexual identity or my sexual orientation, but do not trivialize my life by calling it a lifestyle. My *life* is about something much more profound than 'a style'" (p. 175). Some lesbian and gay individuals and groups are reclaiming terms such as *dyke* and *queer*. These words continue to be offensive when used by people outside the lesbian and gay community.

Relationships: Does the book portray lesbian and gay characters involved in healthy, loving relationships? Are their identities trivialized by the assumption that being lesbian or gay is a bedroom issue only? Is their same-sex attraction depicted as a phase from which they will eventually move toward heterosexuality, read a superior orientation? Is the emphasis always on coming out, or do some of the books in the collection portray young lesbian and gay people whose sexual identities are secondary to the main plot?

Diversity: Does the collection as a whole reflect the diversity of our society? Or are all of the gay and lesbian characters young, white, middle-class, and able-bodied? There is a need for more diversity in the body of literature presently available. Serious omissions exist in young adult fiction portraying lesbian and gay Native Americans, Asian Americans, African Americans, and Latinas and Latinos.

Stereotypes: Does the book promote or debunk stereotypes of lesbian and gay people? One of the most destructive stereotypes is that gay men and lesbian women are seducers of children. Research shows that the vast majority of pedophiles are heterosexual men who molest young girls. Because of the serious nature of this issue, it is imperative that books for young people do not perpetuate the stereotype of gay and lesbian people as pedophiles. Any sexual relationship between a young person and an adult, such as a student and a teacher or a player and a coach, is unequal, inappropriate, and exploitative, even if the author implies that the younger person initiated it. In addition, it is illegal, a serious form of abuse, and harmful to the younger person's sense of self and well-being. Other harmful stereotypes include the myths that gay and lesbian people are preoccupied with sexual liaisons and are unable to maintain lasting relationships.

Erasure: Are biographers honest about the sexual identity of their subjects? In many biographies, the sexual identities of lesbian and gay people have been deliberately obscured. Heterosexualizing, obscuring, erasing, or ignoring the sexual identity of the subject is not only dishonest, it also denies young lesbian and gay people life-affirming access to information about their heritage. Recently, a few courageous biographers are reclaiming the excised past by examining their subjects' lives within the authentic context of their complete identities.

1

Picture Books

Abramchik, Lois. *Is Your Family Like Mine?* Illustrated by Alaiyo Bradshaw. Open Heart, Open Mind, 1993. Paper $11.95 (ISBN 0964714507). Ages 5–9.

Five-year-old Armetha lives with her two mothers, Mom and Mommy, who encourage her to learn something new each day. She asks her friends, "Who lives in your family?" She discovers that they come from all kinds of families, including single parents, foster parents, step-families, and nuclear. Armetha and her friends conclude that although their family constellations are different, it is love that is their common bond. Mommy says, "There are many different kinds of families in the world and it is love that connects everyone together." This appealing book, beautifully illustrated in black-and-white, depicts family diversity in loving terms. Multicultural characters, affectionate interactions, and the sensitive tone, along with the gentle message about love and acceptance of diversity, make this a very special book. *Topics*: Families, Lesbian and Gay Parents.

Alden, Joan. *A Boy's Best Friend.* Illustrated by Catherine Hopkins. Alyson Publications, 1992. Hardcover $12.95 (ISBN 1555832032). Ages 5–8.

Every year since he was four years old, Will has asked for a dog for his birthday. And each year he has been disappointed because, as a person with asthma, a dog would be detrimental to his health. Finally, on his seventh birthday, LeDogg comes into his life and teaches him that to be different is to be distinctive. This is a beautifully written and illustrated story about a boy who makes a magical connection with a stuffed animal. Because of the aggressive behavior of bullies on the playground, this title might be upsetting to preschoolers. But school-age children will be comforted by the fact that LeDogg ends up safely in his human friend's arms. The relationship between Will's mother and their housemate, Jeanne, is so subtle that most children will miss it. By using the word *friend* instead of *companion* or *partner*, the author missed an important opportunity to educate young people. Mom says, "When you don't mind your difference it stops being a problem and becomes your distinction." These words seem rather empty when her relationship with her lover is obscured. Nevertheless, Jeanne is an integral part of the family, and her close relationship with Will's mother is depicted through the lovely handcolored photographs. *Topics*: Asthma, Birthdays, Dogs, Lesbian Mothers.

Arnold, Jeanne. *Amy Asks a Question: Grandma, What's a Lesbian*? Illustrated by Barbara Lindquist. Mother Courage Press, 1996. Hardcover $10.95 (ISBN 0941300285). Ages 8–12.

Grandma Bonnie and Grandma Jo, who have been lovers for over twenty years, respond with clarity and love to their granddaughter's question, "What is a lesbian?" Ten-year-old Amy has been listening to the adults' conversations through the years, so she knows a lot about her grandmothers' lives. But it isn't until she and her soccer teammates are called "lesbians" in a nasty way that she asks for more information. The ensuing discussion is carefully written, with Bonnie and Jo describing the joys and struggles of their life together in warm, candid language. They talk about the isolation of the early years, the fear they experienced when Bonnie lost her job due to homophobia, and the love and support they have shared. This sincere book featuring two admirable lesbians is a valuable resource. Bonnie and Jo are both active, interesting, creative people. Bonnie is an artist, author, musician, and computer expert. Jo enjoys gardening and works at a hospital. When Bonnie lost her job, the two courageously opened a women's bookstore. Brave, resourceful, independent, and passionate, they are women any child should be proud to know. *Topics*: Intergenerational Relationships, Lesbian Grandmothers.

Brown, Forman. *The Generous Jefferson Bartleby Jones*. Illustrated by Leslie Trawin. Alyson Publications, 1991. Paper $7.95 (ISBN 1555831982). Ages 5–8.

Jefferson Bartleby Jones spends weekends with his two fathers, Joe and Pete. Jeff brags to his friends, Kim and Chad, about the great times he has with his dads. When he notices that their fathers are too busy to spend time with their children, Jeff generously offers to loan his dads out. But one day when he finds himself sitting home alone, he realizes that he has been too generous. Happily, his fathers didn't forget him and the foursome arrive home early. They all go to the mall for three-decker ice cream cones. This is a whimsical story about a child of gay fathers who is happy and well-cared-for. Told in energetic verse and lively black-and-white line drawings, this upbeat book featuring multiethnic children is Forman Brown's first book for young children. He completed it the same month as he celebrated his ninetieth birthday. He is also the author of *Better Angel* (1933), one of the first novels to depict gay characters in a realistic and positive way. *Topics*: Gay Fathers, Sharing.

Elwin, Rosamund and Michele Paulse. *Asha's Mums.* Illustrated by Dawn Lee. Women's Press, 1990. Paper $4.95 (ISBN 0889611432). Ages 4–8.

Asha is excited about the trip her class is planning to take to the Science Centre. But when she returns the permission form signed by both her mums, her teacher tells her she can't go unless it is filled out correctly. When Asha explains the situation to her mums, they reassure her that they will talk with her teacher. The next day, Asha shows the class a painting she made of her mummies, Sara and Alice. Soon the children are discussing their feelings about having two mums. Later, the class enjoys their trip to the Science Centre. This is a charming book with a gentle message for teachers, children, and parents. An insensitive teacher created needless worry for a little girl. But because some teachers might make this same mistake, it would be wise for same-sex parents to visit the school early in the school year. The appealing illustrations in *Asha's Mums* show a multicultural cast of interesting characters with expressive faces and body language. This fine book ends with both mums saying they are mummy number one. *Topic*: Lesbian Mothers.

Greenberg, Keith E. *Zack's Story: Growing Up with Same-Sex Parents.* Photographs by Carol Halebian. Lerner, 1996. Hardcover $21.29 (ISBN 082252581X). Ages 7–12.

Narrated by eleven-year-old Zack, this attractive full-color photo essay is part of a series of books on growing up in complex families. Zack lives in New Jersey with his mother, Aimee, and her partner, Margie, whom he calls his second mother. The three of them participate in the

Lesbian/Gay Pride Parade in New York City each year, where Zack wears a rainbow-colored bandanna. Zack discusses his feelings about the anti-gay hecklers who harassed the marchers one year. He also finds the courage to confront one of his friends, who makes a homophobic remark. Vivid photographs show Margie helping Zack practice for Little League, Zack and Aimee making a quilt, Zack playing a board game with a friend, and Zack visiting his dad, who lives nearby. In a well-adjusted, reasonable voice, Zack celebrates his family, dispels some common myths, and tells us that gay people are basically the same as everyone else. The afterword introduces Zack's new sister, Margie's child by artificial insemination. The book ends with additional information about lesbian and gay parents, a glossary, a bibliography, and a list of resources. *Topics*: Lesbian Mothers, Pride Celebrations.

Heron, Ann and Meredith Maran. *How Would You Feel If Your Dad Was Gay?* Illustrated by Kris Kovick. Alyson Publications,1991. Paper $6.95 (ISBN 1555832431). Ages 7–12.

When her teacher invites the students to talk about their fathers, Jasmine proudly tells them that she has three dads—a stepfather, her natural father, and his lover. Her teacher and classmates find this hard to accept. Later her brother, Michael, who has been subjected to name-calling on the playground, complains that Jasmine had no right to reveal something that he wanted to keep secret. The two dads are very supportive and encourage the children to talk about their feelings. Meanwhile, Noah, the boy who had defended Michael on the playground, has a talk with his mother, who is a lesbian. After Jasmine's father confers with the principal, a special assembly is arranged to discuss the different kinds of families there are in the world—and in the school. This solid book does an excellent job of addressing the confusion and prejudice often experienced by children with lesbian and gay parents. The complexity of the issues is gently explored with sensitivity and poignancy. The book will provide support for children who are dealing with the same issues and help their classmates, teachers, and community members understand how to be friends and allies.The black-and-white line drawings depict Jasmine's African-American family and a racially diverse school. *Topics*: African Americans, Families, Lesbian and Gay Parents, Teachers.

Hoffman, Eric. *Best Best Colors/Los mejores colores*. Illustrated by Celeste Henriquez. Translated into Spanish by Eida de la Vega. Redleaf Press, 1999. Paper $10.95 (ISBN 1884834698). Ages 5–10.

Series: Anti-Bias Books for Kids. In this delightful book, Nate has difficulty deciding just which lovely color is his favorite. With the help of his two mammas, Mamma Laura and Mamma Jean, he finally realizes that he does not have to choose a best, best color. Indeed, when he sees the beautiful colors in the rainbow flag his mothers hang on the wall in preparation for the Pride Parade, he understands that each color is pretty by itself, but they are even more special when they are all together. The engaging story is enhanced by lively full-page illustrations depicting a multicultural cast of interesting characters. Mamma Jean and Mamma Laura are shown with their arms affectionately around each other. This charming book is the first bilingual picture book featuring lesbian mothers. In a note to parents, teachers, and other caregivers, the author offers suggestions for ways that adults can help children learn cooperation and respect for diversity. Anti-Bias Books for Kids are designed to help children recognize the biases present in their everyday lives and to promote caring interactions with all kinds of people. The characters in each story inspire children to take a position against bias and injustice and to seek positive changes in themselves and their communities. *Topics*: African Americans, Bilingual—English and Spanish, Colors, Lesbian Mothers, Rainbow Flags.

Jenness, Aylette. *Families: A Celebration of Diversity, Commitment, and Love.* Houghton Mifflin, 1990. Paper $4.95 (ISBN 0395669529). Ages 8–12.

Seventeen young people describe a rich variety of families—each different in composition but alike in caring for each other. As they discuss the benefits and challenges of contemporary family life, they clarify the true definition of family values. Lively black-and-white photographs by the author accompany the multicultural voices of the youngsters, who share their feelings, interests, concerns and hopes. Elliott was adopted at birth by two gay men who plan to adopt more children. Jody recounts her experiences when her parents divorced and her mother became lovers with Carole. At first, Jody hated Carole, even though she didn't know her. She describes how her feelings changed and how she came to love and accept Carole. This book began as a photographic exhibit at The Children's Museum in Boston, Massachusetts. The appended postscript includes quotes from both children and adults who visited the exhibit. A bibliography is also included. *Topics*: Families, Lesbian and Gay Parents.

Johnson-Calvo, Sarita. *A Beach Party with Alexis.* Alyson Publications, 1993. Paper $2.95 (ISBN 155583230X). Ages 3–7.

In this lighthearted coloring book, Alexis celebrates her summer vacation by giving a beach party. The day school is out, she and her mothers start planning the special event. Alexis makes a list of friends to invite to the party, sends out gaily decorated homemade invitations, and counts the days until the party. On July 21 Alexis, her friends, and their parents gather on the beach for a great time in the sun. This buoyant book is special in many ways. Alexis, an African-American girl, is exuberant and outgoing. The multicultural cast of characters is made up of lesbians, their children, and friends. The diversity in size, age, and appearance is refreshing, and the illustrations invite young readers to join the party! *Topics*: African Americans, Lesbian Mothers, Parties, Picnics.

Kennedy, Joseph. *Lucy Goes to the Country*. Illustrated by John Canemaker. Alyson Publications, 1998. Hardcover $15.95 (ISBN 1555834280). Ages 4–7.

Lucy, an adorably rambunctious little cat, spends most of her time in the city with her two human friends. But on weekends the three take the train to the country, where exciting adventures await them. One warm weekend, when the Big Guys invite their friends over for a party, Lucy leads everyone on a caper they will long remember. She tries to tolerate the rude behavior of a little dog named Shmoofy, but soon the two are stranded up in a tree where they knock down a hive of furious bees. Everything turns out fine in the end after a firefighter rescues the frightened duo and returns them safely to the arms of their nervous humans. Lucy's madcap antics are sure to delight young readers. Canemaker's bright illustrations are filled with humorous details, portraying Personality Plus Lucy with all her saucy expressions. Any question about the sexual identity of the two Big Guys is cleared up by an illustration showing two pairs of feet sticking out from under the blankets. Two of the party guests, Pat and Sue, arrive holding hands and accompanied by their daughter, Liza. Two jokes are obviously aimed at adult readers: a train station sign has the sign "Peckerwood" and one of the Big Guys thanks the hunky firefighter with a bit too much enthusiasm while his disgruntled partner watches. This entertaining book ends with Lucy planning more escapades while her two human friends recover. *Topics*: Cats, Feline Friends.

Newman, Lesléa. *Belinda's Bouquet*. Illustrated by Michael Willhoite. Alyson Publications, 1991. Paper $6.95 (ISBN 1555831540). Ages 4–10.

Many people are beginning to understand the damage that racism, sexism, classism, and ableism can do to a child's self-esteem. But few make the connection with size oppression, another difference that can create misery and self-hatred in young people who live in a society that worships thinness. Some adults seem to be concerned about the latest statistics regarding eating disorders among girls in this country, but few books have been written for young readers that address this important issue. Lesléa Newman, who has written elsewhere about her personal experiences with being a chubby child and a fat adolescent, tackles size oppression in *Belinda's Bouquet*. When an insensitive adult makes a cruel comment about her weight, Belinda decides to go on a diet. But then her friend Daniel's lesbian mom tells her, "Your body belongs to you." An experience Daniel's other mother had with fat marigolds and thin irises helps convince Belinda that each person is different and everyone has her or his special kind of beauty. One reviewer wrote, "[W]here was this book when I was a fat little kid? This story eloquently gives a child perspectives on diversity, understanding, tolerance, and self-acceptance" (*The Midtown Times*, date unavailable). Daniel's two mothers are supportive and helpful. Colorful illustrations by Michael Willhoite add to the appeal of this gentle little book. *Topics*: Lesbian Mothers, Size Oppression.

Newman, Lesléa. *Heather Has Two Mommies*. Illustrated by Diana Souza. In Other Words, 1989; Alyson Publications, 1990. Paper $8.98 (ISBN 155583180X). Ages 3–8.

Heather is a happy three-year-old who lives with her two mothers, Mama Jane and Mama Kate. One day at playgroup, Heather becomes aware that she is the only child with two mommies. She is upset until she discovers that one of her classmates has a mother and two fathers (his stepfather and his biological father), another has a mother and a sister, and yet another has two daddies. Molly, their teacher, tells them, "Each family is special. The most important thing about a family is that all the people in it love each other." This charming book was the first to depict a family in which two lesbians choose to have a child together. Newman provides details about artificial insemination, pregnancy, and the birthing process. According to the Intellectual Freedom Office of the American Library Association, *Heather Has Two Mommies* was one of the most frequently challenged titles in school and public libraries in 1993. In spite of the censors, it has been warmly received. Lively black-and-white drawings show an exuberant little girl picnicking with her mothers, building a table with one of them, and playing in the back yard. The adorable drawings depicting Heather's multicultural playgroup were done by Dana Lee Kingsbury, a five-year-old artist. *Topics*: Artificial Insemination, Birthing Process, Challenged Books, Lesbian Mothers.

Newman, Lesléa. *Saturday Is Pattyday*. Illustrated by Annette Hegel. New Victoria, 1993; Women's Press, 1993. Paper $6.95 (ISBN 0934678510). Ages 4–8.

Frankie lives with his two moms, Allie and Patty. But one day, Patty moves out into her own apartment. Allie explains that they had to get divorced because they were fighting too much. Frankie calls Patty to tell her he misses her and she reminds him that they will be spending Saturdays together. "From now on, Saturday is Pattyday." When Saturday finally arrives, Patty shows Frankie a shelf in her closet where he can keep toys, books, or clothes. Then they go to the park for a picnic and before long, Frankie becomes argumentative. He obviously is angry and scared about the breakup of his family. When he tells Patty he doesn't want to get divorced, she reassures him that she loves him and will always be his mom. This tender book captures the feelings of confusion and loss a child feels when his parents separate. Affectionate illustrations show Frankie and his two moms trying to sort out their feelings during a very difficult time in their lives. Newman lovingly weaves a bit of humor into the story through a fourth character: Doris Delores Brontosaurus. This whimsical little stuffed animal comforts Frankie during sleepless nights when his two moms argue. She is the first to nestle down on Frankie's shelf in Patty's new apartment. And as the story ends, Frankie generously leaves Doris Delores with Patty to keep her company until the next Pattyday. *Topics*: Divorce, Lesbian Mothers.

Newman, Lesléa. *Too Far Away to Touch*. Illustrated by Catherine Stock. Clarion Books, 1995. Paper $5.95 (ISBN 0395900182). Ages 6–10.

How can we explain death to young people? Lesléa Newman has written an exceptionally beautiful story that will help adults share information with children about this painful subject. When Zoe and her beloved Uncle Leonard, who has AIDS, go on an adventure to the Hayden Planetarium, he explains that the stars are "Too far away to touch, but close enough to see." Later Leonard and his companion, Nathan, take Zoe to the beach to watch the night sky. When a shooting star flashes across the sky, Zoe knows that it is not really gone because she can always shut her eyes and imagine it again. This gentle story will touch young readers, helping them understand the enduring nature of love. Leonard is portrayed as a loving, thoughtful uncle who plans special activities for his niece to enjoy. Even though he is very tired, he somehow finds the energy to paste glow-in-the-dark stars all over Zoe's ceiling. He generously finds a way to help Zoe understand that even though he may be gone, he will always be in her heart. Soft watercolors accompany this sensitive story about an important topic. *Topics*: AIDS, Dying, Gay Uncles, Stars.

Nones, Eric Jon. *Caleb's Friend.* Farrar, Straus & Giroux, 1993. Hardcover $15.00 (ISBN 0374310173). Ages 7–12.

The bond between two boys, one from land and one from sea, is celebrated through exquisite paintings and lyrical text. When Caleb, who works on a fishing boat, accidentally drops the precious harmonica given to him by his deceased father into the sea, it is miraculously returned to him by an ethereal mer-boy. This is the beginning of a lifelong friendship, during which each character delivers the other from grave danger. The romantic connection between the two is implied through poignant harmonica tunes, sensuous body language, and gifts of wild summer roses. *Caleb's Friend* has been praised for its breathtaking images, quietly elegiac text, and enigmatic tone. Nones is to be commended for portraying two young males who truly care about each other, and whether or not their relationship is sexual, their commitment to each other is expressed with tenderness and affection. *Topics*: Mer-People, Ocean, Ships.

Tax, Meredith. *Families.* Illustrated by Marylin Hafner. Feminist Press, 1996. Paper $7.95 (ISBN 1558611576); Spanish Edition: *Familias.* Translated by Leonora Wiener and Nancy Festinger. Feminist Press, 1998. Paper $7.95 (ISBN 1558611835). Ages 4–8.

Six-year-old Angie introduces readers to her multicultural group of friends and their families. The many forms families take through adoption, divorce, single parenting, stepfamilies, and same-sex parenting are explored in the affectionate, nonjudgmental voice of a young girl. The warm, engaging text highlights what families have in common and encourages an acceptance of the ways in which they are different. The detailed illustrations will appeal to listeners and readers of all ages. Of particular interest is Angie's friend Susie, who lives with her mother and her godmother. Their relationship is not clear but the text tells us that Susie doesn't have any father. The two mothers are shown together with Susie at the roller rink. In a departure from other books featuring nontraditional families, Tax includes animal families such as lions, chickens, and ants. As one of the earliest books on nontraditional families, this title has been revered by librarians, parents, educators, and children, and also attacked by censors. The book's heartfelt message is, in Angie's words, "Families are who you live with and who you love." *Topics*: Nontraditional Families, Spanish Edition.

Valentine, Johnny. *The Daddy Machine.* Illustrated by Lynette Schmidt. Alyson Wonderland, 1992. Paper $6.95 (ISBN 1555831069). Ages 5–8.

In this energetic tale that has been compared to Dr. Seuss' *The Cat in the Hat*, the son and daughter of two lesbians learn the meaning of the saying "Be careful what you wish for!" Overwhelmed with the results of their invention, they finally find a way to solve their unusual dilemma. Told in rhyming verse, the hilarious escapades of the two young geniuses are accompanied by full-page black-and-white drawings. One reviewer wrote, "There is such a playful spontaneity and wholesomeness in the text, that I can't think of a better book to build a loving bridge between heterosexual families and those with gay and lesbian parents" (*Children's Book Review Service*, date unknown). This is one of five books by Johnny Valentine, a pen name for Sasha Alyson, who started the Alyson Wonderland imprint, a line of books about children with lesbian and gay parents. *Topics*: Inventions, Lesbian and Gay Parents.

Valentine, Johnny. *The Day They Put a Tax on Rainbows and Other Stories*. Illustrated by Lynette Schmidt. Alyson Wonderland, 1992. Hardcover $12.95 (ISBN 1555832016). Ages 6 up.

Three original fairy tales celebrate honesty, generosity, courage, kindness, and resourcefulness. In "The Ring of Consequence," a father gives his daughter, Clara, a magic ring on her thirteenth birthday. He cautions her to be careful what she wishes for because with each wish comes a consequence. For him, the consequence had been positive. His wish was to fall in love, and when he did it was with Brendan, with whom he has been happy for many years. Clara uses her wish to save herself from drowning. When she discovers that she is a mer-person, she falls in love and marries a mer-prince and moves into an underwater castle. "The Three Gifts" features three boys who have two fathers. In an imaginative twist on the "kindness rewarded" theme, the brave young protagonists find a chest of gems at the end of the grandest rainbow they have ever seen. In contrast with most fairy tales, where the brothers compete, these boys work together to accomplish their dream. In the title story, a clever boy outwits a greedy king who puts a tax on first sunshine, then rain, and finally rainbows. The tale ends with the boy and his two mothers attending a gala dessert party at the palace. These stories are essentially typical fairy tales with one exception: the protagonists all have same-sex parents. These parents are minor characters who quietly support their children in their endeavors. Enchantingly illustrated with paintings and drawings, this book is a welcome change from traditional fairy tales. *Topics*: Fairy Tales, Lesbian and Gay Parents, Mer-People.

Valentine, Johnny. *The Duke Who Outlawed Jelly Beans and Other Stories*. Illustrated by Lynette Schmidt. Alyson Wonderland, 1991. Paper

$8.95 (ISBN 1555832199). Ages 6 up. *Award*: Lambda Literary Award for Best Children's/Young Adult Book.

Hailed by Robert Hale in *Horn Book Magazine* as one of the outstanding children's books of the season, this fascinating book presents five original fairy tales about the adventures of children who have lesbian or gay parents. In "The Frog Prince," a boy kisses a frog, allowing him to return to his former state as a prince. This magical tale ends happily with the two boys living with their "two wonderful fathers" (unpaged). Scarlett, in "The Eaglerider," yearns to become an Eaglerider and help protect her kingdom, but only boys are accepted. Taking the advice of her mother, who had also experienced discrimination years earlier when she fell in love with a woman, Scarlett finds a way to follow her dream. As the queen gives her a medal for saving the kingdom, she says, "You refused to let prejudice stop you from doing what you wanted. We are all indebted to you." In the title story, the people of the kingdom chafe under the ridiculous decrees proclaimed by a pompous duke. Finally, when the duke proclaims that "any children who have too many mothers or fathers, or not enough, will be thrown into the dungeon," the targeted daughters and sons find a way to outwit the duke and return the kingdom to peace. "Dragon Sense" features a boy who lives with his bookkeeper mother and her female partner, a sorcerer, and "The Ogre's Boots" tells the story of a brave girl who lives with her two moms, Mother Barbara and Mother Josie. These well-crafted tales are about courageous children who take risks, overcome prejudice, solve problems, and save their people. The colorful full-page illustrations are filled with intriguing details. This appealing book is the first of five titles by Johnny Valentine, a pen name for Sasha Alyson, who started the Alyson Wonderland imprint, a line of books about children with lesbian and gay parents. *Topics*: Fairy Tales, Lesbian and Gay Parents.

Valentine, Johnny. *One Dad, Two Dads, Brown Dad, Blue Dads*. Illustrated by Melody Sarechy. Alyson Wonderland, 1994. Hardcover $10.95 (ISBN 1555832539). Ages 4–7.

This light-hearted book features a girl and a boy who compare notes about their fathers. Lou proudly announces that he has two dads and both are blue. Curious, the narrator asks a series of questions about blue dads, trying to ascertain whether or not they are different in other ways. Lou answers each question, explaining that his dads talk, work, play, and laugh like everyone else. When the girl asks how they became blue, Lou tells her that they were always that way. The rhyming, easy-to-read text and appealing illustrations bring humor to the important message that people are basically the same, whatever their skin color or sexual orientation. The good-natured fathers are portrayed doing ordinary things like combing their hair, walking their dogs, and answering the telephone. Their individuality come through when one of them plays the piano and the other makes a mouth-watering chocolate cream pie. Affection among the three members of the family is shown when one of the dads serves the other chocolate chip cookies in bed and they both hug their son. This funny book will help eliminate stereotypes of gay men. *Topic*: Gay Fathers.

Valentine, Johnny. *Two Moms, the Zark, and Me.* Illustrated by Angelo Lopez. Alyson Wonderland, 1993. Hardcover $12.95 (ISBN 1555832369). Ages 5–8.

While his mothers talk with a friend in the park, the narrator wanders over to the zoo where he meets a Zark, a friendly, brontosaurus-like animal. The boy suddenly realizes he is lost and asks a passing couple, the McFinks, for help. But when the McFinks find out that he has two mothers, they are horrified and try to find him a traditional family. The Zark intervenes and the boy is finally reunited with his moms. Valentine's lively verse is complemented by Lopez's zany, cartoon-style illustrations both of which dash across the pages in a humorous way. Explaining that families come in all sizes, forms, and colors, this entertaining book provides several diverse examples. The narrator, an assertive little boy, knows the McFinks are wrong and is able to run away from them. Being lost is one of children's worst fears: this story, with its happy ending, reassures youngsters that if they get lost, they will be able to find help and get back to their parents safely. *Topics*: Families, Lesbian Parents, Lost and Found.

Vigna, Judith. *My Two Uncles.* Albert Whitman, 1995. Hardcover $14.95 (ISBN 080755507X). Ages 5–9.

Elly and her family are happily preparing for her grandparents' fiftieth wedding anniversary party. Her Uncle Ned and his partner, Phil, help her create a diorama as a special gift for her grandparents. But the day before the big celebration, Grampy announces that Phil is not welcome in his house. Elly's father explains the situation to Elly, saying that he disagrees with Grampy. He adds, "I think it's wrong when people hurt gays and lesbians just because of who they happen to be." Uncle Ned refuses to come to the party without his partner and drops the diorama off for Elly to present. When Grampy opens the diorama, he makes a toast to Ned, "who chose not to be here today because of a stubborn old man." His regret for having rejected his son is apparent in subsequent pages, providing hope that he will eventually change. Told through the voice of a child, this is an engaging story about prejudice and the possibility of change. The watercolor illustrations are expressive, depicting the varied emotions of a sad family scenario. Elly's disappointment that her two favorite uncles are excluded is apparent. After talking with her father, she understands Ned's difficult but courageous decision. *Topic*: Gay Uncles.

Wickens, Elaine. *Anna Day and the O-Ring*. Alyson Publications, 1994. Paper $6.95 (ISBN 1555832520). Ages 3–7.

Four-year-old Evan lives with Mama Dee, Mama Gee, and their canine companion, Anna Day. When he and his two mothers try to set up the tent he received for his birthday, they can't find the o-ring needed to hold the tent poles. The missing piece is finally found in the most unlikely place—under Anna Day! The story of the missing o-ring becomes part of the family lore and they enjoy telling it for a long time, affirming their common history. Full-color photographs by Wickens and Mama Gee, attractively framed and well balanced, show Evan at home with his affectionate moms and at school with his classmates. This sweet-spirited book doesn't call attention to the fact that there are two mothers. No explanations, no apologies—they are just there. The simple, appealing story and the charming pictures will be enjoyed by young listeners and readers. *Topics*: Dogs, Lesbian Mothers.

Willhoite, Michael. *Daddy's Roommate*. Alyson Publications, 1990; translated into German by Jan Wandtke as *Papa's Freund*. Magnus, 1994. Hardcover $15.95 (ISBN 1555831788); Paper $9.95 (ISBN 1555831184). Ages 3–7. *Award*: Lambda Literary Award.

A young boy, his father, and the father's lover share life's ordinary activities. Large, full-color illustrations show them cleaning house, shopping for groceries, playing games, and reading. The two dads have a mild argument over a housekeeping mishap, after which they make up. The boy's mother tells him that his father is gay, explaining that "being gay is just one more kind of love." This upbeat, positive book was the first to depict a child with a gay father. The accessible text and bright, framed watercolors portray the relationships with warmth and cheerfulness. *Daddy's Roommate* will be enjoyed by children whose fathers are gay and will help others understand and support them. One of the most challenged books for young readers, it has weathered many storms around the country. Anti-gay groups have tried unsuccessfully to ban it from school and library shelves. *Topics*: Challenged Books, Gay Fathers.

Willhoite, Michael. *Daddy's Wedding*. Alyson Publications, 1996. Hardcover $15.95 (ISBN 1555833500). Ages 3–7.

In this sequel to the often-challenged *Daddy's Roommate*, Daddy and Frank get married. Grandma, Grandpa, Mommy, and many others attend the festive backyard commitment ceremony. Ten-year-old Nick, the narrator, is the best man. After the men read the vows they have written for each other, exchange rings, and kiss, hundreds of balloons float down on the crowd. When everyone heads for the tables filled with food, they discover that Clancy, the dog, has gotten there first. But not to worry, the cake is not completely ruined. This sparkling book ends with the happy couple departing for San Francisco on their honeymoon. Sunny, framed watercolors include interesting details, and the jovial party atmosphere will warm the hearts of readers of all ages. The minister is a large woman, an unusual and refreshing image in children's books. The wedding guests include people from diverse backgrounds, and the young narrator plays an important part in the ceremony. Indeed, his favorite part is when Frank, after vowing to love his father in sickness and in health, says, "And we already have a son to share." *Topics*: Gay Fathers, Gay Marriage.

Willhoite, Michael. *Uncle What-Is-It Is Coming to Visit!* Alyson Publications, 1993. Hardcover $12.95 (ISBN 1555832059). Ages 5–8.

When Tiffany and Igor's mother announces that an uncle they have never met is coming to visit, they ask if he is married. She tells them Uncle Brett is gay but then doesn't have time to explain what that means. The puzzled children turn to a couple of teenage neighbors, who fill their heads with stereotypes. One explains that gay men really want to be women who dress up in frilly clothes. Another regales them with tales of gay men dressed in black leather, zippers, and chains. The children's imaginations run wild, and they aren't sure they want to meet their uncle. But when he arrives, he is an ordinary man who plays catch, wiggles his ears, plays the piano, and makes fancy desserts. He explains that gay men are guys who fall in love with each other. Some of them do wear dresses and some wear black leather. While some reviewers felt that this book does more to galvanize prejudices than to demolish them, others praised Willhoite for courageously confronting negative caricatures head-on. *Topic*: Gay Uncles.

2

Fiction

Barger, Gary W. *What Happened to Mr. Forster?* Clarion Books, 1981. Hardcover 8.95 (ISBN 0395310210). Ages 10 up.

Set in Kansas City, Missouri in 1958, this is the story of an exemplary teacher who is fired for being gay. The book is narrated by Louis Lamb, an eleven-year-old who enters sixth grade determined to overcome his image as the class baby. Louis had spent years being teased and humiliated by his classmates, who called him "sissy" and "crybaby." Last to be chosen for the softball team year after year, he describes his agonizing recesses spent hiding under the kindergarten steps. Mr. Forster, the new teacher in town, patiently mentors Louis in softball and helps him develop his talent for writing. The first male teacher in the school, Mr. Forster rearranges the students' desks in a circle and engages the class in a project to stage a play written by Louis based on Arthurian legends. Meanwhile, parents in the community are becoming suspicious of the bachelor teacher, especially when it emerges that he lives with a male roommate. At the height of Louis' success, Mr. Forster suddenly disappears. Devastated by the loss of his favorite teacher, Louis finds the strength to protest his unfair dismissal. He encourages Mr. Forster to fight for his rights, but the teacher explains that he never did fit in very well at the school. The book ends with Louis writing in the journal Mr. Forster gave him, determined to maintain his newfound independence and strength. Mr. Forster is a warm, caring teacher who brings out the best in students like Louis, although he seems unable to help Ellie, another student who is ostracized and humiliated. Marred by several age, race, and fat-oppressive terms, this book is noteworthy because it is written for a younger audience than most other books featuring gay and lesbian teachers. *Topics*: Gay Teachers, Kansas City, Writing.

Bechard, Margaret. *If It Doesn't Kill You*. Viking, 1999. Hardcover $15.99 (ISBN 0670885470). Ages 12 up.

Freshman Ben Gearhart is part of a football legacy at a high school in Portland, Oregon, where his father was a star quarterback and his grandfather was a celebrated coach. Ben has had a good season, cinching his chances of making the varsity team next year. Everything is great until his dad leaves him and his mom and moves in with a guy named Keith. This is an interesting addition to the literature exploring the belated coming-out process of gay men who have been married and the impact it has on their sons. In this book, football star/college professor Steven Gearhart tells his son, "I just can't go on living a lie anymore, Ben. I can't go on pretending. It's not fair to me or to you or to your mother" (p. 9). Angry and confused, Ben punishes his father by avoiding him. As he tries to sort out his feelings, he remembers his grandfather's words, "If it doesn't kill you, it'll make you stronger" (p. 88). Ben, like the protagonists in *The Eagle Kite* and *Jack*, re-evaluates long-held ideas and finally reaches a better understanding of his father. *If It Doesn't Kill You* has been praised for its realistic descriptions of the stratified society of high school, likeable protagonist, and definitive setting. The two gay men, Steven and Keith, are portrayed as caring, dependable people. Margaret Bechard is the author of five novels for younger readers; this is her first book for young adults. *Topics*: Father/Son Relationship, Football, Gay Fathers, Oregon, Parenting.

Block, Francesca Lia. *Baby Be-Bop*. Demco, 1997. Hardcover $9.60 (ISBN 0606110658). Ages 12 up. *Award*: ALA Best Book for Young Adults.

In this absorbing prequel to *Weetzie Bat*, Dirk McDonald struggles to accept his gayness in a society filled with homophobia. Raised by his Grandma Fifi after his parents are killed, Dirk knows from an early age that he is gay. After being rejected by his first love, he adopts a hard exterior and starts slam dancing at punk joints. When he is severely beaten by skinheads, who call him a faggot, he drags himself home and passes out. While he is unconscious, he is visited by ancestors who share their own stories of struggle, love, and self-acceptance. His visions assure him that his future includes love and companionship. *Baby Be-Bop* has been praised for its extravagantly imaginative settings, finely honed perspectives, and magical, supernatural elements. The power of stories to heal and to help young gays and lesbians understand and accept who they are is beautifully embodied in this engrossing tale. "Stories . . . can carry us into and through our sorrows. . . . Our stories can set us free" (p. 106). Indeed, upon awakening, Dirk embraces his Great-Grandmother Gazelle's words, "Any love that is love is right" (p. 66). *Topics*: Ancestors, Ghosts, Hate Crimes, Punk Culture, Storytelling.

Block, Francesca Lia. *Weetzie Bat*. HarperCollins, 1989, 1991. Hardcover $14.95 (ISBN 0060205342); Paper $4.50 (ISBN 0064470687). Ages 12 up. *Awards*: ALA Best Book for Young Adults; ALA Recommended Book for the Reluctant Young Adult Reader; ALA Booklist Young Adult Editors' Choice.

In her offbeat debut, Francesca Lia Block follows the adventures of a young woman named Weetzie Bat and her friends in a modern fairy tale about punk life and culture in Los Angeles. Weetzie and her best friend, Dirk, who is gay, go surfing and dancing, and ride around in a red 1955 Pontiac named Jerry. Soon Dirk meets Duck, his soulmate, and Weetzie finds her true love, My Secret Agent Lover Man. Weetzie, Dirk, Duck, and My Secret Agent Lover Man, along with Slinkster Dog and two canaries, move into a Hollywood cottage with a fairy tale roof. Soon they are joined by two babies, Cherokee and Witch Baby, and six dogs. After they weather some sad times, Weetzie looks around at her loved ones and thinks, "I don't know about happily ever after . . . but I know about happily" (p. 88). *Weetzie Bat* has been praised for its distinctive voice and emotional honesty, its charm, poignancy, and touches of fantasy, and its beautifully told story of love, friendship, and family. Michael Cart, in *Romance to Realism*, wrote, "For me the single most moving moment in twenty-five years of gay-themed young adult literature is also the simplest. And it occurs in *Weetzie Bat*, when Weetzie's boyfriend, Dirk, comes out to her" (p. 237). "'It doesn't matter one bit, honey-honey,' Weetzie said, giving him a hug" (p. 9). The white fox fur and the feathered headdress are jarring images in a book that otherwise encourages respect for the earth and all living creatures. The inaccurate, negative portrayal of witches is softened somewhat when the group accepts Witch Baby into their family. *Topics*: Alternative Families, Death, Filmmaking, Gay Fathers, Hollywood, Punk Culture.

Block, Francesca Lia. *Witch Baby*. HarperCollins, 1992. Paper $4.95 (ISBN 0064470652). Ages 12 up. *Awards*: ALA Recommended Book for the Reluctant Young Adult Reader, *School Library Journal* Best Book.

In this sequel to *Weetzie Bat*, Weetzie's almost-daughter, Witch Baby, tries to understand who she is and where she belongs. Years earlier Weetzie and My Secret Agent Lover Man found a tiny baby in a basket on their porch. They took her in and named her Witch Baby. Now Witch Baby searches through Los Angeles on her roller skates and finally finds her biological mother living in a Jayne Mansfield Fan Club. Witch Baby returns home with the realization that her heart is with her almost-family. Weetzie and the others tell their adopted child how important she is to them and acknowledge the unique contributions she has made to their family. Block's poignant portrayal of how it feels to be an outsider is beautifully written. Dirk and Duck, accompanied by Witch Baby as a stowaway, travel to Santa Cruz to visit Duck's family. He has spent many painful years hiding his gayness from them. When Witch Baby outs Duck to his mother, he decides to come out to the others. Realizing that they are kindred outsiders, Witch Baby thinks, "Dirk and Duck are different from most people too. . . . Sometimes they must feel like they don't belong just because they love each other" (p. 34). Later, Duck's mother thanks Witch Baby for helping her get her son back. *Topics*: Adoption, Alternative Families, Ecology, Filmmaking, Gay Fathers, Hollywood, Music, Photography, Punk Culture.

Boock, Paula. *Dare Truth or Promise*. Longacre Press, 1997. Paper 14.95 (ISBN 1877135089); Houghton Mifflin, 1999. Paper $15.00 (ISBN 0395971179). Ages 14 up. *Award*: *New Zealand Post* Children's Book of the Year.

"Willa's voice ran through her like warm wind" (p. 180). When Louie and Willa meet, the air stretches, they feel like water, and they fall in love. But when Louie's mother finds them in bed together, their world falls apart. In this beautifully written love story, two teenagers struggle against homophobia, both internal and external, and after much pain and heartbreak finally find their way back into each other's arms. Seventeen-year-old Louie enjoys acting; indeed the stage is "where she had felt the only thing as strong and right as Willa" (p. 93). Willa is new at Woodhaugh High, having been recently kicked out of a nearby school because of her relationship with the daughter of a fundamentalist preacher. In one of the most remarkable scenes in young adult literature, Louie seeks advice from the priest of her church. His response? In words that should be etched on the walls of every church, he replies, "I think that love is a gift. . . . How lucky you are, to love and to be loved in return" (pp. 156–157). Advising her to not be concerned with literal interpretations of the Bible, he adds, "I think love comes from God. And so, to turn away from love, real love, it could be argued, is to turn away from God" (p. 158). *Dare Truth or Promise*, lauded for its frankness and sensitivity, won the prestigious *New Zealand Post* Children's Book of the Year Award. Although both Louie and Willa are well aware of the politics of humor, one fat-oppressive joke remains unchallenged. The Houghton Mifflin edition includes a Kiwi glossary. *Topics*: Fundamentalist Religion, New Zealand Literature, Politics of Humor, Socioeconomic Class, Theatre.

Brett, Catherine. *S. P. Likes A. D.* The Women's Press, 1989. Paper $5.95 (ISBN 0889611424). Ages 10 up.

There is someone who makes thirteen-year-old Stephanie Powell's heart beat so fast that she is afraid it might stop. She doesn't feel anything toward boys, but Anne Delaney makes her nerves stand at attention and her body come alive. She tries to find someone to talk to about her feelings, but she knows that no one would understand. As she tries to decide what to do, she learns that she has won an art contest to build a sculpture that will be erected on the grounds in front of her school. With the help of Kate Burton, a retired paleontology professor, Stephanie draws up plans for an abstract piece made of replicated dinosaur bones. Stephanie soon realizes that Kate and her housemate, Mary, are lovers. As the story progresses, Stephanie finally finds the courage to ask Kate and Mary for advice. Later, Stephanie realizes that Anne is not the person she thought she was. The strengths of this well-written book include an interesting, likeable protagonist who believes in herself. Her mentors are admirable women who generously offer support and guidance to a confused young lesbian. On the down side, one of Stephanie's friends naively outs their art teacher, jeopardizing his job and exposing him to possible harassment and violence. But author Catherine Brett chose to ignore this potential problem, leaving the impression that gay teachers are safe from bigotry. Nevertheless, this is a good book, one of the few written for this age group featuring a young lesbian. *Topics*: Art, Paleontology, Sculpture.

Brown, Forman. *Better Angel.* Alyson Publications, 1995. Paper $9.95 (ISBN 1555832849). Ages 16 up.

First published in 1933, *Better Angel* is the poignant story of a young man's gay awakening. Kurt Gray is a shy, introspective boy growing up in a small town in Michigan. Persecuted by schoolmates, he finds refuge in books, music, and inside his own mind. This edition of the book marks the first time that Forman Brown has placed his real name on the cover. Because of the severe homophobia of the time, he published earlier editions under the pen name Richard Meeker. In the epilogue, he describes the events in his life that inspired the novel. Complete with black-and-white photographs from his life, it is obvious that much of the story is autobiographical. *Better Angel* has been acknowledged as one of the first novels published in the United States to portray male homosexuality in a positive way. Beautifully written, it issues a passionate cry for an end to homophobia. As Kurt grows up, he gradually transcends the shame, remorse, and miserable doubts that plagued his early years. A talented composer, he travels through Europe on scholarship and later breaks into New York's musical world. He finds the love and companionship he so long yearned for and finally finds a way to "bridge that terrific loneliness and uncertainty" (p. 191). *Topics*: Michigan, Music, New York City, Police Entrapment, Gay Teachers.

Brown, Rita Mae. *Rubyfruit Jungle*. Bantam, 1983. Paper $6.99 (ISBN 055327886X). Ages 16 up.

First published in 1973, *Rubyfruit Jungle* has sold millions of copies and is one of the lesbian/gay bestsellers of all time. Rivaling *The Well of Loneliness* as the best-known lesbian novel ever published, this semiautobiographical novel began a new genre of lesbian literature in which lesbians no longer apologize for being themselves. Molly Bolt, the protagonist, refuses to conform to the expectations of society. Born lesbian, poor, and illegitimate, she rebels against the restrictions placed on her by her gender, class, and sexual identity. Adopted by a poor Southern couple, Molly's strong sense of self never allows her to perceive herself as a victim. Armed with remarkable gifts of defiance, resourcefulness, humor, and grit, she storms through childhood with her self-esteem intact. Her adoptive mother tries to beat her into being more feminine, but Molly continues to climb trees and take cars apart. In sixth grade she falls in love with Leota, a classmate. After months of kissing, the two make love one warm May night shortly before Molly's family moves to Florida. Molly experiments with heterosexual sex but concludes that it doesn't hold a candle to Leota. Later, while on full scholarship to the University of Florida, she is kicked out for being a lesbian. She hitchhikes to New York City with the dream of being a filmmaker. *Rubyfruit Jungle* is a protest against lesbophobia, against the narrow, prejudice-ridden world that most young lesbians grow up in. As her name implies, Molly Bolt steadfastly holds on to her identity. Fiery, irreverent, this proud lesbian avenges the wrongs done to lesbians in twentieth-century literature. Although Molly takes a strong position against racism ("I ain't staying away from people because they look different"), the book is marred by looksism, ageism, fat oppression, and anti-Semitism. *Topics*: Adoption, Bisexual Behavior, Child Abuse, Filmmaking, Socioeconomic Class.

Brown, Todd D. *Entries from a Hot Pink Notebook.* Pocket Books, 1995. Paper $10.00 (ISBN 0671890840). Ages 16 up.

Ben Smith copes with his first year of high school in a small town in Maine by recording his innermost thoughts in a hot pink notebook. Brown's lengthy debut novel captures the isolation and pain of growing up gay in a heterosexist society. Ben, who has known that he is gay for a year when the story opens, lives in an apartment above a gas station with his alcoholic father, depressed mother, ultra-religious grandmother, and mercurial older brother. After recovering from a crush on his history teacher, Ben falls in love with Aaron Silver, a new student who has traveled around the world with his liberal parents. Their relationship ends abruptly when a jealous classmate photographs them kissing in the school supply closet. Aaron is sent away to live with his uncle and Ben is beaten, first by his father and then repeatedly by schoolmates. His parents send him to summer camp, where an act of extreme violence toward a gay cabinmate galvanizes him into action. He not only defends his friend, possibly saving his life, but finds the courage to come out to everyone. When he returns home to face his sophomore year, it is clear that he will no longer go along with the crowd, pretending to be het-erosexual and laughing at homophobic jokes. *Entries from a Hot Pink Note-book* has been praised for its solid emotional core, bittersweet, achingly realistic story, and punchy language. The relationship between Ben and Aaron is mutual, providing them with hope that the future will include love, companionship, and self-acceptance. After his first night with Aaron, Ben writes, "I felt so safe. Like I'd just walked through a wild storm and finally made it to a shelter" (p. 165). Strong language. Explicit sex. *Topics*: Alcoholism, Family Violence, Hate Crimes, Maine, Socioeco-nomic Class, Student Council.

Cart, Michael. *My Father's Scar.* Simon & Schuster, 1996. Hardcover $16.00 (ISBN 068980749X); St. Martin's Press, 1998. Paper $11.95 (ISBN 031218137X). Ages 14 up. *Awards*: ALA Best Book for Young Adults, New York Public Library Best Book for the Teen Age.

In his memorable first novel, Michael Cart tells the powerful story of how one gay person survived his anguished childhood to find love and acceptance. During his first year at college, Andy Logan reflects on his early years with an abusive, alcoholic father, an ineffectual mother, and a cruel grandmother in a bigoted community in the 1960's. Haunted by memories of his awkward adolescence, when he was isolated from his peers and relatives by his intellect, weight, and passion for books, Andy finds solace in running and reading. He fondly remembers the lifeline extended to him by his reclusive Uncle Charles, a poet and scholar whose love for books matched his own and who encouraged him to value his differences. Memories of Evan Adams, an older schoolmate, bring back kaleidoscopic feelings of love and sorrow. Evan, a talented gymnast and musician and Andy's only friend, was viciously beaten and driven from town after coming out to the congregation of their church. Andy thinks about his senior-year romance with Billy, about how his father kicked him out of the house when he told him he was gay, and about the scholarship he received as valedictorian of his class. As the title implies, his father's scar from an old football injury symbolizes the childhood wounds that threaten to overshadow Andy's life. This important theme of healing from unforgivable humiliation and pain is handled beautifully. It is to his credit as a writer that Cart is able to weave hope into this heartrending book. *My Father's Scar* has been praised for its convincing first-person narration, well-realized characters, and emotionally satisfying conclusion. *Topics*: Alcoholism, Appearance, Bibliophilism, Child Abuse, Father/Son Relationship, Fat Oppression, Hate Crimes.

Chambers, Aidan. *Dance on My Grave*. HarperCollins, 1982. Paper $5.95 (ISBN 0064405796). Ages 14 up. *Award*: ALA Best Book for Young Adults.

Multilayered and innovative, this engrossing book dissects sixteen-year-old Henry (Hal) Robinson's seven-week relationship with eighteen-year-old Barry Gorman, which ends in tragedy when Barry is killed in a motorcycle accident after the two quarrel. Hal's retrospective in the form of a journal analyzes his kaleidoscopic feelings about the relationship, death, and the future. Filled with guilt, anger, and sadness, Hal struggles to cope while facing charges of desecrating a grave. Compelled to keep his promise to Barry to dance on his grave if he died first, Hal is subsequently arrested and required to meet with a court-appointed social worker prior to the hearing. Introspective, philosophical, and witty, this complex book vividly explores Hal's heart and mind, capturing the breathless intensity of his feelings. Young love, which is often all-consuming and unequal, is portrayed here in all its confusion, heartache, and passion. As Hal struggles to find the right words to express all of what Barry's life and death mean to him, he finds that writing the story has changed him. Indeed, it is the writing itself that helps him survive the loss. The main characters are interesting, likable, and multidimensional. Hal is self-critical, philosophical, and literary beyond his years. Barry, who took over the family business after his father's death, is responsible and reckless, compassionate and cruel. Critics have expressed concern about his characterization, calling him a rake, seducer, and sadist. However, he is grieving the loss of his father and the hope of further education. His fear of intimacy contrasts with the compassion he shows when he rescues Hal from the Thames, defends a drunk in the street, and offers support to a tearful woman after a play. Literary quotations, press clippings, the social worker's report, and footnotes are interspersed throughout this unusual book. First published in 1982, the strengths of this title are diluted by the disturbing number of deaths of gay characters in the genre of the time. *Topics*: Authorship, Death, England, Philosophy.

Coville, Bruce. *The Skull of Truth.* Harcourt Brace & Company, 1997. Hardcover $17.00 (ISBN 0152754571); Simon & Schuster, 1999. Paper $3.99 (ISBN 0671023438). Ages 8–12.

Charlie Eggleston, a sixth grader with a propensity for telling lies, acquires an ancient human skull that forces him and those around him to tell only the truth, with humorous and poignant results. This fast-moving, suspenseful fantasy, the third in the Magic Shop series, has been praised for its solid plot, understandable language, and sensitive mood shifts. Hamlet, talking rats, friendship, endangered species, cancer, and gay issues are all here in an engaging book about the nuances that surround telling the truth. The subplot featuring Charlie's favorite relative, Uncle Bennie, is skillfully blended into the story. One evening at a family dinner, when everyone is suffering from the same mysterious Truth Attack, Bennie comes out of the closet, explaining that his roommate, Dave, is his boyfriend. Predictably, Charlie is upset at first but as the story progresses, he integrates this new information into his image of his beloved uncle. Bennie and Dave are portrayed as interesting, easygoing people with a supportive relationship and with both shared and separate interests. In a touching scene, Charlie and Bennie discuss Truth and agree that love is something to be proud of. Bennie admits that, by staying in the closet, he probably spared himself some grief from a few relatives, but he missed out on important support from others. The epilogue finds Bennie, Charlie, and several friends watching the film version of "The Tragedy of Hamlet," and discussing the differences between telling the truth and Truth itself. *Topics*: Cancer, Ecology, Endangered Species, Gay Uncles, Hamlet, Honesty, Magic, Storytelling.

Crutcher, Chris. *Ironman.* Greenwillow, 1995. Hardcover $15.00 (ISBN 068813503X); Dell, 1996. Paper $4.50 (ISBN 044021971X). Ages 12 up. *Award*: Runner-up for Evergreen Young Adult Award.

While training for a triathlon, seventeen-year-old Bo Brewster's experiences in a before-school anger management group help him not only control and develop his emotional strength, but also provide him with insights into human behavior. This absorbing story is told through both a third-person account and Bo's letters to talk show host Larry King. Bo's struggle to understand the anger he feels toward his emotionally abusive father parallels his growing empathy with the other members of the group. The victims of neglect, molestation, and verbal and physical abuse, they emerge as survivors struggling to cope with a hostile world. The group's wise leader, Mr. Nakatani, deftly draws each youngster into the group, creating a much-needed supportive environment. *Ironman* has been described as powerful, perceptive, and funny, and has been praised for its crackling narration and memorable cast of characters. One of these characters is Mr. Lionel Serbousek, Bo's supportive swimming coach and journalism teacher. When Bo finds out that Mr. S. is gay, he avoids him until Mr. Nakatani confronts him. "Why would you turn on a man stickin' hisself out that far for you? . . . Lionel Serbousek walks with as much integrity as any man I know" (pp. 114–115). After their talk, Bo realizes, "Losing Mr. S. was one of the worst things that ever happened to me, and I didn't even know it because I was stuck in my own stupid head" (p. 116). When Bo apologizes to Mr. S., he responds, "If you learned anything about prejudice—about bigotry—and you pass it on, it was worth a few weeks of losing you, okay?" (p. 121). Many serious issues surface in this sometimes tender, often profound book. Crutcher poses important questions about parenting, belonging, love, loss, security, and integrity. *Topics*: Anger, Child Abuse, Father/Son Relationships, Gay Teachers, Triathlon.

Davis, Deborah. *My Brother Has AIDS*. Simon & Schuster, 1994. Hardcover $15.00 (ISBN 0689319223). Ages 9–13.

Forthright and sensitive, this first novel features Lacy Mullins, a thirteen-year-old avid swimmer whose gay older brother, Jack, returns home because he is dying of AIDS. While the family takes care of him, Lacy struggles to maintain her equilibrium. Chafing under her parents' admonishments to keep Jack's illness a secret, Lacy courageously decides to tell her class how it feels to live with someone who has AIDS. *My Brother Has AIDS* has been praised for its strong dialogue, admirable protagonist, and compassionate integration of information. Jack's pain and physical deterioration are described in unsparing detail, and when he dies his grieving sister doesn't try to hide her feelings. Lacy, unlike her father, has no problem with her brother's sexual identity, and the two siblings have an unusually close relationship. Although Jack's character is never fully developed, we learn that he had been a lawyer in a small town in Colorado. Before his illness forced him to move back to Maine, he took care of his lover, Lincoln, who preceded him in death from AIDS. This sad story is an important addition to the small body of

AIDS fiction for young readers. *Topics*: AIDS, Death and Dying, Gay Brothers, Journals, Swimming.

Dijk, Lutz Van. *Damned Strong Love: The True Story of Willi G. and Stephan K.* Holt, 1995. Translated from the German by Elizabeth D. Crawford. Hardcover $15.95 (ISBN 0805037705); 1998. Paper $6.95 (ISBN 0805057714). Ages 14 up.

Set in occupied Poland during World War II, this powerful novel is based on the true story of the love between Stefan K., a Polish teenager, and Willi G., a young German soldier. Everything about their relationship is damned, but their love for each other is too strong to deny. When the Gestapo discovers their relationship, Stefan is arrested, tortured, and sentenced to prison. After three brutal years, he manages to escape during the chaotic days before liberation. In the appended afterword, the real-life Stefan K. writes that he still doesn't know whether Willi survived. His inquiries to archives in Poland, Germany, and Austria remain unsuccessful to date. Stefan writes, "it is always a crime to punish love and to tolerate violence" (p. 134). Young readers have responded to *Damned Strong Love*, which was first published in German in 1991, by writing to Stefan to tell him that they have learned about the persecution of homosexuals for the first time. They have also learned about the love and tenderness between Stefan and Willi and how important it is to protect people's rights to express their sexual identity. The appended Notes on the Story are not referenced within the text. *Topics*: Bilingualism, Hate Crimes, Holocaust, Poland, Prisons, Nazis, World War II.

Dondy, Farrukh. *Black Swan.* Houghton Mifflin, 1993. Hardcover $14.95 (ISBN 0395660769). Ages 14 up.

This absorbing, idea-packed novel blends a contemporary narrative with a fascinating story of Elizabethan intrigue, which poses a daring question about the true authorship of Shakespeare's plays. Aspiring actor Rose Hassan, who lives with her mother in London, has just graduated from a prestigious secondary school which she attended on full scholarship and where she was the only Black student in her class. When her mother becomes ill, Rose takes over the job of caring for a mysterious elderly Black man, Mr. Bernier, for whom she transcribes the diary of Simon Forman, a contemporary of Shakespeare, Christopher Marlowe and his lover, a Black man known as Lazarus. As her work on the manuscript progresses, Rose soon realizes that both she and Mr. Bernier are under surveillance. Both the contemporary and the fifteenth-century story lines are filled with mystery, cunning, and danger. Lazarus, who was a slave in the Caribbean, survives imprisonment, degradation, torture, and execution to write the plays attributed to Shakespeare. Fast-moving and complicated, this bold novel was written by Farrukh Dondy, who was born in Poona, India and later moved to Great Britain to study English at Cambridge. *Topics*: Authorship, Blacks Britons, England, Mystery, Playwrights, Shakespeare, Socioeconomic Class, Theatre.

Donovan, John. *I'll Get There: It Better Be Worth the Trip.* Dell, 1969. Paper $4.99 (ISBN 0440939801). Ages 12 up. Out of Print.

This much-discussed title was the first gay-themed young adult book to be published in the United States. After his beloved grandmother dies, thirteen-year-old Davy Ross goes to live with his alcoholic mother in New York City. Accompanied by his buddy, Fred the dachshund, he tries to adjust to his mercurial mother, detached father, small apartment, and new school while grieving the loss of his grandmother. He becomes friends with Altschuler, a classmate who is also grieving the loss of a close friend. One afternoon, the two boys kiss and a few days later, after Altschuler sleeps over, Davy muses, "I have a new way of looking at Altschuler because of what we did together last night" (p. 151). Subsequently, Fred is killed by a car and Davy, grief-stricken, blames himself and "all that messing around" (p. 172) for the death of his canine friend. After a period of alienation from Altschuler, the book ends with the two boys trying to sort out everything that happened and wondering if making out with girls will take their minds off "this queer business." *I'll Get There: It Better Be Worth the Trip* has been hailed as a perceptive, funny, remarkable book and has been praised for its beautifully written, poignant depiction of two young boys questioning their sexual identities. At the time it was written, the book was quite revolutionary, but by today's standards it is perceived as overly cautious and even evasive. Critics have expressed concern about the trend in early gay-themed young adult literature in which a character experienced a tragedy in the form of retribution for his/her homosexuality. Nevertheless, this absorbing book is important historically; it helped prepare the way for a body of literature crucial to the lives of young lesbians and gays. *Topics*: Alcoholism, Death, Divorce, Dogs, Grandmothers, Moving, New York City, Parenting.

Donovan, Stacey. *Dive.* Dutton, 1994. Hardcover $15.99 (ISBN 0525451544); Puffin, 1996. Paper $4.99 (ISBN 0140379622). Ages 14 up.

Innovative and compelling, this is a poetic story of painful endings and beautiful beginnings. Fifteen-year-old Virginia "V" Dunn's introspective first-person narrative about her struggle to understand everything that love and loss offer and demand is a powerful commentary on the meaning of life and death. Not only is her beloved canine friend in a cast from a mysterious hit-and-run, but her best friend is avoiding her, her mother is cruel and distant, and her brother is drugged and indifferent. Then her father is hospitalized with an obscure fatal disease and her life slides downhill. Fighting to maintain her balance, V meets Jane and suddenly the world falls into place. Their relationship is strong, grounded, and joyful. "Let our blood laugh in our veins" (p. 103), a line from a poem they share, describes the happiness they find with each other. Their love is the most natural thing in the world, and V finds herself wondering how anyone could think it is wrong. This engrossing book ends with Jane bringing flowers to Mr. Dunn's wake, heralding hope and new beginnings. *Dive* is distinguished by its lyrical first-person narration, extraordinary images, powerful characterization, and depth of emotion. Virginia and Jane are two of the most interesting lesbians in young adult fiction. It is refreshing to find complex characters who never doubt their lesbianism or their love for each other. Their connection is so right, so tender, they feel that they have always known each other. They share a love for books: V notes that books have saved her life and helped her understand herself and life's dilemmas. Betrayal, denial, cynicism, alienation, and silences are all here in this bittersweet exploration of the mysteries of love, life, and death. *Topics*: Acute Milofibrosis, Alcoholism, Animal Companions, Dying and Death, Mother/Daughter Relationships, Poetry.

Durant, Penny Raife. *When Heroes Die*. Simon & Schuster, 1992. Hardcover $15.00 (ISBN 0689317646); 1995. Paper $3.95 (ISBN 0689718357). Ages 9–12. *Award*: Lambda Literary Award.

Twelve-year-old Gary Boyden has a special connection with his Uncle Rob, who has been his mentor ever since his father abandoned the family when he was born. So when his mother tells him that Uncle Rob is gay and has AIDS, Gary is understandably devastated. As his uncle's condition deteriorates, Gary experiences denial, confusion, disillusionment, anger, and grief. Shortly before he dies, Rob apologizes to Gary for not telling him he was gay. *When Heroes Die* has been praised for its frank treatment of a painful issue, potent depiction of the emotions of survivors, and accessible vocabulary. Although it is difficult to understand why Gary puts up with his irritating, homophobic best friend, the other minor characters are helpful and sympathetic. Durant missed an opportunity to present literature study in a positive way; instead Gary suffers through his boring literature classes, never knowing that a good novel can be a wise and compassionate friend. Nevertheless, it is a nonfiction book about AIDS given to him by a neighbor that finally moves Gary out of his denial in time to say goodbye to his uncle. Rob is portrayed as a warm-hearted, charming, and supportive person who goes out of his way to provide guidance for his nephew. Without didacticism, Durant's first novel imparts important information about AIDS, homophobia, secrets, loss, and the grieving process. Durant discussed her reasons for writing *When Heroes Die* in an interview with Michael Thomas Ford in *The Voices of AIDS*, reviewed in the nonfiction section of this guide (Chapter 4). *Topics*: AIDS, Basketball, Dying and Death, Gay Uncles.

Fox, Paula. *The Eagle Kite*. Orchard, 1995. Hardcover $15.95 (ISBN 0531068927); Dell, 1996. Paper $4.50 (ISBN 0440219728). Ages 11 up.

This beautifully constructed, subtly textured story about family secrets, love, and loss opens with Liam Cormac's realization that his father is dying of AIDS. Thirteen-year-old Liam knows his mother is lying when she blames tainted blood transfusions for the disease. He remembers seeing his father embracing a man at the beach several years earlier. Liam's kaleidoscopic feelings of fear, anger, and alienation threaten to overwhelm him at times. When he spends time alone with his father, who has moved to a cabin by the sea, the two finally start communicating and the rift between them begins to heal. The portrayal of Liam's father, Philip Cormac, is sympathetic and multidimensional. A landscape architect, he taught his young son the Latin names of plants long before he knew the common ones. When Philip fell in love with Geoff Chaffee, he decided to keep their relationship a secret from his wife and child. Geoff also died of AIDS and Philip took care of him during his last months. Philip valiantly wages battle against the disease that will eventually kill him at age thirty-eight. *The Eagle Kite* has been praised for its perceptive, even transcendent prose, honest portrayal of tangled emotional issues, and palpable dramatic tension. *Topics*: AIDS, Bisexual Fathers, Dying and Death, Grief.

Futcher, Jane. *Crush*. Alyson Publications, 1981. Paper $5.95 (ISBN 155583602X). Ages 12 up.

It is 1964, and seventeen-year-old Jean (Jinx) Tuckwell is in her senior year at an exclusive boarding school for young women in Pennsylvania. Unsure of herself, Jinx struggles to understand her attraction to her talented classmate, Lexie Yves. Rich in dialogue, this bittersweet book has been praised for its excellent characterization: the passive, confused protagonist; the calculating headmaster; and the enigmatic, destructive Lexie. First published in 1981, *Crush* is important reading because of the thought-provoking way it approaches the confusion that young lesbians often experience. It is a long and compelling book, distinguished by its portrayal of a young woman slowly awakening to her sexuality and growing in her inner strength and confidence. Manipulated and betrayed by Lexie and expelled during the last weeks of school, Jinx graduates later during the summer, determined to follow her dream of going to art school. Futcher somehow managed to weave slender rays of hope and tenderness into this book while exposing the pain and cruelty of homophobia, both internal and external, which sadly continue decades later. *Topics*: Art, Socioeconomic Class, Sports, Teachers, Theatre.

Garden, Nancy. *Annie on My Mind.* Farrar, Straus & Giroux, 1982. Paper $3.95 (ISBN 0374404143). Ages 12 up. *Awards*: *Booklist* Reviewers' Choice, ALA Best Book for Young Adults, ALA Best of the Best 1970–1983, *Booklist* Best Books of the 1980s, Booksellers' Choice List, ALA Best Books for Young Adults for the Past 25 Years.

In this groundbreaking book first published in 1982, two engaging young women fall in love, struggle with both internalized and external prejudice, and ultimately triumph over the forces that threaten to keep them apart. The body of adolescent literature waited a long time for this tender, bittersweet lesbian love story, which is still considered one of the best in the field. Beautifully written, this compelling book is told in retrospect by eighteen-year-old Liza Winthrop during her first semester at Massachusetts Institute of Technology. She reminisces about the magical day she met Annie Kenyon at the Metropolitan Museum, how their relationship developed, and how she struggled to accept her feelings for Annie and to come to terms with her lesbianism. "It was like a war inside me; I couldn't even recognize all the sides" (p. 93). Liza reflects on the day when Annie and she were caught making love in the house of two of Liza's vacationing teachers, who are also lesbians. The ensuing brouhaha led to the dismissal of the teachers, who clearly did not indoctrinate their students. Confusion and guilt prevent Liza from contacting Annie for several miserable months, during which they both leave for college. After much introspection, Liza remembers her teacher's words: "Don't let ignorance win. . . . Let love" (p. 232). Liza telephones Annie and they reaffirm their love for each other. This landmark book not only has a happy ending, it also is one of the few books for young people that actually captures the romance of two lesbians falling in love.

In October of 1993, a copy of *Annie on My Mind* was burned by religious fundamentalists in front of the Kansas City, Missouri school district office. Several months later, the district superintendent ordered the book removed from the nearby Olathe, Kansas school libraries. As a result, a group of students and their parents, in concert with the American Civil Liberties Union, filed a lawsuit to have the title reinstated. On November 29, 1995, United States District Judge Thomas Van Bebber ruled that the Olathe School District violated the First Amendment and ordered the book restored to the library shelves. For more information about this case, see "Annie on Trial: How It Feels to Be the Author of a Challenged Book," by Nancy Garden in *Voice of Youth Advocates* (June 1996), pp. 79–82, 84. *Topics*: Banned Books, Court Cases, Leadership, Lesbian Teachers, Socioeconomic Class, Student Council.

Garden, Nancy. *Good Moon Rising*. Farrar, Straus & Giroux, 1996. Hardcover $16.00 (ISBN 0374327467). Ages 12 up. *Awards*: Lambda Literary Award in the Children's/Young Adult Category, New York Public Library Book for the Teen Age, Notable Children's Trade Book in the Field of Social Studies.

A lesbian love story takes center stage as a high school in New Hampshire prepares a production of *The Crucible* by Arthur Miller. Janna Montcrief, an accomplished actor just back from a rewarding experience at summer stock, is stung when a new student, Kerry Socrides, wins the leading role in the play. Mrs. Nicholson, the drama teacher, assigns Jan a new challenge: Stage Manager and Assistant Director. Her disappointment and resentment evaporate quickly as she and Kerry work together, become close friends, and fall in love. When Mrs. Nicholson is forced by a grave illness to take a leave of absence, Jan realizes that her beloved mentor has been preparing her to step in as Director. Kent, the male lead, spurred by his growing resentment of Jan's new position and his suspicion that the two young women are lesbians, launches a campaign of harassment against them. Like Liza and Annie, who were the targets of homophobia in Garden's landmark book, *Annie on My Mind*, Jan and Kerry must decide whether or not to remain silent about their love for each other. Garden skillfully draws parallels between the hysteria of the Salem Witch trials in *The Crucible* and the homophobic attacks on the two young lesbians. She takes the reader inside the dynamics of homophobia, exposing its foundation of ignorance, intolerance, and cruelty. This is Garden at her finest: strong writing, powerful characterization, and most of all, a message of hope for young lesbian and gay readers who may be facing hostility, violence, and erasure. *Topics*: Teachers, Theatre.

Garden, Nancy. *Holly's Secret*. Farrar, Straus & Giroux, forthcoming. Hardcover $16.00 (ISBN 0374332738). Ages 10 up.

Seventh grader Holly learns the value of truth—and of real friendship—when her plan to take on a new identity and to pretend she has a mom and a dad instead of two moms backfires. *Topic*: Lesbian Mothers.

Garden, Nancy. *Lark in the Morning*. Farrar, Straus & Giroux, 1991. Hardcover $14.95 (ISBN 0374343381). Ages 12 up.

Seventeen-year-old Gillian Harrison spends a summer with her family at their vacation home in Rhode Island. She is clear about her love for her best friend, Suzanne, and their lesbianism, although she hasn't told her parents yet. She stumbles across the thieves who broke into their vacation home but they turn out to be young runaways who have fled an abusive father. When they tell her their story, especially about fourteen-year-old Lark's suicide attempt, Gillian decides she must help them, secretly. Garden has created an admirable lesbian protagonist who follows her own ethics in making important decisions. Although this book has not received the praise garnered by Garden's earlier book, *Annie on My Mind*, it has a number of notable strengths. It features a young lesbian who is perfectly comfortable with her sexual orientation, a rare occurrence in literature for young readers. The love story between Gillian and Suzanne feels authentic and they are both likeable, interesting characters. The ethical question of lying to family and friends in order to protect others is explored in a responsible way. And in a welcome turn of events, it is the not the lesbian who is running away and suicidal. Indeed, this level-headed, mature young woman is the one who saves the day! Readers searching for positive images of young lesbians will feel affirmed by this well-written book. *Topics*: Child Abuse, Runaways, Suicide (attempted).

Garden, Nancy. *The Year They Burned the Books*. Farrar, Straus & Giroux, 1999. Hardcover $17.00 (ISBN 0374386676). Ages 12 up.

In 1993, Nancy Garden's landmark book, *Annie on My Mind*, was burned by a fundamentalist minister in front of the building housing the Kansas City, Kansas school board, and school officials in several districts ordered it removed from library shelves. A group of students and parents in Olathe, Kansas successfully sued to have it returned to circulation. Her feelings about censorship in general, along with the attempts to ban *Annie on My Mind*, led Garden to write *The Year They Burned the Books*. Dedicated "To the courageous plaintiffs, librarians, and lawyers who saved ANNIE ON MY MIND from being permanently banned in the Olathe, Kansas, School District, with thanks and love!," this important novel examines issues related to censorship, prejudice, and morality. High school senior Jamie Crawford, who is in the process of coming to terms with being a lesbian, has attained her dream of being editor-in-chief of her school newspaper. But when a powerful conservative is elected to the school board, Jamie finds herself embroiled in a controversy that polarizes her small coastal New England town. The debate centers around the new health education curriculum, which includes making information about homosexuality available to students. *The Year They Burned the Books* has been praised for its fair-minded, believable, and courageous treatment of important themes; well-developed and sympathetic characters; and probing examination of a white-hot contemporary battleground. Jamie and her gay friend, Terry, are appealing, ethical people whose struggles will interest young readers and help them think through First Amendment issues. Garden notes that the events in this story are not based on events in any one specific town. *Topics*: Banned Books, Censorship, Depression, Fundamentalist Groups, Harassment, Journalism, School Newspapers, Sex Education.

Greene, Bette. *The Drowning of Stephan Jones*. Bantam Doubleday, 1991. Paper $4.99 (ISBN 0440226953). Ages 14 up.

Frank Montgomery and Stephan Jones, antique dealers, move from Boston to a small town in Arkansas, where they are subjected to harassment, vandalism, and violence. Carla Wayland, high school senior and daughter of a liberal librarian, struggles throughout the book to reconcile her attraction to her all-American boyfriend with her conviction that all people deserve to be treated with respect. She vacillates while he harasses the gay couple until, in a brutally vivid scene, he and his friends torture and drown Stephan. Finally, all her mother's lessons make sense and she is galvanized into action. But her testimony as chief witness at the trial is discredited and the murderers are found guilty of involuntary manslaughter and given probation. Frank, devastated and grief-stricken, exacts an unusual but problematic revenge. This heartbreaking, disturbing, and important book analyzes hate crimes, censorship, religious hypocrisy, peer pressure, and flaws in the judicial system. Greene's powerful book is undermined by uneven writing and phrases like "to make any Apache wince with envy" (p. 8) and "blacker than a witch's heart" (p. 129). Frank and Stephan are unbelievably naive and Carla is a weak sycophant. Nevertheless, the book traces Carla's moral reawakening, even though it is too little, too late. Most important, the book issues a loud and clear wake-up call to ethical people everywhere. Chilling and thought provoking, it will compel young people and adults to scrutinize their values and re-examine the true meaning of freedom and justice for all. *Topics*: Censorship, Fundamentalist Religions, Hate Crimes, Judicial System, Murder, Peer Pressure.

Guy, Rosa. *Ruby*. Dell, 1991. Paper $3.99 (ISBN 0440211301). Ages 14 up. Out of Print.

First published in 1976, *Ruby* is the poignant story of how Ruby Cathy and Daphne Duprey fall in love during their senior year of high school. When the novel opens, Ruby is desperately lonely. Her mother, who sustained her when the family first arrived in Harlem from the West Indies, has been dead for a year. Her father is emotionally and physically abusive, her sister has buried herself in books, and her classmates reject her because of her kindness to a racist, disabled teacher. Ruby initiates a friendship with Daphne, a Black Nationalist classmate who describes herself as "cool, calm, collected, poised, sophisticated, cultured, and refined" (p. 61). In spite of their differences, they embark on a passionate relationship that ebbs and flows for most of the school year. When Daphne ends the relationship, Ruby is devastated and tries to commit suicide. The book ends with Ruby thinking about an old boyfriend. *Ruby* has been praised for its finely drawn, complex characters; poetic, stylized language; and emotional honesty. However, the ableism and looksism in the portrayal of the teacher are inexcusable, even for a book that was written in the early 1970s. A teacher who has a disability is no more or less likely to be a bigot than one who is able-bodied and physically attractive in the traditional sense. This book has been criticized because the ending implies that lesbianism is just a phase. Another concern is that the relationship between Daphne and Ruby is so unequal. Although Daphne has her tender moments, she often belittles her lover. Nevertheless, the connection between the two young women is very strong. "She could never again love so completely" (p. 138). *Ruby* is historically important because it was one of the first young adult novels to deal with lesbianism. *Topics*: Acculturation, Black Nationalism, Child Abuse, Harlem, Immigrants, Socioeconomic Class, Suicide (attempted), Teachers, West Indies.

Hamilton, R. J. *Who Framed Lorenzo Garcia?* Alyson Publications, 1995. Paper $5.95 (ISBN 1555836089). Ages 11 up.

Dedicated to "gay kids everywhere, whose humanity, vulnerability, and courage make them the real-life Pride Pack," this mystery stars sixteen-year-old Ramón Francisco Angel Torres, whose father beat him up and kicked him out of the house when Ramón told him he was gay. After several years of living on the streets and being bounced from one foster home to another, Ramón has finally found a safe haven with gay police sergeant Lorenzo Garcia, who plans to adopt him. When Officer Garcia is framed for dealing drugs, Ramón and his friends from the Gay and Lesbian Community Center form the Pride Pack and catch the real crooks. His name cleared, Lorenzo adopts Ramón. *Who Framed Lorenzo Garcia?* is filled with suspense and lively action, and the characters are from diverse cultures. Ramón and Lorenzo are a welcome addition to young adult literature which suffers from a scarcity of gay Latino characters. The members of the Pride Pack work together well, bravely tackling difficult situations. This title reassures young gay people who have been disowned by their parents that there are safe, loving places for them. *Topics*: Adoption, Community Centers, Disownment, Family Violence, Foster Homes, Homelessness, Mexican Americans, Mystery, Police, Puerto Ricans.

Hines, Sue. *Out of the Shadows*. Random House (Australia), 1998. Paper $14.95 (ISBN 0091837650). Ages 14 up. *Award*: Nominated for The Children's Book Council of Australia Children's Book of the Year Award.

"Sometimes I think it's the way you handle the absolute crap in your life that shows the real you, and yet that's the one you always try to hide" (p. 20). In this first novel by Australian author Sue Hines, two teenagers struggle to maintain their friendship while hiding secrets they fear will destroy their connection. Rowanna Preston, whose mother was recently killed by a drunken driver, is living with Deb, her mother's lover. Jodie Waters, a new student, is not only in the closet about her sexual identity but also hiding her attraction to Ro. *Out of the Shadows* has been praised for its strong characterization, well-sustained plot, and compelling tensions. By alternating the voices of Ro and Jodie in reflective narratives, Hines provides insights into both characters. She demonstrates clearly the damage a homophobic society wreaks on young people. When Ro first discovers that her mother and Deb are lovers, she reacts with such extreme anger and hatred that she not only jeopardizes her relationship with them but ends up living on the streets. Starving and sick, she returns home only in time to apologize before her mother dies in the accident. The unrelenting guilt and anguish she experiences finally begin to dissipate when she writes her story in a special hand-made journal crafted by Deb and shares it with Jodie. Some readers will wonder why Deb and Sara, two wise and courageous lesbians, didn't come out to their daughter and teach her how to cope with a homophobic society. After her lover dies, Deb lovingly cares for Ro while living with an enormous loss she cannot grieve openly. In one of the most hopeful scenes in the book, Jodie sees two women holding hands in public. She has long imagined what a world would be like in which all kinds of love are accepted, and in this moment, she knows there is a place for her. *Out of the Shadows* is an engaging book about the ripple effect of discrimination, "so that it isn't just the minority group that suffers, but anyone close to them . . . with so much unnecessary pain and suffering" (p. 167). However, it is marred by oppressive language: *moron*, *old hag*, *tank-arse*, *bitch*. *Topics*: Australian Literature, Death, Lesbian Mothers.

Homes, A. M. *Jack*. Vintage, 1989. Paper $10.00 (ISBN 0679732217). Ages 12 up.

Stuck somewhere between being a child and an adult, Jack struggles to understand his father's sexual identity. With generous doses of irreverence and exaggeration, this engaging book traces several years in the life of a teenager who is coping with his parent's divorce and his father's homosexuality, in addition to all the usual challenges young adults face. When his father takes him out in a rowboat on Lake Watchmayoyo and tells him he is gay, Jack feels that nothing will ever be the same again. He goes through the usual stages of trying to prove his own heterosexuality by dating, going to the library to research homosexuality, and worrying about AIDS, transvestism, and perversion. His best friend, Max, tells everyone at school and Jack's nickname becomes "fag baby." Then Jack meets Maggie, whose father is also gay, and things start to improve. When Max's "perfect" family crumbles after his father batters his mother, Jack is forced to re-evaluate long-held ideas. As he thinks about Max's violent father, "the Cub-Scout leader, the baseball fan, the complete heterosexual" (p. 154), he reaches a new understanding of his own father. This book has been praised for its humor, panache, and charm. Critics have described the protagonist as a doggedly funny, endearing, and attractive human being. Each of the gay characters is portrayed as an individual, and Jack's father is a multidimensional person who is trying to do his best to be a good parent. The book is marred by repeated references to cripples and retards and an oppressive scene at Frontier Town, including the use of the offensive term "squaw." It ends with Jack hoping to learn from the mistakes of others and planning to do something different with his life. *Topics*: Divorce, Family Violence, Gay Fathers.

Jenkins, A. M. *Breaking Boxes*. Delacorte Press, 1997. Hardcover $14.95 (ISBN 0385325134). Ages 14 up. *Award*: Delacorte Press Prize for a First Young Adult Novel.

Charlie Calmont's father abandoned the family when he was born and his mother drank herself to death. His best friend recently moved away, and at sixteen he is a loner, having learned early how to "shut off wishing." The one constant in Charlie's life is his gay older brother, Trent, who has taken care of him most of his life. In this disquieting novel of self-discovery, Charlie begins to break out of the boxes he has built around his emotions. Early in his sophomore year he spends four days in detention after a fight when one of the rich kids from the "in crowd" taunts him about his shoes. This is the beginning of an unlikely friendship with the popular Brandon Chase, who turns out to be less phony and superficial than Charlie thought. Most of the book is about their friendship. They actually have a few serious conversations while playing one-on-one hockey in a parking lot, riding around in Brandon's fancy car, and hanging out at Charlie's apartment. When Charlie tells Brandon that Trent is gay, Brandon reacts with horror and disgust and tells the other kids at school. Devastated by Brandon's betrayal and harassed by classmates, Charlie reaches a breaking point. When Trent tries to talk with him, he lashes out, calling his brother a pervert. All these distressing events collide and Charlie finally admits to himself that he does care, perhaps too much. This book has been praised as a finely crafted teen novel with barbed, conversational, first-person narration. The ending leaves hope that Charlie will overcome his callous treatment of women and learn how to have respectful, meaningful relationships in the future. Trent is an admirable character who is working his way through college while raising his kid brother. He has an easygoing personality and does his best to be supportive to his troubled sibling. Profanity, explicit language, objectification of women. *Topics*: Alcoholism, Child Abuse, Socioeconomic Class.

Kerr, M. E. *Deliver Us from Evie*. HarperCollins, 1994. Hardcover $15.00 (ISBN 0060244755); Paper $4.95 (ISBN 0064471284). Ages 12 up. *Awards*: ALA Best Books for Young Adults, *Booklist* Editors' Choice, ALA Recommended Books for Reluctant YA Readers, *Horn Book* Fanfare Honor List, *School Library Journal's* Best Books; Michigan Library Association Best Book Honor Award.

Among the most inspiring lesbian characters in young adult fiction is eighteen-year-old Evie Burrman, who lives with her family on a farm in Missouri. Strong and handsome, with short, slicked-back hair and dressed in jeans and boots, Evie is a mainstay on the farm, repairing machinery and working in the fields. Apologizing to no one, Evie has remained true to herself through eighteen years of pressure from family, church, and community. Her mother tries to force femininity and heterosexuality on Evie, urging her to wear dresses and date a local boy. Evie's brother, Parr, who narrates the story, concludes that trying to change Evie is "like trying to change the direction of the wind" (p. 4). Evie's father accepts her appearance until the day she falls in love with Patsy, the daughter of the town banker, who holds the loan on the Burrman farm. Then he wants to kick her out of the house but he depends on her too much to keep the farm going. In spite of increasing pressure from their parents, Evie and Patsy develop a strong relationship and eventually escape the confines of their narrow-minded community and move away to New York City. Kerr does a beautiful job of juxtaposing Evie's and Patsy's stable relationship with those of her brothers, who both become in involved in shallow, albeit socially sanctioned relationships. The body of young adult literature is strengthened by the presence of Evie, one of the few young lesbians who knows and accepts who she is. She is a likeable, multidimensional character who writes poetry, enjoys books, repairs tractors, and cracks everybody up with her jokes. This fast-paced, well-plotted story examines lesbophobia against a backdrop of farm life, natural disasters, and economic realities. *Topics*: Appearance, Farm Life, Floods, Religious Intolerance, Sibling Issues, Socioeconomic Class.

Kerr, M. E. *"Hello," I Lied*. HarperCollins, 1997. Hardcover $15.95 (ISBN 0060275294); Paper $4.50 (ISBN 0064471284). Ages 14 up.

Just when seventeen-year-old Lang Penner is trying to be more open about his homosexuality, he experiences unexpected feelings for a young woman and becomes more confused than ever. He is spending his seventeenth summer on Long Island, where his mother is cooking for a retired rock icon. Separated from his lover, Alex, Lang tries to sort out his feelings. He hates the homophobic treatment he and Alex are subjected to wherever they go, whether it is to a family gathering or a restaurant for dinner. As he tries to find the right time to come out to his friends, he becomes increasingly aware of his attraction to Huguette. He is also aware of the difference in people's reactions to him when he is with Huguette as opposed to when he is with Alex. As the title implies, this is a book about the masquerading, artifice, and subterfuge that gay people sometimes internalize in a homophobic society. As usual, Kerr is sharp, fast-paced, and thought-provoking. *Topics*: Bisexuality, Internalized Homophobia, Music, Socioeconomic Class.

Kerr, M. E. *Night Kites*. Harper and Row, 1986. Paper $4.95 (ISBN 0064470350). Ages 14 up. *Awards*: ALA Best of the Best Books, ALA Best Books for Young Adults, *Booklist* Best of the 80's, ALA Recommended Books for Reluctant YA Readers, California Young Reader Award, Cited for Margaret A. Edwards Award.

Night Kites, the first young adult novel about AIDS, was written in 1985 before there was much information available about the disease. Interestingly, it is still one of the best books available. Seventeen-year-old Erick Rudd tells the story of how his family reacts when they find out about his older brother Pete's homosexuality and debilitating illness at the same time. Individually and as a family, they struggle to find ways to understand and support Pete during what may be his last months. For Erick, Pete will always be a night kite, an adventurer, not afraid to be different, to go out into the world alone. While teaching French and English at a private school in New York City, Pete writes science fiction. The book ends with Pete reading from one of his stories to Erick, a story about a planet where there are no scents except in the year before death. Just when Erick needs support the most, he betrays his best friend, dumps his girlfriend for a new relationship with the worldly Nicki, and suffers the loss of Oscar Wilde, his canine friend. Later on, when he also loses Nicki after she finds out about Pete's illness, Erick reaches an understanding of his brother's courage and convictions. *Night Kites* has been praised for its sympathetic, believable characters and sensitive treatment of a serious social issue. *Topics*: AIDS, Authorship, Death and Dying, Internalized Homophobia, Music, Socioeconomic Class.

Ketchum, Liza. *Blue Coyote*. Simon & Schuster, 1997. Hardcover $16.00 (ISBN 0689807902). Ages 13 up.

In this engrossing sequel to *Twelve Days in August*, which the author wrote under the name Liza Ketchum Murrow, seventeen-year-old Alex Beekman searches for his lost friend, Tito Perone, and finally accepts his own sexual identity. *Blue Coyote* opens with Alex still in Vermont, suffering from isolation and harassment because of his differences. He survives the humiliation and threats of physical violence by dreaming of going back to California, finding Tito, moving with him to Hawaii, and surfing the Pipeline. Alex finally discovers the truth behind Tito's disappearance, and with it, the truths they have both been hiding from themselves. During the year that Alex was in Vermont, Tito came out of the closet, and as a result, his father savagely slashed him with a knife, broke his leg, kicked him out of the house, and disowned him. At first Alex is in denial, but a forest fire that threatens Tito's life galvanizes him into action and he finally acknowledges his feelings. Ketchum does an excellent job of portraying the solid, heavy closet Alex had constructed to hide his sexual identity from himself. Equally powerful is the way she writes about the crumbling of that closet as Alex accepts the fact that he is gay and has always been gay. He realizes that Tito and he fell in love six years ago in sixth grade. The intensity of his emotions is magnified by the heartbreak of finding Tito too late because Tito is now in another relationship. Once Alex comes out to himself, he courageously comes out to his twin sister, friends, and parents. This is an important book that tells the truth about the violence and threat of violence that gay and lesbian people suffer, sometimes from their own relatives. *Topics*: Art, Disownment, Family Violence, Hate Crimes, Latinos, Tattoos, Surfing.

Kincaid, Jamaica. *Annie John*. NAL/Dutton, 1986. Paper $6.95 (ISBN 0452260167); Farrar, Straus & Giroux, 1997. Paper $10.00 (ISBN 0614272769). Ages 14 up. *Award: Library Journal*'s Best Book Award.

Annie John is a powerful autobiographical novel about a girl growing up in Antigua in the 1950s. Praised as magical, gripping, vibrant, and exquisite, this book beautifully captures the anguish a young girl experiences when she separates from a mother who insists she follow the straight and narrow path society dictates. Much has been written about this extraordinary book but interestingly, most critics have ignored or trivialized Annie's relationship with her classmate Gweneth Joseph, instead focusing on the mother/daughter split. But the connection between Annie and Gwen is a significant one, well worth examining and celebrating. When Annie and Gwen fall in love, they are inseparable, "joined at the shoulder, hip, and ankle, not to mention heart" (p. 48). As Annie meets Gwen each morning to walk to school arm in arm, her heart beats fast and she feels as if she will "explode with happiness" (p. 47). "Sometimes when she spoke to me, so overcome with feeling would I be that I was no longer able to hear what she said" (p. 51). "Since in the world we occupied and hoped forever to occupy boys were banished," (p. 50) Annie and Gwen plan to live together when they grow up. Indeed, Annie has already picked out a gray house with many rooms. Meanwhile, the chasm between Annie and her mother is widening each day. Finally, when she is seventeen, Annie leaves the island, determined to live her own life. She plans to never return to the island and "never to marry at all" (p. 132). Annie is an admirable protagonist, brilliant, endearing, and strong-willed. After a close, loving relationship with her mother as a child, adolescence takes her into open rebellions and secret discoveries. She lies, plays marbles and volleyball, makes farting noises when she is forced to curtsy, and eats the plums on her teacher's piano. Annie is appalled when Gwen suggests she marry Gwen's brother and soon the Little Lovebirds, as their friends call them, go their separate ways. *Annie John* is a memorable book about a young woman whose liveliness of spirit and determination to lead an independent existence will intrigue and inspire. *Topics*: Antigua, Mother/Daughter Relationship, West Indies.

Klein, Norma. *Now That I Know*. Bantam, 1988. Hardcover $13.95 (ISBN 0553054724). Ages 12 up.

Nina Calder, thirteen-year-old editor of the school newspaper, is used to being a joint custody kid who spends part of the week with each parent. But when her father tells her that he is gay and that his lover, Greg, is moving in with him, she decides to stay at her mother's full-time while she sorts through her feelings. She grapples with the fear that she will be displaced in her father's affections, discomfort with gayness, and resentment that her father didn't talk to her first before inviting Greg to move in. Nina's reconciliation with her father is gradual and credible, and the book ends with her returning to the joint custody arrangement. *Now That You Know* has been praised for its light touch to what could be a heavy topic, sharp observations of relationships, and demonstration that homophobia is something that can be overcome with thoughtful reflection. The two gay characters, Duncan and Greg, are the only stable couple in the book. Duncan, an editor of a medical newsletter, is a caring father whose fear of losing his daughter's love and respect keeps him from coming out to her until the last minute before his lover moves in. Greg, a former teacher, runs a gourmet health food store in Upper West Side Manhattan, where the story takes place. The healthy relationship between Duncan and Greg contrasts with the dysfunctional heterosexual relationships depicted in the story. *Topics*: Divorce, Father/Daughter Relationship, Gay Fathers, Joint Custody, Journalism.

Koertge, Ron. *The Arizona Kid*. Avon Books, 1989. Paper $3.99 (ISBN 0380707764). Ages 12 up. *Award*: ALA Best Book for Young Adults.

After spending the summer in Arizona with his gay Uncle Wes, Billy, sixteen-year-old greenhorn and all-around nice guy, finds that he's not only learned a lot about gay issues, horses, and love, but he's gained a better understanding of himself. He finds romance with a spirited horse rider named Cara Mae, re-evaluates his dream of becoming a veterinarian, and begins to accept the fact that he is short. This book has been praised for its believable characterizations, fast pace, hysterically funny situations, and lighthearted treatment of serious themes. Billy's self-deprecatory humor, open-mindedness about differences, and desire to be a supportive romantic partner for Cara Mae have endeared him to many readers. The portrayal of Uncle Wes is essentially positive: he is a warm person who talks openly with his nephew about feelings, relationships, problems, and safe sex. As an AIDS activist, Wes speaks, writes, hosts fundraisers, and organizes hotlines and healing services. He is a complex person with strengths, faults, fears, and a great sense of humor. However, his house is a bit too neat, with an overabundance of mirrors, and he drinks too much when he gets depressed. A major concern with the book is the cavalier way it deals with Native American culture. Wes has obviously made a huge profit from his business selling Native blankets, rugs, jewelry, and baskets. When Billy first walks into his elegant house, he picks up a statue with an engorged penis that he later concludes must be a fertility symbol. Another concern with the book is the mostly unacknowledged exploitation of the racehorses. Although Billy goes back home to Missouri with an increased awareness about some issues, he has learned little about respect for indigenous cultures or the ethical treatment of animals. Explicit sex and strong language. *Topics*: AIDS, Appearance, Death, Drugs (Marijuana), Gambling, Horseracing, Horses.

Larson, Rodger. *What I Know Now*. Henry Holt, 1997. Hardcover $15.95 (ISBN 0805048693). Ages 11 up.

It is the summer of 1957 in Stockton, California, when Dave Ryan turns fourteen and falls in love with a man named Gene Tole, although he doesn't recognize it as love at the time. This well-crafted novel opens with Dave's mother leaving her abusive and adulterous husband and settling into her childhood home. Dave spends the summer helping Gene, a landscaper designer, build a garden around the neglected old place. As the two work together, Dave discovers not only the fascinating world of plants but learns a great deal about love and life. This is a multilayered portrayal of self-discovery, healing, and growth. Dave is introspective and sincere. Gene is a thoughtful mentor: gentle, empathetic, and willing to listen. One of the most touching scenes takes place after Dave's older brother joins the Marines to escape his violent father. Gene, along with Dave and his mother, plants a tree to commemorate this important life passage. Gene muses, "Planting a tree seems to me to be the most optimistic thing in the world we can do" (p. 197). Evocative passages celebrate the California countryside and tenderly depict a boy's dawning sexuality. At the end of the book, Dave is still trying to sort out his feelings for Gene. "I'd figure love out and I'd live by the kind of love that was right for me" (p. 262). *Topics*: California, Divorce, Domestic Violence, Landscaping.

Maguire, Gregory. *Oasis*. Houghton Mifflin, 1996. Hardcover $14.95 (ISBN 0395670195); Disney, 1998. Paper $4.95 (ISBN 0786812931). Ages 11–14.

When thirteen-year-old Mohandas "Hand" Gandhi Gunther finds his pacifist father dead of a heart attack on the floor of their rundown motel in Massachusetts, he searches for a way to cope with his grief. Abandoned by his mother three years earlier, Hand fiercely resents her when she moves back and takes over the family and the motel. Maguire handles the teen's feelings of shock, denial, guilt, and anger with insight and sensitivity. *Oasis* has been praised for its multilayered, beautifully written story, well-defined characters, and sharp, frank narration. A subplot about Hand's Uncle Wolfgang is of interest to readers searching for gay and lesbian characters in young adult literature. Wolfgang, who is dying of AIDS, spends his last months at the Oasis Motel with Hand and his mother. Wolfgang recently suffered the loss of his lover, Bernard, "whom he loved dearly" (p. 138). As Wolfgang and Hand discuss death, grieving, and Emily Dickinson's poetry, the young teenager moves toward a more compassionate sensibility. Taking his uncle's advice ("There's not enough time for all the forgiveness that's needed in life" [p. 162]), Hand makes peace with his mother. *Topics*: AIDS, Dying and Death, Gay Uncles, Mother-Son Relationship.

McClain, Ellen Jaffe. *No Big Deal.* Penguin, 1994. Paper $4.99 (ISBN 0140380469). Ages 11 up.

Thirteen-year-old Janice Green's favorite teacher is Mr. Padovano, whose innovative teaching strategies breathe life into the social studies curriculum at West River Junior High in a small town in New York. When rumors surface that Mr. Padovano is gay, Janice supports him even when it means confronting her own mother. As a large, intelligent, divergent thinker, Janice has learned how to deal with closed-minded people. After an explosive community meeting, petitions are circulated in support of Mr. Padovano and the controversy wanes. Fast-paced and humorous, this well-written book debunks many commonly held myths and stereotypes about gay people. Mr. Padovano is an admirable character who not only brings out the best in his students but shows great restraint while waiting to find out if he is going to be fired. Later he writes an article about the bigotry he experienced and how it put a chill on his interactions with his students. The characterization of the narrator is also praiseworthy: Janice does not give in to ridicule, peer pressure, or admonishments from her mother. However, the portrayal of Kevin, the class bully and one of the most hostile homophobes in the book, is puzzling. His beloved brother is dying of AIDS and supposedly this is what drives him to participate in the attack on Mr. Padovano with so much venom. *No Big Deal* is a thought-provoking book that takes an unflinching stance against homophobia. The way it deals with looksism is good but not excellent: Janice and Kevin, the two fat characters, both participate in fat oppressive name-calling. But the most disappointing flaws in an otherwise sensitive book are two glaring examples of ageism and the use of the derogatory term "greaser." *Topics*: AIDS, Appearance, Fat Oppression, Gay Teachers, Looksism.

Mullins, Hilary. *The Cat Came Back.* Naiad Press, 1993. Paper $9.95 (ISBN 156280040X). Ages 14 up. *Award*: ALA Quick Picks: Recommended Title for Reluctant Young Adult Readers.

During her last five months at a posh prep school, seventeen-year-old Stephanie (Stevie) Roughgarden falls in love with her classmate, Andrea Snyder, and all the fragile pieces of her life gradually start falling into place. Fighting off depression, Stevie struggles to free herself from a three-year sexually exploitative relationship with a male teacher at her school and from childhood memories of sexual abuse by her uncle. Anguished, suffering from self-hatred, and grieving the loss of her beloved feline friend, she finds solace in the pages of her journal. Encouraged by her writing teacher, Stevie writes poetry, stories, and a play which help her sort through her confusion, denial, and despair. But it is when she reads *Rubyfruit Jungle* by Rita Mae Brown that she begins to understand and accept herself. Mullins' first novel beautifully demonstrates the power of books and of writing to touch the lives and hearts of young readers and writers. Vividly written, this poignant book explores a number of important, complex issues. Although the book has been criticized because the perpetrator is not punished, the reality is that in 1980 there *was* a conspiracy of silence surrounding sexual abuse of students by teachers. Hopefully that has changed.*Topics*: Authorship, Cats, Family Rape, Sexual Abuse, Socioeconomic Class, Sports, Teachers.

Murrow, Liza Ketchum. *Twelve Days in August*. Holiday House, 1993. Hardcover $15.95 (ISBN 0823410129); Avon, 1995. Paper $3.99 (ISBN 0380723530). Ages 12 up. *Awards*: ALA Quick Picks: Recommended Title for Reluctant Young Adult Readers, New York Public Library Book for the Teen Age.

In twelve short days, sixteen-year-old Todd O'Connor gains a better understanding of himself, relationships, gay people, and bigotry. The changes begin when twins Alex and Rita Beekman move to Todd's small Vermont town just as soccer practice begins. As the players watch Alex move like a dancer on the field, they know that he is a sure bet for the starting lineup in the fall. Both Todd and Randy Tovitch, the star of last year's squad, fear that Alex is a rival for their positions. When Randy wages a homophobic campaign to get Alex to quit, most of the players participate by sabotaging his plays. Randy hurls insults at anyone who hesitates, using age-old tactics to intimidate and control the other players. Although several players ignore Randy, the protagonist's fence-sitting makes him a target of homophobic remarks. Finally, when Todd learns that his beloved Uncle Gordo is gay, he finds the compassion to dismantle his prejudices and take a position against bigotry. *Twelve Days in August* has been praised for its careful scrutiny of human nature; engaging, high-caliber writing; and terrific pacing. It is successful in spite of the less-than-admirable protagonist who objectifies women, gives in to his anger, and disrespects his younger sister. Murrow makes the important connection between racism and homophobia when Craig, the only African American in the book, tells Todd, "Calling Alex a fag might be like calling me nigger. It doesn't matter which insult you use, it's still hate" (p. 103). Uncle Gordo is portrayed as a positive, supportive person who genuinely cares about his nephew and niece. The fact that Todd's father required his brother and wife to keep Gordo's sexual identity a secret clearly creates problems for everyone. Although Alex's sexual identity is unconfirmed, his relationship with his friend back in Los Angeles is very close and tender. In the sequel, *Blue Coyote* (written under the name Liza Ketchum), Alex realizes that he is, indeed, gay. *Topics*: Gay Uncles, Soccer.

Nelson, Theresa. *Earthshine*. Orchard Books, 1994. Hardcover $17.00 (ISBN 0531087174). Ages 11 up. *Awards*: Best Books for Young Adults, Notable Books for Children, Quick Picks.

Earthshine is one of the most sensitive books about AIDS that has been written for young adults. Twelve-year-old Margery (Slim) McGranahan narrates this poignant story of her last months with her beloved father, Mack, who is dying of AIDS. They live in the Hollywood Hills with Mack's lover and devoted companion, Larry, who manages the household. At a support group for children who are living with Persons with AIDS or PWAs, Slim meets Isaiah, whose father died of the disease and whose pregnant mother is infected with the virus. Isaiah's faith in miracle cures leads them all on a quest to the Hungry Valley deep in the mountains north of Los Angeles in search of the Water of Life. Although the mishap-plagued trip does not produce the results they had hoped for, the transcendent beauty of the earthshine does give them strength to face the difficult times ahead. Nelson's characters, rich in individuality, draw the reader into the story. Slim is an admirable young woman who packed up her bags one day in the middle of sixth grade and left her mother and latest stepfather to live with her father. Mack, an actor and mischievous extrovert, is an irresistible force who brings life into a room just by entering it. The author touches on the homophobia that surrounds AIDS when a fundraising event Slim's support group has organized is attacked by bigots. This is a sad story but it includes healthy doses of humor, and the heart breaking times are interspersed with lighter moments. One of its most important contributions to literature is the way it portrays the love and tenderness among the three members of the McGranahan household. *Topics*: AIDS, Dying and Death, Father/Daughter Relationship, Gay Fathers.

Revoyr, Nina. *The Necessary Hunger*. Simon & Schuster, 1997. Hardcover $22.50 (ISBN 0684832348); St. Martin's Press, 1998. $13.95 (ISBN 0312181426). Ages 16 up.

In this extraordinary debut novel, two young lesbians grapple with the pressures of competitive high school basketball, the ambiguities of their intense relationship, and the uncertainties of the future. Nancy Takahiro, a Japanese-American basketball star, reminisces about her senior year of high school in South Central Los Angeles in 1986, when she fell in love with Raina Webber, an African-American All-State shooting guard. *The Necessary Hunger* has been praised for its subtle exploration of the mysteries of the human heart; engaging subplots; and sensitive handling of contemporary issues of race, socioeconomic class, and sexuality. Revoyr's strong portrayal of young lesbians who are comfortable with their sexual identity is refreshing in a genre where many are still struggling to speak love's name. Nancy, Raina, and their friends embraced their lesbianism several years earlier and now, as "members of the family," they support and nurture each other. The title refers not only to their degree of commitment to basketball, but the kind of hunger Nancy feels for Raina. Her unrequited passion is portrayed with all the yearning, sweetness, and complexity of first love. "It wasn't simply that I loved Raina; it was that she filled my life, she flowed through my veins, she splashed out into every corner of my body" (p. 279). Tender passages about "how it feels to hold the woman you love" (p. 340), "feeling the warmth of her presence spread through my body like wine" (p. 312) honor the beauty and magnitude of lesbian love. Nina Revoyr is a gifted and original new voice, and her remarkable first book is one of the best in its field. Strong language. *Topics*: African Americans, Basketball, College Recruiting, Coaches, Interracial Relationships, Japanese Americans, Los Angeles, Parenting, Socioeconomic Class, Unrequited Love.

Salat, Cristina. *Living in Secret.* Bantam, 1993; Marcus, 1999. Paper $7.95 (ISBN 0916020029). Ages 10 up.

When Amelia Monet's parents got a divorce, she wanted to live with her mother, but a homophobic judge awarded her father custody. Finally, after years of living apart, Amelia, her mother, and her mother's lover, Janey, run away and start a new life. Eleven-year-old Amelia tells the story of how she moved from New York to San Francisco, changed her name, frosted her hair, and met a number of unexpected challenges. After nine months, she is heartbroken when her father finds her and, under threat of prosecution, forces her to return with him to Long Island. Undefeated, Amelia contacts her mother and they consider reopening the custody question in court. *Living in Secret* has been praised for its candid first-person narration; courageous, thought-provoking examination of lesbian custody issues; and realistic depiction of the ups and downs of Amelia's new life. The relationship between Amelia's mother and Janey is affectionate, committed, and mature. They both choose to give up their comfortable lives and jobs to move across country so that Amelia can live with them. Their strength of character enables them to live with hardships and secrecy so that they can establish a supportive home for the child they love. Amelia's mother treats her with respect, unlike her father, who ignores her wishes and even though he claims to care about her, chooses to spend most of his time away from home.

Living in Secret makes the point that it is personal integrity and not sexual identity that determines whether or not individuals will be good parents. This engaging book addresses important social issues including racism, children's legal rights, family values, civil disobedience, and lesbian custody cases. *Topics*: Custody Cases, Lesbian Mothers, San Francisco.

Scoppettone, Sandra. *Happy Endings Are All Alike*. Harper and Row, 1978; Dell, 1979; Alyson Publications, 1991. Paper $6.95 (ISBN 155583177X). Ages 12 up. *Awards*: ALA Best Book for Young Adults.

Eighteen-year-old Jaret Tyler feels very happy and clear about her lesbian relationship with Peggy Danziger, but she knows that there are plenty of people in this world who harbor prejudice toward people like them. Even though Jaret and Peggy are comfortable about their love for each other, society (represented by various relatives, "friends," and community members) constantly tries to undermine their relationship. One day a friend of Jaret's brother sees Jaret and Peggy in the woods together. Realizing he knows a secret he can use for his own brutal purposes, he savagely rapes and beats Jaret, assuming she won't report the crime in order to protect her "secret." The resulting "scandal" puts pressure on Jaret's and Peggy's relationship. But Jaret is very sure and strong about who she is. In this poignant love story, Scoppettone explores an array of prejudices and fears about lesbianism, about rape, and about women. Many of the "issues" about a lesbian relationship are woven skillfully into the story so that each page increases the awareness of the reader. Although most of the characterizations are excellent, the way in which Peggy's sister, Claire, is portrayed diminishes the story. Authors should re-examine their characterizations of so-called unattractive people (by society's standards) and treat them with more dignity and complexity. Another concern is with the depiction of the rapist as disturbed. Research shows that most rapes are committed by ordinary men. In spite of these reservations, I recommend this well-written book for the positive way it deals with lesbianism and for the way it exposes the brutality that often accompanies bigotry. Although the book has been criticized because of this violence, the reality is that in a homophobic society, lesbians and gay men are vulnerable to hate crimes. To her credit, Scoppettone has shown how one young lesbian survived and fought back. *Topics*: Hate Crimes, Rape.

Scoppettone, Sandra. *Trying Hard to Hear You*. Harper and Row, 1974; Alyson Publications, 1991, 1996. Paper $6.95 (ISBN 1555831966). Ages 12 up. *Award*: ALA Best Book for Young Adults.

Camilla, the sixteen-year-old narrator, tells of a critical summer in the lives of her friends when her close-knit summer theatre group learns that two of its male members are gay. This discovery leads to heartbreak and terror, a time that reveals the group in all its strengths and weaknesses. Scoppettone examines the underlying prejudice that some teenagers harbor toward lesbians and gays. She also deals with relationships between the African-American and white communities and between Camilla and those around her. Teenage as well as adult characters are well developed, and the plot threads are skillfully interwoven. Camilla gradually educates herself and comes to a more enlightened view of homosexuality. Scoppettone based this book on her experience during the summer of 1973, when she directed a production of "Anything Goes" with about sixty teenagers. The book was criticized because of the death of one of the gay characters, a disturbing trend in the genre at the time when this book was published. Scoppettone explained that her intention was to show that he died not because he was gay, but because he was trying to be something he wasn't (he had gone on a date with a young woman). The negative portrayal of one of the characters who is fat and racist portrayals of African-American women as not being able to figure out that they are being conned by a character who predicts the gender of their unborn children mar what is otherwise a good book. *Topics*: Death, Theatre.

Shannon, George. *Unlived Affections*. HarperCollins, 1989. Hardcover $12.95 (ISBN 0060253045); Alyson Publications, 1995. Paper $8.95 (ISBN 1555832997). Ages 12 up.

When eighteen-year-old Willie Ramsey finds a box of old letters written by the father he thought was dead, he discovers his hidden family history. This painfully honest novel opens shortly after Willie's grandmother died, leaving him with a house full of secrets. As he pores over the letters his father wrote his now-deceased mother, he finds out that his father was gay. In his first novel, Shannon explores how two young men of different generations struggle to understand themselves and the deceptions society forced upon them. As Bill Ramsey's words leap from the page, a picture of a compassionate, sensitive person emerges. His realization that he is gay is built slowly and credibly, until with deep emotion he composes the words to his wife, "I love you . . . like a friend, like my best friend, but not like a lover. I love men" (p. 67). During the hours Willie spends reading the letters, he experiences all the emotions he was denied during his early years. By the last letter, he begins to feel a kinship with the father he never knew. *Unlived Affections* is an intriguing, uncompromising novel about the secrets, lies, and silences that often accompany homophobia and the damage they can do to everyone involved. *Topics*: Abandonment, Death, Gay Fathers, Grandmothers, Swimming, Woodworking.

Sinclair, April. *Ain't Gonna Be the Same Fool Twice*. African American Images, 1996. Hardcover $19.95 (ISBN 0614223555); Avon Books, 1997. Paper $12.00 (ISBN 0380727943). Ages 16 up.

April Sinclair introduced Jean "Stevie" Stevenson in her widely acclaimed debut novel, *Coffee Will Make You Black*. Now she follows Stevie through her early twenties during her search for her sexual identity in the San Francisco Bay Area. The first in her family to get a college degree, Stevie goes to San Francisco with two friends on a post-graduation trip and decides to stay. At a women's dance she meets Traci, who invites her to sublet a room in her house and introduces her to lesbian culture. Soon they become lovers and Stevie has her first orgasm, attends her first potluck, and eats her first tofu burger. The year is 1975—a time of personal growth, women-only space, and analysis of racism, sexism, classism, and the patriarchy. After months of searching for a job, Stevie reluctantly applies for food stamps. When her relationship with Traci goes sour, Stevie moves in with a gay man and has a one-night stand with his blatantly heterosexual brother. She then has a short relationship with Cythnia, a white bisexual. The book ends with Stevie realizing that for her, sexuality is a journey and that she is "still on the road." Sinclair's appealing protagonist, crackling dialogue, and hilarious scenes make this a captivating book. Explicit sex and strong language. *Topics*: African-American Literature, Bisexuality, Interracial Relationships, Drugs, Lesbian Culture.

Sinclair, April. *Coffee Will Make You Black*. Avon Books, 1994. Paper $12.00 (ISBN 0380724596). Ages 14 up. *Awards*: ALA Book of the Year, Carl Sandburg Award in Fiction from the Friends of the Chicago Public Library.

April Sinclair's debut novel has been described as adventurous, brilliant, bold, earthy, heartwarming, feisty, and humorous. Like Sinclair, protagonist Jean "Stevie" Stevenson is an African American who grew up in a working class neighborhood in Chicago in the 1960s. Stevie's mother is a bank teller, her father is a janitor, and her grandmother owns a popular South Side chicken stand, and all are striving to provide a loving home for their children. Stevie narrates the story of five years of her life, starting when she is eleven years old. Told against the backdrop of the emergence of the Civil Rights Movement, this well-crafted book provides a moving portrayal of personal and political awakening. It also vividly documents powerful societal pressures on Stevie to be heterosexual. Bombarded with heterosexist messages, Stevie dates boys, trying to convince herself that she isn't "funny" (a lesbian). This memorable book ends with Stevie questioning her sexual orientation, knowing that her life might not be easy and hoping that she will have the strength to be herself. As the title implies, this novel unflinchingly explores color prejudices among African Americans and illustrates how deeply white racism was internalized by some Black people. Never shying away from the damage caused by this bigotry, Sinclair finds ways to heal the wounds. References to skin color—fudge, pecan, taffy, chocolate, peanut butter, penny, caramel, bronze, eggplant, and walnut—all evoke positive images, replacing the hurtful terms from the past. This funny, fresh novel with its rich cast of characters is full of sass, vitality, and food for thought. Explicit sex and strong language. The sequel, *Ain't Gonna Be the Same Fool Twice*, follows Stevie through her early twenties during her search for her sexual identity in the San Francisco Bay Area. *Topics*: African-American Literature, Alcoholism, Appearance, Internalized Racism, Mother-Daughter Relationship, Socioeconomic Class.

Stoehr, Shelley. *Tomorrow Wendy*. Delacorte Press, 1998. Hardcover $15.95 (ISBN 0385323395). Ages 14 up.

Seventeen-year-old Cary is secretly in love with her boyfriend's twin sister, Wendy. On the surface she seems to fit right in: she has a popular, drug-dealing boyfriend, a wealthy family, an aptitude for calculus, and a distinctive sense of style. But on the inside, she is a very scared, confused young woman. Hiding behind eccentric clothes, sex with Danny, drugs, and alcohol, she attempts to deny her sexuality. Distancing herself from her parents, her cousin Jen, and the out lesbians at her school, she sinks in and out of depression. Desperate, she invents a wraithlike confidante, Rad, who offers advice through song lyrics. Enter Raven, a new student and proud lesbian, who falls in love with Cary and helps her make sense of the mess her life has become. After much anguish and self-destructive behavior, Cary takes Rad's advice: "Feet on ground, heart in hand/Facing forward, be yourself." This gritty book is awash with crude language, explicit sex, and privileged, alienated teens living life in the drug lane. Nevertheless, it explores the pain and confusion that young lesbians and gays often experience in a homophobic society. The narrator, self-absorbed and callous as she often is, clearly is searching for her identity. As she stumbles along, no book, no teacher, and no relative offer to guide her along the way. Instead, it is a peer, another young lesbian, who provides support and direction. Well-written and bold, this book is disconcerting, forceful, and thought-provoking. *Topics*: Alcohol, Bisexual Behavior, Cross-Class Relationships, Drugs.

Sweeney, Joyce. *Face the Dragon*. Delacorte Press, 1990. Hardcover $14.95 (ISBN 0385302061). Ages 12 up.

Eric and Paul, best friends since fourth grade, along with four other fourteen-year-olds, are selected to participate in an accelerated program. After reading *Beowulf* as their first English assignment, they each struggle to overcome their personal dragons. Much of the story focuses on the conflicts and issues that test the friendship between Eric and Paul. In a poignant scene, Paul finally finds the courage to come out to his best friend. Shocked, Eric avoids Paul until the actions of a sadistic teacher compel him to follow the example of Beowulf's comrade, Wiglaf. In the gripping conclusion, Eric remembers what kinship really means and valiantly defends his friend. *Face the Dragon* has been praised for its portrayal of complex internal struggles, provocative ideas about loyalty, courage, and ambition, and firm grasp of the feelings and actions of teenagers. Paul is talented, generous, honorable, and humorous. He is the only one who has the courage to defend a classmate against the devastating criticism of a teacher. It is Paul who cares enough to ask the hard questions needed to help a friend confront her anorexia. By the book's end, he has also learned to be compassionate with himself. "I have to live with myself all my life, and if this is the way I'm going to be, I want to understand it and be ready for it" (p. 231). *Topics*: Anorexia, Appearance, *Beowulf*, Competition, Debate, Gymnastics, Paraplegia, Socioeconomic Class, Teachers.

Taylor, Sheila Ortiz. *Coachella*. University of New Mexico Press, 1998. Paper $14.95 (ISBN 0826318436). Ages 16 up.

This intriguing novel, set in Palm Springs in the Coachella Valley of California, takes place in 1983 when blood bank authorities were still interpreting post-transfusion AIDS as minor accidents and refusing to draw appropriate inferences from it. Yolanda Ramírez, a lesbian, works as a phlebotomist at the Palm Springs hospital, where she notices that it is not only gay men who are dying of AIDS. Wealthy women who have had plastic surgery are also suffering from similar symptoms. As she studies the data, she tries to warn the hospital administrators that the blood supply may be tainted. Meanwhile she becomes lovers with Marina Lomas, who has recently changed her identity in a desperate attempt to escape her violent husband. Marina finds a job at a guest house for gay men, where she meets the people who will later provide a safe place when her life is threatened. Elsewhere in Coachella, Yolanda's father, Crescensio, a gardener, plants flowers outside the window of Eliana Townsend, who is dying of an unknown illness. Gradually truths rise to the surface in this community of false fronts and deep roots. Taylor skillfully draws parallels between the contouring of women's bodies and the exploitation of natural resources. Her characters are interesting, her writing is both suspenseful and lyrical, and her analysis of issues is sharp.

Yolanda is a strong, resourceful Latina lesbian who worked her way through college and has learned to listen to both her heart and head while planning her future. *Topics*: AIDS, Battered Women, Death and Dying, Desert, Ecology, Euthanasia, Latina Literature, Phlebotomy, Plastic Surgery.

Taylor, William. *The Blue Lawn.* Alyson Publications, 1999. Paper $9.95 (ISBN 1555834930). Ages 14 up. *Award*: New Zealand AIM Fiction Award.

First published in New Zealand in 1994, *The Blue Lawn* is an unusual story about first love, self-discovery, and abstinence. The beauty of the book builds slowly as Taylor explores the confusion, angst, and desires experienced by gay teens living in a society that has denied them information about who they are. The mutual attraction between David Mason and Theodore Meyer vacillates from curiosity to hostility to denial to acknowledgment. In spite of their confusion, they find the courage to talk to each other about their feelings. David tells Theo, "If I touched you right now, well, first off, I wouldn't know much what to do and, second, I wouldn't know how to stop what it is I didn't know what to do if I did get started" (p. 50). Interesting sub-themes revolve around Theo's grandmother, who is a Holocaust survivor, avid gardener, and owner of a Porsche. *The Blue Lawn* is a poignant book with an interesting mixture of tenderness, vulnerability, and irreverence. Although Theo is initially a rather irritating person, his admirable qualities are gradually revealed as the story unfolds. Even though David experiences his share of confusion, he is more accepting of his sexual identity. "Bloody hell, Theo. . . . If you're made this way, you go on being this way. . . . Just let things be as they are for as long as it is, well, as long as it seems right" (p. 72). Readers who survive the duck hunting scenes and the oppressive jokes will be glad they stayed for the second half of this engaging book. Strong language. *Topics*: Gardening, Holocaust, New Zealand Literature.

Velásquez, Gloria. *Tommy Stands Alone.* Arte Público Press, 1995. Paper $7.95 (ISBN 155885147X). Ages 12 up

Tomás Montoya is becoming increasingly uncomfortable at school, especially with his friends' expectations that he date. But he finds himself going along with them to keep from being noticed, even going so far as to laugh at their homophobic jokes. When a classmate finds a note Tommy accidentally dropped, he confronts him in front of all their friends. "Are you a faggot or what, Tommy?" Hurt and confused, Tommy runs away and tries to commit suicide. Luckily he calls his friend Maya, who calls 911, and Tommy's life is saved but his problems are far from over. Maya convinces him to see Ms. Martínez, a psychologist who not only works with Tommy but also counsels his mother, who has convinced herself that it was an accident and told her husband that Tommy has pneumonia. When his father learns the truth, he kicks his son out of the house. As the story unfolds, Tommy struggles through the long, painful, coming-out process that reveals not only his inner resources but who his real supporters are. Passages narrated by Tommy are juxtaposed with those narrated by Ms. Martínez, who has just learned that her gay brother-in-law is HIV positive. She also has painful memories of her brother's suicide years before and of her parents' subsequent denial. The double narration works well, opening windows on important issues from two perspectives. Velásquez does a superb job of portraying Maya as an incredibly strong ally to the suffering Tommy. She valiantly goes against the pressure from the group to stand alone with Tommy, leading the way for others to change their homophobic attitudes and behaviors. *Topics*: Latino Literature, Peer Allies, Peer Pressure, Suicide (attempted).

Walker, Kate. *Peter*. Houghton Mifflin, 1993. Hardcover $13.95 (ISBN 0395647223). Ages 12 up. *Awards*: ALA Best Book for Young Adults, ALA Notable Children's Book, ALA Quick Pick—Recommended Title for Reluctant YA Readers, Australian Human Rights Award. Out of Print.

First published in Australia in 1991 by Omnibus Books, *Peter* is a memorable novel about a teenager's struggle to discover his sexual identity. Peter Dawson is a fifteen-year-old aspiring photographer who hides his sensitivity from his macho friends, overbearing father, callous older brother, and understanding mother. He spends his free time dirt-biking with a group of cruel boys who constantly challenge, taunt, and hurl insults at each other. The pejoratives include *poofter*, Australian slang for homosexual, which they use to intimidate and control each other and to enforce heterosexuality. Goaded to prove his manhood, Peter engages in death-defying feats on his dirt bike. When he is attracted to David, his brother's gay friend, he begins to question his own sexual identity. At one point, after he is injured in a fight with one of the gang, David gently comforts him. "It was like coming home, like finding a place you've always wanted to be, and I could have stayed there forever holding on to him" (p. 124). Confused, Peter later calls a teen counseling hotline for advice, tests himself with pictures in a gay magazine, and finally decides to seduce David. In a moving final scene, the older man refuses his advances but tenderly advises him to give himself more time. Heavily salted with Australian slang, this sensitively wrought book has been praised for its likeable characters, emotional accuracy, and frank exploration of sexual identity. Some of the minor characters are stereotyped (Peter's friend, Tony, is described as an Italian who gets emotional very easily), and old people are trivialized. However, David's character is multidimensional: he is a warm, ethical person who dresses in immaculate designer clothes, has a knack for fixing cars, dirt bikes, and lawnmowers, and is studying engineering at the university. *Peter*, Kate Walker's first novel, was inspired by the experiences of a young male friend and is the product of eight years of research, writing, and rewriting. Strong language. *Topics*: Australian Literature, Dirt Bikes, Photography.

Wersba, Barbara. *Crazy Vanilla*. HarperCollins, 1986. Hardcover $11.95 (ISBN 0060263687). Ages 12 up.

Photographing birds is much more than a hobby for privileged fourteen-year-old Tyler Woodruff. His passion for birds is the only thing that makes him happy, even though it adds to his isolation. His father is a tyrant, his mother is an alcoholic, and his beloved older brother, Cameron, who is gay, has been banished from the family. Lonely and depressed, Tyler meets Mitzi Gerrard, a strong, streetwise, uniquely individual fifteen-year-old who not only shares his love for wildlife photography but challenges and expands his way of thinking. By the time Mitzi moves away, Tyler is ready to confront his father, accompany his mother to AA, and mend his relationship with Cameron. *Crazy Vanilla* has been praised for its strong characterizations, perceptive writing, and commendable pace and structure. Cameron is a very caring person who years earlier helped his younger brother with his homework and taught him how to swim and play tennis. When Tyler started photography, Cameron was the only one who understood. But when Tyler was twelve, the family discovered that Cameron was gay, and their relationship was never the same. In an attempt to understand, Tyler immediately bought six books on homosexuality. He and Cameron started meeting secretly in the city, where they went to museums, plays, and photography shows. But when Cameron falls in love and Tyler realizes that he has a life of his own and is never coming home, his feelings escalate. Kaleidoscopic feelings of jealousy, abandonment, and alienation combine, and Tyler considers running away. When Cameron brings his new lover, Vincent, to visit the family, Tyler wants to hate him. But when he meets the charming, genuinely friendly Vincent, he is confused. Mitzi helps him sort through these feelings and encourages him to forgive his brother. This sensitive book ends with a wiser, more confident, optimistic Tyler reaching out to Cameron, leaving hope that their relationship can be repaired. *Topics*: Alcoholism, Birding, Photography, Socioeconomic Class.

Wersba, Barbara. *Just Be Gorgeous*. HarperCollins, 1988. Hardcover $11.95 (ISBN 0060263598). Ages 12 up.

Even though she knows he is gay, Heidi Rosenbloom falls in love with Jeffrey Collins the first time she meets him. Growing up with wealthy, shallow parents who have no idea who she is, Heidi is searching for herself when she befriends Jeffrey, a homeless dancer who is trying to break into show business. He is the only person who has ever told her that she is a totally unique and charming person. The two develop an unlikely friendship until Jeffrey has an opportunity to move to Hollywood. Wersba juxtaposes the problems of an affluent teenager whose mother is obsessed with her daughter's hair, figure, and wardrobe with the issues facing a former foster child who is dealing with poverty, homelessness, and gay-bashing. She skillfully shows that while Heidi can give Jeffrey food and clothing, he can teach her about compassion, determination, and hope. Jeffrey, with his bleached hair, blue eyeshadow, and old fur jacket, is gentle, kind, funny, and talented. He is a sympathetic and lovable character whose optimism changes the life of a disillusioned, directionless young woman. When Jeffrey is attacked on the street, Heidi accompanies him to the emergency room, where the doctor adds insult to injury. The open discussions the two have about his childhood, his homosexuality, and his special love, David (who died in a car accident) are deeply touching. By the time Jeffrey leaves, Heidi is a different person. She knows that she is all that he said she was. *Topics*: Divorce, Foster Homes, Hate Crimes, Homelessness, Socioeconomic Class.

Wersba, Barbara. *Whistle Me Home*. Holt, 1997. Hardcover $14.95 (ISBN 0805048502). Ages 12 up.

This beautifully written book has a powerful message for every parent who is trying to force heterosexuality on his or her son or daughter and for anyone who believes gay people can change if they just try hard enough. Seventeen-year-old Thomas Jerome "TJ" Baker, pressured by his parents and therapist, makes a serious attempt to change when he enters into a relationship with his classmate, Noelle (Noli) Brown. Instead, he not only deceives himself but breaks her heart. The warning signs are there early on but Noli ignores them, dazzled by the sensitive, sophisticated, gorgeous soulmate who has come into her life. Noli narrates this intense story of how she meets TJ, falls in love, and tries to make the relationship work. When he can no longer go on hiding the fact that he is gay from himself or from Noli, she responds first with anger and harsh words, and then with despair. Her tendency to escape through drinking escalates and she finds herself spying on TJ and his new companion, a young man from a nearby school. But she also checks out books on homosexuality from the local library, some of which confirm what TJ had said: homosexuality is not a choice. Noli joins AA and gradually

becomes a stronger, more independent person. Wersba whistles a poignant song about young people searching for a home amidst ruins built on
secrets, delusions, and bigotry. *Topics*: Alcoholism, Appearance, Dogs,
Poetry, Unrequited Love.

Wieler, Diana. *Bad Boy*. Doubleday, 1992. Hardcover $12.95 (ISBN
0385307063); Firefly, 1997. Paper $5.95 (ISBN 0888990839). Ages 13
Up. *Awards*: The Canada Council Governor General's Literary Award,
Canadian Booksellers' Association's Ruth Schwartz Award, Canadian Li-
brary Association's Young Adult Book Award, International Board on
Books for Young People Honour List.

The friendship between two sixteen-year-old hockey players takes
some unexpected turns after they are selected to play on a Triple A team.
Self-absorbed, hot-tempered, and aggressive, A. J. Brandiosa experiences
kaleidoscopic feelings when he discovers that his best friend, Tulsa
"Tully" Brown, is gay. Tully knows he cannot keep his sexual identity
a secret forever, but he still isn't prepared for A. J. 's reaction. After much
inner turmoil, A.J. admits to himself that he is attracted to Tully. When
he finally finds the courage to tell Tully, his friend realizes that even
though the attraction is mutual, an intimate relationship would not work:
A. J., who is probably bisexual, is not yet ready to become involved in
a gay relationship. Set in a small town in Saskatchewan, *Bad Boy* has
been praised for its fast-paced hockey action, carefully delineated main
characters, strong supporting cast, believable sub-plots, and delicate approach to homosexuality and peer pressure. It exposes the way in which
the hockey coach and fans groom A. J. to become an "enforcer," someone
whose role is to make violent hits against opposing players. It is difficult
to understand why Tully's sister, Summer, who doesn't have a maso-
chistic bone in her body, is interested in A. J., especially after his rough
treatment of her at a party. Tully, a more sensitive, caring person, is
impulsive, charming, and outwardly happy-go-lucky. Living in a society
that persecutes gay people, he has had plenty of practice pretending to
be heterosexual. Wieler raises important questions about homophobia,
heterosexism, violence in sports, parenting, male sexism, and friendships
among male teenagers. *Topics*: Canadian Literature, Hockey.

Williams, Bett. *Girl Walking Backwards*. St. Martin's Press, 1998. Paper
$12.95 (ISBN 0312194560). Ages 16 up.

Raw and anguished, this story about a young lesbian's circuitous quest
for a home is not for the faint of heart. Praised for its authentic portrayal
of pain and humor and its brilliant mixture of Southern gothic with punk
rock, *Girl Walking Backwards* stars Skye Berringer, a high school senior in

Santa Barbara, California. Alienated in bland suburbia, the only thing she is sure of is her sexual identity. Her mother is an abusive New Age fanatic who threatens to withhold support for Skye's college education if she doesn't rid herself of her lesbianism by participating in encounter group confrontations. Her self-absorbed father is too involved with his world as an independent filmmaker in Los Angeles to offer any support. As Skye walks backwards trying to find herself, she uncovers information about possible cult abuse when she was a child, drugged by her now divorced parents. She is drawn to Jessica, whose self-mutilation becomes deeper and more frequent until she is finally sent away to a long-term psychiatric hospital. *Girl Walking Backwards* is a disturbing book about experimentation with drugs and sex, New Age charlatans, predatory adults, neighborhood cybercafes, wild parties, and self-destructive behavior. Skye is an appealing young lesbian whose search for a lesbian soulmate is the only stable component of her world. As she wanders around studying the architecture of the houses in surrounding neighborhoods and struggles to write her senior paper, "Images of Madness As a Response to Childhood Trauma in the Writings of Virginia Woolf," this vulnerable young lesbian emerges as the most sane person in a chaotic, insane world. Explicit Sex. *Topics*: Bisexual Behavior, Child Abuse, Drugs, Mental Illness, Mother/Daughter Relationships, New Age Culture, Self-Mutilation.

Winterson, Jeanette. *Oranges Are Not the Only Fruit.* Grove Atlantic, 1997. Paper $12.00 (ISBN 0802135161). Ages 14 up. *Award*: England's Whitbread Prize for Best First Fiction.

First published by Pandora Press in London in 1985, this fictionalized autobiography vividly portrays the absolutism of Christian fundamentalism and the concomitant homophobia of the members of the congregation. Adopted as an infant into a evangelical household in the Midlands of England, the narrator is raised to believe that she was chosen by God to save the heathens of the world. Her dominating mother taught her to read from the Book of Deuteronomy, and soon she is winning Bible quiz competitions and stitching samplers with apocalyptic themes. When she is accused of terrorizing her classmates at school with stories of hell, she consoles herself with the thought that in ten years she will be able to go to missionary school. Her first theological disagreement develops during a sermon on perfection. And when she becomes lovers with Melanie (a recent convert), her mother, the pastor, and the flock try to rid her of her demons, denouncing her "Unnatural Passions." Finally, she leaves the church and moves away. Humorous parables interspersed throughout the narrative serve as allegories for the narrator's journey toward self-knowledge and liberation. Delightfully original and quirky, this is an unforgettable story of how one young lesbian listened to the truths of her own heart and mind. Winterson's voice, with its subtle hilarity and idiosyncratic wit, distinguishes this rite of passage into adulthood. The author later wrote the screenplay for the 1990 British television film version of *Oranges Are Not the Only Fruit*, which won the British Academy of Film and Television Arts Award for Best Drama. It is available at 1–800–438–9653. *Topics*: Absolutism, Adoption, England, Religious Fundamentalism.

Wittlinger, Ellen. *Hard Love*. Simon & Schuster, 1999. Hardcover $16.95 (ISBN 0689821344). Ages 14 up.

Since his parents' divorce six years earlier, sixteen-year-old John "Gio" Galardi, Jr. has been immune to emotion. Stuck in neutral, he finds solace in homemade zines (magazines) like the amazing "Escape Velocity" by Marisol Guzman, a self-proclaimed Puerto Rican Cuban Yankee Lesbian. The two forge an unlikely friendship based on zines, alienation, and dreams of escape. Even though Marisol makes it very clear from the beginning that she is a lesbian, John finds himself falling in love with her. It is this unrequited love that enables him to break out of his shell and start experiencing his emotions again. *Hard Love* is an absorbing book about loss, love, trust, family, transformation and, interestingly, authorship. Wittlinger's young characters explore their thoughts and feelings through writing. John says, "That's what I love about writing. Once you get the words down on paper, in print, they start to make sense. It's like you don't know what you think until it dribbles from your brain down your arm and into your hand and out through your fingers and shows up on the computer screen, and you read it and re-alize: That's really true: I believe that" (p. 7). Interspersed throughout this intriguing book are pages designed to look like zine excerpts, hand-written poems, and letters. Marisol, who was adopted at birth by an aristocratic white social worker and her Cuban-born college professor husband, writes electric pieces that leap from one subject to another. After her first lover leaves her, she writes a letter to her birth mother, whoever and wherever she is. "It's almost impossible for me to trust anyone. . . . if I let [people] see that I like them (as I did with Kelly), they'll run away (as she did, as you did)" (pp. 120–121). Finally, at a zine conference, Marisol reaches "escape velocity" and flees to New York City with a group of lesbians. The lyrics to the song "Hard Love" are appended. *Topics*: Adoption, Authorship, Divorce, Unrequited Love, Zines.

Woodson, Jacqueline. *The Dear One*. Delacorte, 1991. Hardcover $9.00 (ISBN 0606025898); Dell, 1992. Paper $3.99 (ISBN 0440214203). Ages 12 up.

Twelve-year-old Afeni (Swahili for "the Dear One") and fifteen-year-old Rebecca develop a warm friendship after they learn to enjoy each other's differences. Afeni, an only child living in an affluent town in Pennsylvania, is coping with her grandmother's death, her parents' divorce, and her mother's recovering alcoholism. Afeni's mother invites Rebecca, the daughter of a college friend who now lives in Harlem, to share their home during the last three months of her pregnancy. Afeni and Rebecca, who end up sharing a room, are determined to dislike each other. How their initial animosity gradually melts away and blossoms into a beautiful friendship makes for a very special story. *The Dear One* has been praised for its rich, memorable characterizations, warm, humorous style, and original, life-affirming story. This book is unique because all the characters are African-American females. Of particular interest are the two lesbian characters, Marion and Bernadette, who have been lovers for eight years. Marion, a classmate of Afeni's and Rebecca's mothers at Spelman College, is a legal-aid attorney who defends people who can't afford a lawyer. Bernadette, who was Afeni's teacher in fifth and sixth grade, generously offers to tutor Rebecca so she can keep up her studies. Marion and Bernadette have a warm, loving relationship; they shower Rebecca and Afeni with tender, loving care. Woodson's valuable novel addresses a number of important issues and topics including tensions between working-class and middle-class African Americans and teenage pregnancy. *Topics*: Adoption, African-American Literature, Alcoholism, Death, Divorce, Grandmothers, Single Mothers, Socioeconomic Class.

Woodson, Jacqueline. *From the Notebooks of Melanin Sun.* Scholastic, 1995. Hardcover $14.95 (ISBN 0590458809); 1997. Paper $3.99 (ISBN 0590458817). Ages 12 up.

A thirteen-year-old African-American boy struggles to accept the fact that his mother is a lesbian and has fallen in love with a white woman. Melanin Sun, an only child, and his single mother, Encata Cedar, have always been very close. She has taught him to be tolerant of differences, even taking him to a memorial service for Audre Lorde, the lesbian author of many excellent books. Melanin read her biomythography *Zami: A New Spelling of My Name* in which Lorde combines elements of history, biography, and myth. But somehow none of this prepared him for the truth about his mother. His reactions range from shock to rage to bewilderment to alienation, and finally, after he has slowly sorted out his feelings, acceptance. *From the Notebooks of Melanin Sun* has been praised for its astute, perceptive insights, brave, thought-provoking story, and sensitive analysis of racism and homophobia. Encata, a law student, is loving, courageous, and intelligent. Her lover, Kristin, lost her family when they found out that she was a lesbian. She has wisely created a new family, a family of choice made up of close friends. Encata and Kristin have found their way to each other across color lines and enjoy each other's differences. Woodson has written another strong novel that encourages readers to push beyond walls of hatred, secrets, and lies to find the common bonds that connect us all. *Topics*: African-American Literature, Endangered Animals, Interracial Relationships, Journaling, Lesbian Mothers.

Woodson, Jacqueline. *The House You Pass on the Way*. Delacorte Press, 1997. Hardcover $14.95 (ISBN 0385321899); Bantam Doubleday Dell, 1997. Paper $4.50 (ISBN 0440227976). Ages 11 up.

Staggerlee has always felt different, isolated by the tragic deaths of her famous grandparents, by her parents' interracial marriage, and by something lonely inside herself. Her parents named her Evangeline Ian Canan, but when she was nine she took on a fiercer name, one that tells about her need to break out of the narrow definitions society imposes. Staggerlee's only close friend back in sixth grade was Hazel, the first and only girl she ever kissed. After Hazel rejected her, she has had no one to share her feelings with until her fourteenth summer when her adopted cousin, Trout, comes to visit. From the moment they meet, they are drawn to each other by their family history, their common interests, and most of all, by a magical feeling growing inside them. When they talk about these feelings, Trout confides that she couldn't deal with the ridicule if everyone knew she was a lesbian. Staggerlee responds, "If I loved someone enough, I would go anywhere in the world with them" (p. 76). Months later, Staggerlee learns that Trout has a boyfriend, that she finally succumbed to the pressure to try to be heterosexual. This richly layered novel ends with Staggerlee wondering about the future, about who they both will become. *The House You Pass on the Way* is a book to savor, to let the beauty of the words and images slowly sink in. It has been praised for its understated, lyrical writing, complex examination of emerging sexual identity, depth and complexity of minor characters, and gentle exploration of questions regarding racism and homophobia. The portrayal of Staggerlee is beautifully wrought. Introspective and sensitive, she possesses the kind of quiet strength that will enable her to be true to herself. The same qualities that moved her to think her own thoughts, to ignore the dictates of the fashion industry, and to take on a proud name like Staggerlee will empower her to embrace her lesbianism. *Topics*: Adoption, African-American Literature, Cousins, Mixed-Race People.

Yamanaka, Lois-Ann. *Name Me Nobody*. Hyperion, 1999. Hardcover $14.99 (ISBN 0786804521). Ages 13 up.

Set in Hawaii, this novel is about identity, friendship, loss, sexuality, body image, and fitting in. Fourteen-year-old Emi-Lou "Louie" Kaya often feels like a nobody—her young unmarried mother abandoned her when she was three, and her grandmother adopted her. In the absence of a mother and father, Emi-Lou made a family for herself. Since preschool, Yvonne has been her closest friend, like a sister. When they were nine, they took a vow: "Us against the world. . . . We will always be together" (p. 10). But five years later, Emi-Lou feels Von slipping away. The book covers a year in their lives, when Von falls in love with Kris and Emi-Lou struggles to understand what this means for their friendship. Finally, she accepts the wisdom of her grandmother's words: "Yvonne is who she is. You cannot change that. She was born the way she is. . . . Best you think open-minded. Best you and me be there for Yvonne, no matter what" (pp. 184–185). As a young lesbian, Yvonne not only faces the possibility of losing her best friend, but is forced by her father to break up with Kris and to meet with a psychologist. Apologizing to no one, she embraces her sexual identity and remains true to herself. *Name Me Nobody* has been praised for its biting dialogue, vivid images, and rich, complex voice. One of the many issues explored is body image. After Emi-Lou loses weight by starving herself and using appetite suppressants, diuretics, and laxatives, she thinks, "I was nobody fat. Am I somebody skinny?" (p. 52). This is Lois-Ann Yamanaka's first book for young adults, although she has written several award-winning books for adults. *Name Me Nobody* is written in Pidgin, or Hawaii Creole English, the language of Yamanaka's childhood. The term "Japs" is used frequently. *Topics*: Adoption, Fat Oppression, Hawaii, Japanese-American Literature.

Yolen, Jane. *Briar Rose*. Tor Books, 1992. Hardcover $17.95 (ISBN 0312851359); Paper $4.99 (ISBN 0812558626). Ages 14 up.

In a book that has been described as both imaginative and grim, Jane Yolen retells the story of Sleeping Beauty as a Holocaust memoir. Twenty-three-year-old journalist Becca Berlin's promise to her dying grandmother to solve the mystery of the castle leads her on a poignant journey to the site of a Nazi extermination camp in Poland. Alternating chapters juxtapose Grandmother Gemma's unique version of the tale of Sleeping Beauty with Becca's investigation of her beloved grandmother's early life. This a powerful tale of life and death, of love and hate, of roses and barbed wire. *Briar Rose* was one of the books burned on the steps of the Kansas City Board of Education because one of the characters is gay. The jumbled pieces of the puzzle finally fall together when Becca meets Josef Potocki, a non-Jewish elderly gay man in Poland. His gripping story of his part in saving Gemma's life begins with his own persecution as a gay man during the Holocaust. He describes his early aptitudes for the theater, for political amnesia, and for love; his sudden political awakening during the war; and later, his years of grieving, of trying to comprehend the incomprehensible. As his words spill forth, questions arise as to how one becomes a person of honor. "How does one redeem a life?" Those searching for positive images of gay characters in young adult literature will be heartened by Potocki's existence. He is multidimensional, complex, and for the most part an honorable person. In the introduction, editor Terri Windling writes that fairy tales were originally created for an adult audience. *Briar Rose*, the sixth in the Tor Fairy Tale Series, transforms Sleeping Beauty into a contemporary tale both excruciating and inspiring. *Topics*: Fairy Tales, Holocaust, Intergenerational Relationships, Jews, Journalism, Poland, Storytelling, World War II.

3

Short Stories

Anderson, Gina. "Carta a una compañera" (Letter to a Female Companion). In *Compañeras: Latina Lesbians*, edited by Juanita Ramos. Routledge, 1994. Paper $14.95 (ISBN 0415909260). Ages 14 up.

First published in 1987 by the Latina Lesbian History Project, *Compañeras: Latina Lesbians* is a collection of oral histories, essays, poems, short stories, letters, and artwork by forty-seven women born in ten different countries. Gina Anderson, in her piece, "Carta a una compañera," writes a powerful coming out letter to Marta, a close friend from her teenage years. Anderson reminds Marta of the night seven years earlier when they shared a passionate kiss. She reminisces about the longing looks they often gave each other and the jealousy she experienced when Marta danced with boys. Now, after seven years of drinking and one of sobriety, Anderson writes, "Yes, I am a Cochona, a Maricona, a Nicaraguan dyke" (p. 82). She wonders if Rossana, another childhood friend with whom she shared her first kiss, has also grown up to be a lesbian, or whether she betrayed herself and gave in to the pressures to live as a heterosexual. Anderson issues a plaintive cry, "Can I be the only Nicaraguan cochona in New York City?" (p. 81). Where are the others who severed the patriarchal umbilical cords and embraced their lesbianism? Anderson writes that although it took her years to overcome her fear of being rejected, she has found self-acceptance and self-love. This is a compelling letter filled with anger, pain, loneliness, love, and joy. Gina Anderson was born in Puerto Cabezas, Nicaragua and raised in Nicaragua and the United States. *Topics*: Latina Literature, Letters, Nicaragua.

Bauer, Marion Dane, editor. *Am I Blue? Coming Out from the Silence.* HarperCollins, 1994. Hardcover $15.00 (ISBN 0060242531); Paper $5.95 (ISBN 0064405877). Ages 12 up. *Awards*: ALA Best Book for Young Adults, ALA Recommended Book for Reluctant Young Adult Readers, ALA Gay-Lesbian-Bisexual Book Award for Literature, Lambda Literary Award for Children and Young Adults, Minnesota Book Award for Older Children.

Sixteen original short stories by noted young adult authors speak of love, self-discovery, acceptance, identity, survival, and hope. Marion Dane Bauer conceived of the idea and mobilized the authors for this unique collection out of a conviction that those who write for young people have a responsibility to speak out on subjects, such as homosexuality, that society attempts to shroud in silence. Each piece is followed by an afterword by its author that tells the story behind the story. The title story by Bruce Coville features a camp fairy godfather who mentors Vince, a sixteen-year-old victim of gay-bashing. When every lesbian and gay person turns blue for a day, myths and stereotypes are shattered and Vince is able to get on with his life. "We Might as Well All Be Strangers" by M. E. Kerr is an engaging coming-out story that draws parallels between the outsider experiences of Jews and lesbians/gays. A young lesbian finds that her grandmother is the most sympathetic member of the family because "she had seen more than enough prejudice in her lifetime" (p. 27). In Jacqueline Woodson's poignant story, "Slipping Away," a young lesbian is devastated when she realizes that homophobia is driving her dearest friend away. As she feels her slipping away, she wants to scream, "Remember, Maria, how we said we'd grow old together? Just you and me and forever and ever, amen?" (p. 57). A Gay-Straight-Bisexual Alliance is formed by the students in "Parents' Night" by Nancy Garden. This is the heartening story of two young lesbians, Karen and Roxy, who are in love, and how their courage educates and changes Karen's parents. Lesléa Newman writes about two girls who help each other develop their kissing skills in "Supper." Cristina Salat's story, "50% Chance of Lightning," finds a young lesbian longing for a lover and trying to decide what to do with her life. This fine collection of stories ends with Marion Dane Bauer's piece, "Dancing Backwards," in which two young lesbians are expelled from a boarding school. It is during the final meeting with Sister Stephan Marie that they make a life-changing discovery. "For the first time in my life I saw that love, the actual, corporeal love, of another woman was something to be desired" (p. 271). Other stories are by C. S. Adler, Francesca Lia Block, Bruce

Coville, James Cross Giblin, Ellen Howard, Jonathan London, Lois Lowry, Gregory Maguire, William Sleator, and Jane Yolen. *Topic*: Anthology.

Birtha, Becky. "Johnnieruth." In *Lovers' Choice*. Seal, 1994. Paper $10.95 (ISBN 1878067419). Ages 12 up.

Becky Birtha is the author of two collections of short stories, *For Nights Like This One: Stories of Loving Women* and *Lovers' Choice*, and a collection of poetry, *The Forbidden Poems*. "Johnnieruth" is the delightful story of a fourteen-year-old's determination to be herself. At eight, after years of wearing "all them ruffly dresses" (p. 4), Johnnieruth puts her foot down and starts dressing in blue jeans and Wrangler jackets. She shovels snow, washes cars, and delivers papers to earn money to buy a bicycle so that she can escape the confining contours of her neighborhood. One night she rides to her favorite park, where she sees two women kissing. Birtha beautifully captures the elation Johnnieruth experiences at the discovery that there are grown-up women like herself. As Johnnieruth rides away, everything suddenly makes sense. "I'm sailing down the boulevard laughing . . . and then I'm singing at the top of my lungs" (p. 9). The narrator's liveliness of spirit and physical exuberance soar through the pages of this captivating story. Johnnieruth is one of the few young lesbians in adolescent literature who apologizes to no one for being who she is. She doesn't care what people think: "I guess everybody got it figured out by now that I ain't gonna be like nobody else" (p. 6). She prefers her own company to that of "dumb boys" (p. 7) and girls who sit around watching babies and talking. She knows that someday she will find others like herself. *Topic*: African-American Literature.

Block, Francesca Lia. "Winnie and Cubby." In *Girl Goddess #9: Nine Stories*. Demco Media, 1998. Hardcover $10.05 (ISBN 0606129448); HarperCollins, 1998. Paper $4.95 (ISBN 006447187X). Ages 12 up.

From the author of *Weetzie Bat* comes a collection of nine tales in Block's lush jacarunda style. "Winnie and Cubby" was previously published in slightly different form as "Winnie and Tommy" in *Am I Blue? Coming Out from the Silence*, edited by Marion Dane Bauer (reviewed elsewhere in this chapter). Seventeen-year-old Winnie is in love with the hottest skateboarding guy ever, and they are celebrating their graduation from high school by spending the weekend in San Francisco. They hang out at the Haight, eat croissants and drink cappuccinos, and dance to blues at a small bar. But Winnie feels Cubby pulling away from her. Finally, he comes out to her, saying, "I've always liked guys. I kept waiting for it to stop. . . . You're the only person I can tell" (pp. 168–169).

During that night, while Cubby is out dancing, Winnie grieves the loss of her boyfriend but gradually realizes that Cubby will still be her friend. When he returns, they hug each other, "wrapped in each other's arms like little children, until they fall asleep" (p. 172). Block fills her story with the smell of muffins baking, hoarse voices singing on the radio, chunky puppy shoes, and angel face roses. Before finding each other, Winnie and Cubby were lost, searching for love. Winnie's father had been killed in a motorcycle accident and her mother closed their house up like a tomb. Cubby's abusive father had beaten him and broken his arm before abandoning the family. Now they discover that friendship is precious no matter where you find it. Once again Block reminds her readers that the world is not a simple place and that there is more than one way to live. *Topics*: Family Violence, Gay-Straight Friendship.

Brant, Beth. *Food and Spirits.* Firebrand Books, 1991. Paper $8.95 (ISBN 0932379923). Ages 16 up.

In her second book, gifted Mohawk writer Beth Brant offers eight powerful stories of survival and endurance. The book opens with "Telling," a poem in which Brant writes, "What good is this pen, this yellow paper, if I can't fashion them into tools or weapons to change our lives?" (p. 14). She writes as a lesbian, a Mohawk, a mother, and as a working-class person. In "Swimming Upstream," Anna May grieves the death of her six-year-old son, Simon. Several years earlier, his father had been awarded custody because Anna May was a lesbian and because she had a history of alcoholism. When she learns that Simon drowned after falling out of a boat, she blames herself. This is the poignant story of how she overcomes the compulsion to start drinking again and regains her strength. "This Place" is the sad story of David, a young gay man with AIDS who goes home to die. Joseph, a medicine man, brings a snakeskin, a feather, and words from David's ancestors. As they talk about life and death, David realizes that Joseph, too, is gay. He learns that his father defended Joseph against the homophobic attacks years earlier at the residential school. This is a sensitive story about death and dying, homophobia, and racism. In the title story, an eighty-year-old man takes a seven-hour bus trip to visit his granddaughters in the city. Other stories cry out against violence toward women, mourn the death of a mother killed by a hit-and-run-driver, celebrate the creation of the earth, and weigh the joys and sorrows of coming home. Beth Brant is a Bay of Quinte Mohawk from Tyendinaga Mohawk Territory in Ontario, Canada, who has lived much of her life in Michigan. *Topics*: AIDS, Death and Dying, Mohawk Literature, Native Americans.

Brant, Beth. *Mohawk Trail.* Firebrand Books, 1985. Paper $6.95 (ISBN 0932379028). Ages 16 up.

The cover of this first book is based on a quilt design, "Mohawk Trail," created by Beth Brant's grandmother, Margaret Brant, almost fifty years before the book was published. Several stories celebrate grandmothers and the beauty of quilting, "Stitch by stitch, block by block. Hands moving across the boards" (p. 26). "A Simple Act" tells the story of two girls who were best friends from third to seventh grades. "Spending nights at each other's houses, our girl bodies hugging tight" (p. 88). Then one day a neighbor looked through the bedroom window and saw them together. Their parents forbade them to see each other again. Their rebellions failed and gradually "something hard, yet invisible, had formed over our memories. We went the way of boys, back seats of cars, self-destruction" (p. 89). Twenty-five years later, the narrator writes about her memories. "Sandra, I am remembering our loss" (p. 90). She tells Sandra that she now has a woman lover and that she is a writer. This is a poignant story about two young women torn apart and shamed into denying their love for each other. Another story, "Coyote Learns a New Trick," features a trickster who learns that it is better to be a real woman than an imitation man. Brant's stories are intensely personal and reflect her strong sense of tribal identity. Her acknowledgments include Denise, her "lover and mate," and "My mom and dad I want to thank for giving me just the right blend of Indian spirit and Irish/Scots practicality." *Topics*: Intergenerational Relationships, Mohawk Literature.

Chiu, Christina. "Rain." In *Not the Only One: Lesbian and Gay Fiction for Teens*, edited by Tony Grima. Alyson Publications, 1994. Paper $7.95 (ISBN 155583275X). Ages 12 up.

This story is special not only because of the writing but also because it is one of the few pieces about Chinese-American lesbians written for young adults. When the unnamed narrator discovers that her twin, Rainy Chang, is a lesbian, she tries to understand why she didn't confide in her. As she reminisces about their relationship, she analyzes their connections and conflicts, and their shared dreams and separate interests. She remembers her parents' homophobic reaction to two women who were holding hands one night when they all went out to dinner and realizes how this must have hurt Rainy. She wonders why she didn't notice that her sister wasn't interested in the guys at school or that she chose to spend the night with her close friend, Jade, instead of attending the prom. As the narrator puts the pieces together, she imagines what it would be like to make love with a woman. "Something in me was starving to feel every bone, every muscle, every pinch of my flesh" (p. 212). Suddenly, she knows that her parents are wrong, her boyfriend is wrong, and that she, too, is a lesbian. This is a beautifully written story about a young woman awakening to her sexual identity. It also examines family dynamics, favoritism toward male children, and the determination to follow one's dreams. *Topics*: Chinese-American Literature, Sibling Rivalry, Twins.

Cofer, Judith Ortiz. "White Balloons." In *An Island Like You*. Orchard, 1995. Hardcover $15.95 (ISBN 0531068978); Viking Penguin, 1996. Paper $4.99 (ISBN 014038068X). Ages 10 up.

Twelve interconnected stories explore the experiences of Puerto Rican–American teenagers in a New Jersey barrio. One of these stories, "White Balloons," tells the story of Rick Sanchez, a gay man who had grown up in the barrio, escaped to Broadway to become a celebrated actor, and returned to his old neighborhood to try to start a theater group for young people when he discovered he was HIV-positive. This story is narrated by Doris, who in an earlier story, "The One Who Watches," struggled with feeling invisible and scared. Now, inspired by Rick, she plays a major role in coordinating the theater group and gradually starts feeling fully multidimensional. As she thinks about the way Rick has been ostracized by the community, she realizes, "I could identify with him as an outsider" (p. 152). When Rick dies, Doris finds the courage to organize the birthday party for him that bigotry denied him while he was living. As Mami sings "Las Mañanitas," Doris knows that by taking a risk, she has made a difference; she has changed the way some people think about gay people. Rick and his lover, Joe Martini, who have a strong, stable relationship, are portrayed as caring, supportive individuals. They sincerely care about the young people in the barrio and talk to Doris as equals. Even when he is very sick, Rick's telephone conversations with Doris show his concern for her. "After a while I started thinking of him as an older brother" (p. 156). "White Balloons" is a beautifully written, poignant story about identity, loss, dignity, and hope. *Topics*: AIDS, Dying and Death, HIV, Puerto Rican–American Literature, Theater.

Crutcher, Chris. "In the Time I Get." In *Athletic Shorts: Six Short Stories*. Greenwillow Books, 1989, 1991. Hardcover $13.95 (ISBN 0688108164); Bantam Doubleday Dell Books, 1992. Paper $4.99 (ISBN 0440213908). Ages 12 up.

Six powerful short stories chronicle bits of the lives of characters, major and minor, who inhabited the rough terrain of Chris Crutcher's earlier works. Louie Banks from *Running Loose* confronts another challenge in "In the Time I Get," this time in the form of his own bigotry toward a gay man who is dying of AIDS. During the past school year, after his football coach had ordered an illegal hit on an African-American player from another team, Banks found the courage to oppose racial bigotry and as a result was stripped of his starting position on the team. In time, he became proud of his conduct, knowing that he was stronger for having resisted the pressure to conform. Now, in this memorable story, he befriends a stranger during the last months of his life. Twenty-five-year-old Darren, disinherited by his homophobic parents, moves across country to live with his uncle. When Banks finds out that he is gay and has AIDS, he panics and retreats until he remembers the lesson he learned when his girlfriend died. "I knew there isn't time to hesitate or be squeamish about death. It comes when it wants, and whether you're the one going or the one staying, you better have your shit in order, or you're going to wind up hating yourself for all you wish you'd done" (p. 149). Banks asks more of himself than he realized he could give and is transformed by the experience. His heart grows and he emerges determined to "see how far I can go in the time I get" (p. 154). In the preface to the story, Crutcher states, "We're all bigots" (p. 127). What he doesn't say but demonstrates beautifully in the story is that we are each capable of expanding our hearts and minds and overcoming our bigotry. *Topics*: AIDS, Dying and Death.

Dines, Carol. "LezBoy." In *Talk to Me: Stories and a Novella*. Bantam, 1999. Paper $4.50 (ISBN 0440220262). Ages 12 up.

Each story in this collection features a teen narrator who finds a way to speak up loud and clear. In "LezBoy," sixteen-year-old Wes lives with his mother and her lover, Liz, in a small town in Minnesota. The subject of schoolyard taunts, Wes copes by being silent. "I don't deny it, and I don't advertise it" (p. 49). That changes when Wes goes to Paris to participate in a six-week French immersion summer program for accelerated language apprehension. Thriving in the anonymity of the city, Wes finds a girlfriend, studies French, and gains a better understanding of his mothers. "For the first time, I begin to feel what Liz and my mother have sacrificed to put me in the center of their lives" (p. 72). During his last week in France, his mothers arrive for their long-postponed honeymoon. When an admirer becomes too attentive to his mother, Wes finally finds the courage to speak up and explain that his mother and Liz are partners. Later, Wes reflects on how new places and experiences shape our lives. "I feel it: How many lives are possible, how many distances there are to cover, and maybe for the first time the future feels large enough to embrace them all" (p. 82). *Topics*: Lesbian Mothers, Paris.

Dixon, Melvin. "The Boy with Beer." In *In the Life: A Black Gay Anthology*, edited by Joseph Beam. Alyson Publications, 1986. Paper $8.95 (ISBN 0932870732). Ages 16 up.

On a cold Friday night, a young gay man searches for a way to overcome the voices of his past and find companionship, love, and hope. Willis summons his courage and walks into a club while being bombarded with negative words, images, and feelings from his childhood. As he sorts through memories of schoolyard threats, playing the piano, baptism, and his first love and rejection, he settles into a booth in the back of the bar. He remembers his father's ridicule when he found him in the kitchen making a cake. He thinks about his mother's shame when she caught him looking at the other boys after the baptism. "He wanted to ask someone, anyone, if he was always to be lonely" (p. 29). When Willis meets Jerome, a friendly stranger, he struggles to remain in the present. This haunting story aches with the misery, loneliness, and doubts many young gay and lesbian people experience. It captures the chilling way memories of a childhood filled with homophobia cut through Willis' veins, keeping him frozen in the past, icing out the present, and numbing him to future possibilities. And yet, there is hope that he will be able to reach out to Jerome and find the warmth he needs to reclaim his life, his identity. *Topics*: African-American Literature, Childhood Memories.

Donoghue, Emma. *Kissing the Witch: Old Tales in New Skins*. HarperCollins, 1997. Hardcover $15.95 (ISBN 0060275758). Ages 12 up.

In this mesmerizing collection of thirteen reimagined fairy tales, Donoghue avenges the wrongs done to female characters in a genre rife with misogyny. At last, females of all ages break out of their pumpkin shells and embrace life as full human beings. Cinderella says no to the handsome prince and makes a home with the fairy godmother. Beauty discovers the Beast behind the mask is a woman who refuses to do what women are supposed to do. In the title story, it is the witch who is transformed by kissing a woman from the nearby village. As she ponders the magic of the kiss, she muses, "Perhaps it is the not being kissed that makes her a witch; perhaps the source of her power is the breath of loneliness around her" (p. 226). Snow White, Gretel, the Little Mermaid, Rapunzel, and others valiantly refuse to follow the paths mapped out by their parents and set out to discover who they can become. As they untangle the knotted ropes of their minds, they open up a whole new way of thinking about the world. By magicking these old stories into innovative shapes, Donoghue rebuts the traditional messages drummed into every girl's head: "Keep your horizons narrow, your expectations low" (p. 14). Each story is cleverly nested into the next through an intriguing literary device so that they become one long tale. *Kissing the Witch* has been praised for its lyrical, exquisite writing, creative, almost musical structure, and unconventional, dazzling images. However, the magical spell is broken by the gratuitous murder of a horse, the slaughter of a donkey, and the drowning of a kitten. If given the opportunity to reinvent ourselves, wouldn't we choose to end the violence toward gentle creatures great and small? *Topic*: Fairy Tales.

Gage, Carolyn. "Becca and the Woman Prince." In *Love Shook My Heart*, edited by Irene Zahava. Alyson Publications, 1998. Paper $10.95 (ISBN 1555834043). Ages 8 up.

Once upon a time there was a princess named Becca who was like no other princess. She "showed not one shred of passivity, helplessness, or submissive behavior" (p. 93). Her father, the king, tried to marry her off but all the likely suitors found her behavior quite disconcerting and soon found excuses to disappear. Then one day, Ymoja, an African Woman Prince, announced her intention to court the Princess Becca. This fairy tale is their love story, told with humor, wisdom, and poignancy. Multi-layered, gentle, and witty, it will be enjoyed by children, teenagers, and adults. Gage captures the feelings of difference and not fitting into a family—feelings that many young lesbians will recognize. Undaunted by the pressures to conform, Becca remains true to herself and apologizes to no one. She is content with her scientific experiments, building projects, paintings, books, and music. When she meets Ymojo, who had left her kingdom because of similar constraints, the two talk, laugh, wrestle, argue, and play soccer. These strong young lesbians who refuse to internalize the traditional roles expected of them will inspire, educate, and empower. This refreshing story would be an excellent choice for a picture book. The author, Carolyn Gage, is a lesbian feminist playwright, writer, and performer. *Topic*: Fairy Tales.

Grima, Tony, editor. *Not the Only One: Lesbian and Gay Fiction for Teens*. Alyson Publications, 1994. Paper $7.95 (ISBN 155583275X). Ages 16 up.

Twenty-one short stories explore the experiences of teenagers who are dealing with lesbian and gay issues, either personally or as they learn that a relative or friend is lesbian or gay. Even though most of the stories are appropriate for early adolescents, a few are so explicit and/or disturbing that this book is best suited for older teens. One of the best, "Rain" by Christina Chiu, is reviewed separately in this chapter. In another excellent story, "About Zan" by Jenny Pausacker, a young lesbian finally finds the courage to come out to her parents, only to be met with silence. They don't cry, kick her out of the house, or send her to a psychiatrist, but they don't want to talk about her life. In "It Feels Great" by Pam McArthur, a young lesbian attends her first meeting of the local Gay and Lesbian Youth Alliance. As she says no to all the homophobic messages that have threatened to drown her, she realizes, "I'm saying yes to my life and it feels—great" (p. 143). In Emily Ormand's piece, "Seeing Ellie," two young women postpone dealing with their attraction to each other because one of them is overwhelmed with her parents' divorce. "Loving Bobby" by Bill Huebsch is written in an interesting prose style called per cola et comata. Tommy, the eight-year-old narrator, adopts Bobby, a doll given to his sister by their Aunt Sara. As the story unfolds, he struggles with his parents, who want him to play with trucks. "In befriending Bobby I'd befriended some silent, deep inner part of myself (p. 197). Aunt Sara is anything but dainty and says whatever is on her mind. She wears trousers and a red work shirt, drives a pickup truck, and cusses. "To me, she was the model of freedom. She said and did whatever she wanted and nobody stopped her or even stepped in her way" (p. 192). In other stories, a boy falls in love with his sister's boyfriend, a girl develops a crush on a camp counselor, a young lesbian struggles against pressures to become heterosexual while attending her sister's wedding, and a young man falls in love with a classmate while on a trip to New York City. *Topics*: Anthology, Coming Out.

Lim-Hing, Sharon, editor. *The Very Inside: An Anthology of Writing by Asian and Pacific Islander Lesbian and Bisexual Women.* Sister Vision Press, 1994. Paper $29.94 (ISBN 0920813976). Ages 17 up.

The Very Inside is a 450-page anthology of short stories, interviews, poetry, and essays. Sixty-four contributors to this comprehensive work originate from or identify their heritage to Bangladesh, Bengali, Cambodia, China, Hawaii, India, Indonesia, Japan, Korea, Laos, Malaysia, the Philippines, Singapore, Taiwan, Thailand, and Vietnam. The book is divided into five sections: Origins, Departures; Finding/Founding Community; Waking from a Dream of Love; Life Struggle; and Out of Fire, Grace. Editor Sharon Lim-Hing writes, "this book speaks of our many oppressions but it also speaks of our strength, our beauty, our dynamism, and our creativity. We are escaping and resisting, extending and enriching what it means to be Pacific Islander and Asian, bisexual and lesbian, and what it means to be alive, what it means to create. . . . The work in this collection will challenge, perplex, entertain, and enlighten" (unpaginated introduction). In "New Mexico APL," Tze-Hei Yong remembers having dreams about holding other girls' hands and kissing them when she was fifteen. Juliana Pegues/Pei Lu Fung, in her piece titled "White Rice: Searching for Identity," writes, "My best friend Lisa and I practiced kissing inside that broken down clubhouse/when we weren't pretending we were Wonder Woman or riding/our invisible horses" (p. 31). In "Slowly but Surely, My Search for Family Acceptance and Community Continues," Susan Y. F. Chen writes about the family meetings with her parents during which she tries to help them understand her lesbianism. "One of my dreams was to see my parents become PFLAG [Parents, Families, and Friends of Lesbians and Gays] parents, for them to hold signs (such as, Proud Parents of a Lesbian Daughter) and march in a huge gay and lesbian parade" (p. 81). In "Solitary Bravo,"

Darlena Bird Jimenes writes, "the anger from the seething homophobia that I experienced during high school enabled me to graduate with a sense of strength I had never felt before. I gave myself the gift of the determination to live on the edge, to be personally responsible for my own well-being as a gay person and politically active, and to realize my voice and vision through personal celebration" (p. 136). The array of voices, themes, and visions in this powerful book is challenging, tender, intellectual, passionate, exploratory, and sensual. Explicit sex. *Topics*: Anthology, Asian and Pacific Islander Lesbian Writers.

McKinley, Catherine E. and L. Joyce DeLaney, editors. *Afrekete: An Anthology of Black Lesbian Writing.* Doubleday, 1995. Paper $14.00 (ISBN 0385473559). Ages 17 up.

Afrekete is a collection of twenty pieces—fiction, essays, and poetry— written in a variety of styles and addressing a range a significant themes. Writers represented are Jamika Ajalon, Cynthia Bond, Michelle Cliff, Malkia Amala Cyril, L. Joyce DeLaney, Alexis De Veaux, Jackie Goldsby, Jewelle Gomez, Carolivia Herron, Melanie Hope, Helen Elaine Lee, Audre Lorde, Catherine E. McKinley, Sharee Nash, Pat Parker, Michelle Parkerson, Sapphire, Jocelyn Maria Taylor, Linda Villarosa, Evelyn C. White, and Jacqueline Woodson. Because some pieces are very explicit, this collection is best suited for older teens and adults. The book opens with "Tar Beach," an excerpt from Audre Lorde's celebrated memoir, *Zami: A New Spelling of My Name,* which introduces the character Afrekete. "Ode to Aretha" is Evelyn C. White's nostalgic recollection of family life in Gary, Indiana in the 1960s. In "Revelations," Linda Villarosa writes about her experiences with homophobic Bible-thumpers after she came out in an article in the May 1991 issue of *Essence* magazine. "Dear Aunt Nanadine" by Alexis De Veaux confronts color prejudices among African Americans, exposing the painful ways in which racism has been internalized by some Black people. Jewelle Gomez examines her complicated relationship with Black men in "Wink of an Eye." Melanie Hope, in "Dare," discusses the contradictions, struggles, and boundaries she has encountered in her relationships with white lovers. She pays tribute to writers Pat Parker, Audre Lorde, and James Baldwin, each of whom also had non-Black lovers. This anthology celebrates the words of a group of writers often relegated to the margins. Inspiring and provocative, this collection will inform and delight. *Topics*: African-American Lesbian Writers, Anthology.

Mohr, Nicholasa. "Herman and Alice." In *El Bronx Remembered.* Peter Smith Publishers, 1994. Hardcover $18.50 (ISBN 084466779X); HarperCollins, 1993. Paper $4.95 (ISBN 0064471004). Ages 12 up.

The novella, "Herman and Alice," first published in 1975, was one of the earliest Puerto Rican–American stories to deal with the topic of homosexuality. It is part of a collection of eleven short stories set in the Bronx in New York City. When gay thirty-eight-year-old Herman Aviles and pregnant fifteen-year-old Alice get married, they agree that they are not interested in a physical relationship. But after the baby is born, Alice starts going out with her teenage friends and her feelings change. Eventually, they separate and Herman decides to return to Puerto Rico and to try to contact his former lover, Daniel. Mohr portrays Herman as a respected member of the neighborhood where no one knows that he is gay. He left his small town in Puerto Rico seven years earlier where "life had become a nightmare. . . . Everyone trying to get him married" (p. 133). But after his relationship with Daniel ended, he had given up looking for that special someone. So when he meets Alice, he decides to enter into a marriage of convenience for both of them. "At last he could think about his own parents and feel right, not ashamed of his feelings" (p. 145). This is a sad story of a gay man searching for acceptance and respect in a homophobic world, but it ends with Herman thinking about "beautiful Daniel, so sweet, so loving" (p. 133). *Topics*: Marriage of Convenience, Puerto Rican Literature.

Mohr, Nicholasa. "The Perfect Little Flower Girl." In *In Nueva York*. Arte Público Press, 1994. Paper $9.50 (ISBN 0934770786). Ages 14 up.

Set during the Vietnam War, this story is part of a moving collection of eight interrelated short stories. Johnny Bermudez and Sebastian Randazzo are two gay Puerto Rican men living together in Losaida, New York City. They met at a rehabilitation center where Sebastian went after being released from a state hospital, where he was being treated after several suicide attempts. Johnny, who as a child had been shuttled around to various foster homes, was sent to the rehabilitation center after being released on probation for drugs. Now Johnny has just been drafted and he is searching for a way to provide for Sebastian, who is disabled with asthma and migraine headaches. They find a way around the homophobic system by arranging for Johnny to marry a lesbian friend with the agreement that his benefits will go to Sebastian. Mohr portrays the two gay men and the two lesbians, Vivian and Joanna, as stable couples who respect and care about each other. Vivian, a social worker, and Joanna, a teacher, have secure incomes and believe that they should help their "brothers" survive in the mainstream society. Except for a few neighborhood gossips, who disapprove of the relationship between Johnny and Sebastian, the community agrees with a character who says, "for them it's a normal thing. They're happy. Besides, it's not other people's business what they do" (p. 89). At the reception after the mock wedding, Hilda, the flower girl, dedicates "You've Got a Friend" by Carole King to Johnny and Sebastian. Originally published in 1977, this story was one of the earliest Puerto Rican–American works with a gay theme. *Topics*: Marriage (Mock), Puerto Rican Literature.

Moore, Lisa C, editor. *Does Your Mama Know? An Anthology of Black Lesbian Coming Out Stories*. Redbone, 1997. Paper $19.95 (ISBN 0965665909). Ages 16 up.

By turns funny, angry, passionate, and joyous, *Does Your Mama Know?* reflects the complexity of emotions that 41 Black lesbians experienced during the coming-out process. These 49 short stories, poems, interviews, letters, and essays—fiction and nonfiction—make up a powerful collection of original writing by contributors who identity as African American, Jamaican Canadian, and Haitian American. Editor Lisa C. Moore, who realized she was a lesbian when she was thirteen, felt that Black lesbians would be strengthened and affirmed by reading these stories and becoming aware of their history. In "From a Lesbian Womb Into a Lesbian World: Coming Out," Laura Irene Wayne writes "As far as I can remember, I have always been out and treated as out. . . . Maybe I'm an out Lesbian because I take pride in uniqueness and myself" (pp. 103–104). In "I Lost It at the Movies," Jewelle Gomez writes, "To be a lesbian is part of who I am, like being left-handed" (p. 123). She writes about the process of integrating her Black identity and her lesbian identity: "The different faces came together as one, and my desire became part of my heritage, my skin, my perspective, my politics, and my future" (p. 125). The importance of lesbian literature is discussed in several pieces. "If it wasn't for the books I'd read, I'd have probably come out a much harder way, and in shame and disgrace. . . . I hope that today the wealth of queer-positive literature will give other lesbian and gay male kids the necessary knowledge of self to know this crucial component of who they are" (p. 152) writes Donna Allegra in "Lavender Sheep in the Fold." This powerful book is dedicated "In memory of Terri Jewell, who lit a fire in my heart and under my butt and kept me going." Jewell, who died in 1995 at the age of 41, contributed several pieces to this anthology, including interviews of Ruth Ellis and Stephanie Byrd. Ellis, who was over ninety years old when Jewell interviewed her in 1990, talks about her lover, Ceciline, with whom she lived for thirty years. Byrd, who knew she was a lesbian when she was seven, talks about the time she was sent to the school office when she was in the seventh grade. "I had put down that my goals were to be a brain surgeon, a lawyer, and a lesbian" (p. 130). In her review of *Does Your Mama Know?* titled "No Longer Orphaned by Silence," Dale Edwyna Smith wrote, "They are beautiful poems and stories, yes, but more than that, they are proof of our existence and show how essential it is that we have a literature of our own" (*The Lesbian Review of Books*, Fall 1997, p. 16). Strong language and explicit sex. *Topics*: African-American, Haitian-American, and Jamaican-Canadian Literature, Anthologies, Coming Out.

Muse, Daphne, editor. *Prejudice: Stories About Hate, Ignorance, Revelation, and Transformation.* Hyperion, 1995. Hardcover $16.95 (ISBN 0786800240); Paper $7.95 (ISBN 0786813105). Ages 12 up.

This eclectic mix of short stories and excerpts from novels examines the many facets of prejudice. In the introduction, Muse writes about the experiences that helped her "understand how racism, sexism, homophobia, anti-Semitism, and classism have negated the accomplishments of millions of people" (p. x). She selected fifteen pieces for this anthology, hoping to inspire young people to join the struggle to create an equitable and just society. "So's Your Mama" by Julie Blackwomon is an engaging story featuring Kippy, a young African-American girl whose mother is a lesbian. She says, "[This] means mostly that my mother has a bunch of women friends and works for the women's bookstore and goes to lots of meetings and demonstrations and stuff" (p. 50). One day, when Kippy is hanging out with her friends after school, one of them calls her mother's friend a "bulldagger." Kippy, who has known that this moment would come someday, tries to decide what to do. Should she fight back with words or her fists? The conflict is defused when one of her friends intervenes and suggests that the namecaller go home. This piece is also available in *Voyages Out 2* by Julie Blackwomon (Seal Press, 1990). Other stories that have lesbian or gay characters include "A Brief Moment in the Life of Angus Bethune" by Chris Crutcher and an excerpt from *Peter* by Kate Walker (reviewed in Chapter 2 of this book). *Topic*: Prejudice.

Newman, Lesléa. "Right Off the Bat." In *Speaking for Ourselves: Short Stories by Jewish Lesbians,* edited by Irene Zahava. The Crossing Press, 1990. Hardcover $23.95 (ISBN 0895944294); Paper $8.95 (ISBN 0895944286). Ages 12 up.

Right off the bat, twelve-year-old Ronnie wants prospective friends to know that her mother is a lesbian so that they won't reject her later when they find out. Better to weed out the homophobes early so that she won't have to go through what she did with her best friend, Brenda. "She said go away, my mom says I can't talk to you anymore. Your mother's a dyke." Ronnie explains, "Dyke is a bad word for lesbian, like Yid is a bad word for Jew. I'm Jewish too, which is another thing that makes me different" (p. 13). This clever story, told from the perspective of the daughter of a lesbian, is written with humor, insight, and poignancy.

Ronnie, who lives with her mother and her mother's lover, Linda, makes sure that new friends know that she doesn't have a father. She matter-of-factly explains how she was conceived through alternative insemination. Ronnie shares the ups and downs of their lives. One year her mother and Linda got all dressed up and went out to celebrate their anniversary. When they left the restaurant, they discovered that their truck had four slashed tires. Ronnie's anger erupted and she told them that these things wouldn't happen if they would quit holding hands. Her mother explained, "if I only teach you one thing in your whole life, it's be yourself. . . . be whoever you are and be proud of it, okay?" (p. 19). This is an engaging piece, filled with images of lesbian culture: bumper stickers, t-shirts, and more. Even though it was written for adults, teenage children of lesbian and gay parents will enjoy it, too. *Topics*: Jewish Literature, Lesbian Mothers.

Roscoe, Will, editor. *Living the Spirit: A Gay American Indian Anthology*. St. Martin's, 1989. Paper $10.95 (ISBN 031203475X). Ages 16 up.

Living the Spirit celebrates the rich heritage of lesbian and gay Indians and examines the double challenge of racism and homophobia in contemporary society. Compiled by Gay American Indians (GAI) of San Francisco, this exciting anthology includes short stories, poetry, interviews, excerpts from novels, essays, photographs, art, and anthropological reports. GAI was founded in 1975 by Barbara Cameron (Lakota) and Randy Burns (Northern Paiute) and has been instrumental in ending the isolation of lesbian and gay Native People. Programs include referral services, cultural and educational projects, and active involvement within local networks of Indian organizations and agencies. Writers included are Paula Gunn Allen, Beth Brant, Randy Burns, Chrystos, Ben the Dancer, Janice Gould, Nola M. Hadley, Daniel Little Hawk, Maurice Kenny, Richard LaFortune, Carole LaFavor, Joe Dale Tate Nevaquaya, Lawrence William O'Conner, Debra S. O'Gara, M. Owlfeather, Erna Pahe, Kieran Prather/Jerry, Will Roscoe, Tala Sanning, Daniel-Harry Steward, Midnight Sun, Mary TallMountain, and Anne Waters. The book opens with "Some Like Indians Endure," a poem by Paula Gunn Allen in which she writes, "dykes remind me of indians/like indians dykes/are supposed to die out . . . go away/to nowhere (p. 12). In "Children of Grandmother Moon," M. Owlfeather writes about his first love and the loneliness and sadness he felt when his lover moved away. "Speaking Up" is Will Roscoe's interview of Erna Pahe, who served as Executive Director and President of GAI. She discusses GAI's involvement, visibility, and advocacy in the Indian community. She says that gay people are caring, aware, and sensitive, adding, "we are special, because we're able to deal with all of life in general" (p. 114). Appended resources include contact addresses, a table of North American tribes with berdache and alternative gender roles, contributor notes, sources, and suggested reading. *Topic*: Native-American Literature.

Ruff, Shawn Stewart, editor. *Go the Way Your Blood Beats: An Anthology of Lesbian and Gay Fiction by African American Writers*. Holt, 1995. Hardcover $30.00 (ISBN 0805047360). Ages 17 up.

This powerful collection of short stories and excerpts from novels presents a critical discussion of race, culture, and sexual identity while delivering thought-provoking images of love realized or frustrated. The list of contributors includes both established and emerging writers: James Baldwin, Amira Baraka (a.k.a. Leroi Jones), Becky Birtha, Bennett Capers, Samuel R. Delaney, Max Gordon, E. Lynn Harris, Charles W. Harvey, Carolivia Herron, Cary Alan Johnson, Gayl Jones, Randall Kenan, Audre Lorde, Catherine E. McKinley, Toni Morrison, Bruce Morrow, Gloria Naylor, Alice Dunbar Nelson, Richard Bruce Nugent, Maude Irwin Owens, Shawn Stewart Ruff, Carl Hancock Rux, Sapphire, Reginald Shepherd, Brooke M. Stephens, Wallace Thurman, Alice Walker, Orian Hyde Weeks, Artress Bethany White, John Edgar Wideman, Jacqueline Woodson, and Richard Wright. The title was inspired by an interview of James Baldwin with the *Village Voice* in 1984 in which he said, "The best advice I ever got was from an old friend of mine, a Black friend, who said you have to go the way your blood beats." Editor Ruff adds, "live life instinctively, intuitively, with integrity and an awareness of consequences, and without self-deception" (p. xxii). Through thirty-two stories, nearly half in print for the first time, writers from the Harlem Renaissance to the present examine a wide variety of themes and issues such as love, homophobia, self-acceptance, AIDS, gender, and class. This anthology has been described as surprising, fierce, sensual, eloquent, grim, rich, painful, and brave. Explicit sex and strong language. *Topic*: African-American Literature.

Singer, Bennett L, editor. *Growing Up Gay, Growing Up Lesbian: A Literary Anthology*. New Press, 1994. Paper $9.95 (ISBN 1565841034). Ages 12 up.

This eclectic collection includes short stories, poems, diary entries, letters, essays, rap lyrics, and excerpts from novels by teenagers and established writers. Presented in sections on self-discovery, friends/relationships, family, and facing the world, the 56 pieces represent diverse ages, races, and viewpoints. The material ranges from fiction by Rita Mae Brown, James Baldwin, and Jeannette Winterson to autobiographical essays by Audre Lorde, Martina Navratilova, and Quentin

Crisp, to poetry by Pat Parker, Kitty Tsui, Essex Hemphill, and Dorothy Allison. Excerpts from young adult writers Nancy Garden (*Annie on My Mind*) and M. E. Kerr (*Night Kites*), a bibliography, and an extensive resource directory round out this excellent introduction to lesbian and gay literature. In a letter to his aunt and uncle, Tom Shepard, a recent graduate from Stanford University wrote, "I think by trusting young people with honest information, as opposed to protecting them from what is taboo and controversial, we empower them to make educated and non-bigoted choices in their lives" (p. 222). By making books like this available to young readers, we help them find the self-acceptance and respect to live a joyful, full life. *Topics*: Anthologies, Interviews, Letters, Poetry, Short Stories.

Trujillo, Carla, editor. *Chicana Lesbians: The Girls Our Mothers Warned Us About*. Third Woman Press, 1991. Paper $12.95 (ISBN 094321906X). Ages 16 up. *Awards*: Lambda Best Lesbian Anthology Award, Out/Write Vanguard Best Pioneering Contribution to the Field of Lesbian/Gay Literature.

Composed of creative and theoretical works and art by twenty-four Chicanas, this collection documents the diversity in class, color, region, education, and language found in Latina lesbian literature. Distinctive styles and topics are featured, including fictional explorations of interracial relationships and critiques of gender bias and homophobia in Latino and U.S. cultures. The book is divided into four sections: "The Life," "The Desire," "The Color," and "The Struggle." Contributors include Carmen Abrego, Diane Alcalá, M. Alvarez, Gloria Anzaldúa, Angela Arellano, Cathy Arellano, Martha Barrera, Ana Barreto, Ana Castillo, Yan Maria Castro, Terri de la Peña, Karen T. Delgadillo, Diane C. Gómez, E. D. Hernández, Natasha López, Gina Montoya, Cherríe Moraga, Marta A. Navarro, Monica Palacios, Emma Pérez, Juanita M. Sánchez, Lidia Tirado White, Carla Trujillo, Marie-Elise Wheatwind, and Yvonne Yarbro-Bejarano. In "La Frontera," Diane Alcalá writes about her childhood growing up in Del Rio, Texas. She came out to her sisters when she was eighteen years old. One of them is also a lesbian. In a letter, her mother wrote, "Because of my religion, I have a hard time understanding (but) you are my hija, I love you" (p. 196). In her biographical sketch, Natasha López wrote, "Being lesbian is not 'abnormal'; what is abnormal and unnatural is being totally straight. Society creates heterosexuals. Most people are not naturally heterosexual—I encourage every woman to explore her sexuality" (p. 199). *Topics*: Anthologies, Chicana Literature.

Tsui, Kitty. "Skinner and Choy." In *To Be Continued*, edited by Michele Karlsberg and Karen X. Tulchinsky. Firebrand, 1998. Paper $11.95 (ISBN 1563411040). Ages 16 up.

Everywhere Jean Choy goes, she is taunted by racist ditties and assumptions. One day she is attacked by the local bullies, who throw her in a mud puddle. Just when a foot threatens to come down on her face, a voice calls out, "Stop that, you bully!" (p. 140). This is the beginning of a friendship between Alison Skinner and Jean Choy that lasts through high school, when Jean moves from England to the United States. The two form a gang, Skinner and Choy, which has one rule: Only tomboys allowed. They both hate dolls and love exploring in the park. Alison helps Jean overcome her fear of heights as they climb their first tree together. The story ends twenty years later in San Francisco, when Jean sees a poster saying "Lost: Alison Skinner" (p. 147). The second part of this story will appear in *To Be Continued: Take Two*. "Skinner and Choy" is one of eleven stories in an anthology of page-turning writing by contemporary lesbian authors. Kitty Tsui is an Asian Pacific lesbian writer whose poetry and short stories have been widely anthologized. *Topic*: Chinese-American Literature.

4

Nonfiction

Bass, Ellen and Kate Kaufman. *Free Your Mind: The Book for Gay, Lesbian, and Bisexual Youth and Their Allies*. HarperPerennial, 1996. Paper $14.00 (ISBN 0060951044). Ages 12 up.

This fantastic book is one of the most comprehensive resources available to young lesbian, gay, and bisexual people and their families, teachers, counselors, and friends. It has been described as practical, refreshing, lively, truly readable, groundbreaking, thoughtful, lifesaving, forthright, and user-friendly. An empowering guide, it is divided into six sections: "Self-Discovery," "Friends and Lovers," "Family," "School," "Spirituality," and "Community." Key points are summarized in boxes, and cartoons, photographs, graphs, jokes, and interviews with over fifty teenagers are scattered throughout. Inspiring quotes and biographical profiles of notable lesbian and gay people are highlighted in sidebars; diagrams accompany directions for how to use a condom and how to create safe barriers for oral sex with women. In the school section, information for educators includes curriculum ideas, a sample school non-discrimination policy, and a sample school code of behavior. The thirty-three-page state-by-state resource section includes agencies, services, organizations, hotline numbers, videos, books, and more. This reasonably priced, extraordinary guide ends with a comprehensive index. The authors, both lesbians, write, "Our goal . . . has been to contribute to making the world a safer, happier place for lesbian, gay, and bisexual youth and those who love them. We hope to help families come together in love and understanding, to affirm loving and respectful relationships, to lessen despair and isolation, to honor the fabulous youth who are leading this vital liberation movement, and to validate the worth of all young people, nurturing self-esteem, pride, and joy" (p. xxi). *Topics*: Coming Out, Community, Health, Religion, Schools.

Berzon, Betty. *Setting Them Straight.* Penguin, 1996. Paper $10.95 (ISBN 0452274214). Ages 16 up.

This empowering book was written to help lesbian and gay people of all ages confront homophobia, challenge bigotry, and create change. Berzon, an activist, writer, and therapist, writes, "You and I are diminished by discrimination when the value of our very existence is questioned. When . . . we don't fight back, our integrity as gay and lesbian human beings is further compromised. Talking back to bigotry is posing the issue of our right to love versus their right to hate" (p. 8). She suggests ways to overcome the fear of speaking out and includes typical scenarios of encounters with homophobia. In Part I, "Defining the Problem," Berzon analyzes the origins of prejudice, offers ideas for ways to understand and manage one's own anger, and discusses ways to deal with scapegoating. Part II, "Finding Solutions," offers guidelines for encounters with family, friends, acquaintances, and strangers; suggests ways to challenge messages and messengers; and discusses referendums on lesbian and gay people in American life, including the military ban, legal marriage, and anti-gay ballot initiatives. Berzon weaves her personal experiences into the chapters, sharing how she overcame forty years of denial to embrace her lesbian identity. She writes, "Every social movement is born of anger over injustice" (p. 42). Her suggestions for how to get our anger to work for us are especially helpful. "I channeled my own anger into useful action, and one product of that action is this book" (p. 45). The result is a readable, timely, and important resource. Berzon is also the author of the lesbian and gay self-help classic *Permanent Partners* and the editor of *Positively Gay*. This book includes short profiles of noteworthy lesbian and gay people, a reading list, and an index. *Topic*: Self-Help.

Bono, Chastity with Billie Fitzpatrick. *Family Outing.* Little, Brown, 1998. Hardcover $24.00 (ISBN 0316102334); 1999 Paper $14.95 (ISBN 0316115967). Ages 12 up.

This helpful coming-out guide weaves Chastity Bono's own dramatic story with those of other young lesbian and gay people and their parents. Bono generously shares painful memories of her early years, when she lived under a cloud of disapproval because of her mother's attitude toward her appearance and behavior. She clearly remembers the day she "vowed never to wear anything girlie again" (p. 6). Using a caring tone, she helps young people plan their coming-out process: begin by making sure you are really ready; then tell someone you know you can trust. As she elaborates on the process, she moves from one interview to another, analyzing recurring themes. She writes, "The goal of *Family Outing* is not only to guide gay women and men through the closet door but also to give them the tools with which they can complete the process by bringing their families, especially their parents, along with them" (p. x). Bono's book is readable and interesting. As with most books, there are some problems. Bono writes, "a family's acceptance of a gay or lesbian child or sibling is directly tied to the gay person's ability to accept him- or herself. As gay people we can't expect acceptance from those close to us and the world at large until we are completely comfortable with being gay ourselves" (p. viii). Many readers will disagree, feeling that it is the parents who should protect and empower their children. In spite of apologist statements like this and several oppressive terms such as "mannish" and "sexual intercourse," this is a well-intentioned, ultimately reassuring book. No bibliography or index. *Topics*: Coming Out, Hollywood.

Borhek, Mary. *Coming Out to Parents: A Two-Way Survival Guide for Lesbians and Gay Men and Their Parents.* Pilgrim, 1993. Paper $15.95 (ISBN 0829809570). Ages 14 up.

In her first book, *My Son Eric*, Mary Borhek wrote about her struggle to understand and accept her gay son. Drawing on that profound experience, she now offers heartfelt advice to lesbians and gay men and their parents. She explores the fears and misgivings that young people often have about coming out to their parents, and provides suggestions for how, when, and where to come out, what reactions to expect, and how to deal with the initial responses. She includes information on how to prepare for the possibility of being disowned, emotionally and/or legally. She examines the feelings of confusion, disappointment, and guilt that can beset parents and explains that the initial reactions of grief and loss can be overcome through understanding and love. She also includes information about religious issues for those readers who are concerned about what the Bible says about homosexuality. Using a warm, reassuring tone, Borhek encourages all parties to avoid wounding each other and to focus on the positive aspects of their relationships. She writes, "I am sad that such elaborate preparation is necessary in order for a gay or lesbian child to be open with his or her parents about the person that child really is" (p. xi). Extensive notes, a sample coming-out letter, a list of organizations, and a bibliography are appended. *Topic*: Coming Out.

Brimner, Larry Dane. *Being Different: Lambda Youths Speak Out.* Franklin Watts, 1995. Hardcover $24.00 (ISBN 0531112225). Ages 14 up. *Award*: New York Public Library Best Book for the Teen Age.

Series: The Lesbian and Gay Experience. Dedicated "To lambda youths everywhere—know that there is a rainbow," this compelling book explores the issues that young lesbian and gay people face at home, school, church, and community. The voices of courageous teens speak out about their experiences, confront ignorance and bigotry, and demand to be treated with dignity and respect. In the foreword, Patricia Nell Warren writes, "we are all injured by the guilt, terror, and deviousness that are fostered in our children as a result of extremist efforts to keep homosexuality criminalized" (p. 12). In his poignant introduction, Larry Dane Brimner writes about his early years, during which he remembers a blur of psychiatric appointments, electroshock treatments, and three suicide attempts. He writes, "In every school, in every city, in every state, in every country, there are sexual-minority youth who are wishing desperately to find themselves portrayed in books" (p. 23). Brimner divides this important book into four chapters: On Being Different, On Coming Out, On High School, and On the Issues. He introduces each chapter with an excellent overview of the issues involved, followed by interviews with the teenagers. In "Contemplations of the First Year Out," sixteen-year-old Trey writes, "I've been harassed by teachers and cruel students, and been 'outed' by a faculty member at my high school. . . . I spent hour upon hour talking to one of my teachers, who began to attend P-FLAG (Parents, Families, and Friends of Lesbians and Gays) meetings as my friend" (p. 57). All in all, he reports that it has been the best year of his life. Other teenagers talk about letters they wrote asking for advice, hiding in heterosexual relationships, attending Gay Youth Alliance meetings, and waiting for high school to end so they could start their real lives. Several give advice to young readers. "Above all, don't give up. Don't compromise who you are. Be honest with yourself" (p. 113). This book includes one of the most comprehensive resource lists available, listing social service agencies for every state, bookstores, archives and libraries, religious organizations, and Internet addresses. Also included are photographs, chapter notes, bibliographies, and an index. *Topics*: Coming Out, Interviews.

Brimner, Larry Dane. *Letters to Our Children: Lesbian and Gay Adults Speak to the New Generation.* Franklin Watts, 1997. Hardcover $24.00 (ISBN 0531113221); Paper $9.95 (ISBN 0531158438). Ages 14 up. *Award*: New York Public Library Best Book for the Teen Age.

Series: The Lesbian and Gay Experience. "Don't give up, and don't give in. Fight for your dignity. . . . Believe that you are worthwhile and life is worthwhile" (p. 97) writes poet Ron Norman in this collection of letters and essays designed to provide support for young lesbians and gay people. Seventeen writers of diverse experiences and perspectives responded to the need young gay people have for mentoring from their elders. They share the mistakes they made, the ways they solved problems, and the actions they took. Several provide suggestions for paths young people might follow if they wish to make an impact on the social and political climate. They encourage youngsters to become familiar with our history and culture, our music and art, and our political work in order to dismantle internalized homophobia and gain strength and freedom. Gary Mallon writes about checking out the Kinsey study on sexuality when he was eight years old, and David D. Clark shares the coming-out letter he wrote to his nieces. In "Celebrate Your Sexual Orientation," Ronni Sanlo, the director of the Lesbian Gay Bisexual Programs Office at the University of Michigan, unflinchingly writes about the pain and anger she experienced as a young lesbian. She advises, "Dear young people, as hard as it may be at times, look in your mirror and love that person looking back at you. . . . read some books and find out who our heroes and forebears are. . . . and you are glorious!" (pp. 42–43). In the most lyrical piece in the collection, "Elemental Wanderer," S. E. Gilman writes about love, loss, struggle, and hope. She tells young people that knowledge and integrity are within, grounding her piece in the four elements—air, earth, fire, and water. "The path we are on is like no other. This is why I hope you'll leave a marker too, a marker at the elemental corners of your life" (p. 85). Editor Larry Dane Brimner introduces each section with an overview and discussion of terms. He discusses the need young lesbian and gay people have for mentors and explains that elders have been hesitant to respond to that need for fear of being labeled "recruiter" or "molester." This unique book shows one way elders can mentor from a distance and hopefully touch many young lives and hearts. Black-and-white photographs, brief biographical profiles of the contributors, a short resource list, chapter notes, and a bibliography are included. *Topics*: Elders, Mentoring, Role Models.

Brimner, Larry Dane. *The NAMES Project*. Children's Press, 1999. Hardcover $20.00 (ISBN 051620999X). Ages 8 up.

Series: Cornerstones of Freedom. This informative book traces the origins and growth of the NAMES Project AIDS Memorial Quilt. Through color and black-and-white photographs and accessible text, Larry Dane Brimner tells the story of how the quilt has called attention to a devastating disease, exposed governmental neglect, promoted healing, and spurred action. Striking aerial views show the quilt displayed in its entirety on the National Mall in Washington, D.C. As of April 1999, the quilt weighed 52 tons and was made up of more than 41,000 panels. It contained almost 80,000 names and spread out over twenty-five football fields. Brimner writes, "The panels speak their own language. Some are sad. Some are funny. Some are defiant" (p. 27). The panel that honors children's book author Arnold Lobel was created by schoolchildren in Santa Cruz, California. Through the National High School Quilt Program any high school can receive sections of the quilt to use with their AIDS prevention program. This well-researched book concludes with a glossary, a timeline, and an index. *Topics*: AIDS, Art, The NAMES Project, Quilts.

Carlip, Hillary. *Girl Power: Young Women Speak Out.* Warner, 1995. Paper $13.99 (ISBN 0446670219). Ages 12 up.

This spirited collection celebrates the potential of writing to explore, empower, heal, and transform. The thoughts, fears, and dreams of young women between the ages of thirteen and nineteen from all across the United States are by turns insightful, courageous, fiery, poignant, disturbing, funny, and entertaining. These stirring voices of females from diverse backgrounds are divided into thirteen chapters featuring gang members, riot grrrls, teen mothers, queers, cowgirls, Native Americans, farm teens, rappers, surfers, sorority sisters, homemakers, and pageant queens. The chapter featuring the writings of young lesbians and bisexuals speaks out loud and strong against homophobia in all its destructive forms. Lony Nelson writes, "I'm a seventeen year old lesbian . . . writer, and the words I put on paper are the purest, most honest connection I can have with the world around me. I want to be understood. I want my anger, pain and frustration to make someone who has never even met me see red" (p. 113). Some young lesbians write about the anguish of being constantly bombarded with the disapproval of parents, peers, teachers, media, and religious institutions. Others write about the pride, love, and happiness they have found with other lesbians. Whitney Morrison shares her experiences starting a Sexual Minority Young Group in a rural part of Virginia, where there are many conservative people who think that it's a sin to be a homosexual. "I'm eighteen years old and proud to say I've been a lesbian all my life. . . . In whatever lies ahead I'm with my 'family,' and we are armed and ready for battle" (pp. 114–115). Resource and referral list appended. *Topics*: Authorship, Writing.

Chandler, Kurt. *Passages of Pride: Lesbian and Gay Youth Come of Age.* Times Books, 1995. Hardcover $23.00 (ISBN 0812923804); Alyson Publications, 1997. Paper $11.95 (ISBN 1555834175). Ages 14 up.

Six Minneapolis–St. Paul teenagers speak eloquently about their experiences of realizing at an early age that they were different, of learning how to hide, of facing ostracism, harassment, and depression, and ultimately of coming out and finding community, self-acceptance, and hope. Also included are briefer profiles of dozens of teens from across the country who face similar challenges. Interspersed throughout the book are sidebars: "The Roots of Homosexuality," "Networks of Hope," and "A Shining Resiliency," and insights from notable pediatricians, psychologists, and educators. *Passages of Pride* has been praised for its textured perspective, compelling narratives, and illuminating discussions. It has also been criticized for its reductive approach to sexuality, trite descriptions, and pitying tone. Nevertheless, Chandler, who is heterosexual, handles the material with good intentions and open-mindedness. The voices of his interviewees are the real strength of this book. One of them, Amy Grahn, is also featured through photographs and personal narrative in *Growing Up Gay: The Sorrows and Joys of Gay and Lesbian Adolescence* by Rita Reed, reviewed in Chapter 5 of this book. Amy survived isolation, rejection, and depression, embraced her lesbianism, and found community. Chandler includes her parents' story of how they battled their own homophobia, pushed for reforms in their church and school district, and marched with their daughter in a Lesbian/Gay Pride March. Chandler's analysis isn't as clear as Linnea Due's in *Joining the Tribe*, but the words of the teenagers are just as compelling. *Topics*: Coming Out, Interviews.

Cobain, Bev. *When Nothing Matters Anymore: A Survival Guide for Depressed Teens*. Free Spirit Publishing, 1998. Paper $13.95 (ISBN 1575420368). Ages 12 up.

This much-needed resource offers helpful information for depressed teens and their friends, relatives, and teachers. Author Bev Cobain wrote the book after her cousin, Kurt Cobain, ended his struggle with depression and chemical dependency by taking his life in 1994. His suicide stunned millions of teens who identified with the music of his band, Nirvana. This book is Bev's way of trying to make sense of his death and of reaching out to teens who are sad, discouraged, or depressed. She describes the causes and types of depression and the connections between depression, suicide, and drug and alcohol abuse. Then she discusses ways to stay healthy, different kinds of professional treatment, and resources to turn to for more information, advice, and support. Interspersed throughout the book are the first-person stories of teens who have grappled with depression, found help, and survived to offer suggestions to young readers. Cera, an eighteen-year-old lesbian, says, "Hang in there. There *are* resources; there *are* people who care and can help, even if they don't know you. Find them. Use the Internet. Keep the hope" (p. 53). Highlighted survival tips include: get some exercise, take a break, have some fun, eat good food, talk about it, stick with it, and feed your spirit. Quotes from well-known people are offered, such as the words James Baldwin wrote: "Not everything that is faced can be changed. But nothing can be changed until it is faced" (p. 103). This well-designed, readable book also includes a letter Bev wrote to Kurt after his death, a note to parents, a mood chart, illustrations, an index, and much more. *Topics*: Depression, Suicide Prevention.

D'Angelo, Laura. *Hate Crimes*. Chelsea House, 1997. Hardcover $19.95 (ISBN 0791042669). Ages 12 up.

Series: Crime, Justice, and Punishment. Through careful historical analysis and horrifying example, this title examines hate crimes against people from racial, ethnic, religious, and sexual-identity minorities. *Hate Crimes* traces the origins of bigotry and describes the psychology of hatred, exposing the ways in which particular groups seek to mobilize and direct violence. The Ku Klux Klan, Aryan Nation, Christian Identity, and Nazi skinheads are among the most prominent of the estimated 275 organized hate groups in the United States. But experts say that most hate crimes are committed by people with no hate-group affiliation. D'Angelo analyzes a range of bias-motivated acts—what causes them, who commits them, and what can be done to stop them. She discusses Supreme Court decisions that distinguish between verbal or symbolic expressions of hatred, which are frequently referred to as hate speech, and actual conduct. "Words may be weapons, but they are protected by the Constitution. Actions are not" (p. 18). According to hate crime experts Jack Levin and Jack McDevitt, lesbians and gays are the most frequently targeted victims of thrill-seeking hate criminals. The attackers are often teenage males with an irrational fear and hatred of homosexuals. Most of the cases discussed in this book are against racial minorities but D'Angelo does provide information about the 1990 murder of Julio Rivera, a gay man from the South Bronx. This important book ends on a hopeful note with a discussion about what can be done to stop the hatred. Includes photographs, a bibliography, and an index. *Topic*: Hate Crimes.

Duberman, Martin, Martha Vicinus, and George Chauncey, Jr., editors. *Hidden from History: Reclaiming the Gay and Lesbian Past*. NAL/Dutton, 1990. Paper $17.95 (ISBN 0452010675). Ages 16 up. *Awards*: Lambda Rising Best Gay Anthology, Lambda Rising Best Lesbian Anthology.

This informative anthology brings together scholarly studies of lesbian and gay life in places as diverse as the Athens of Plato, Renaissance Italy, Victorian London, Jazz Age Harlem, Revolutionary Russia, Nazi Germany, Castro's Cuba, and post–World War II San Francisco. Twenty-nine essays by prominent historians explore the lives of South African miners, Chinese courtiers, Japanese samurai, Native Americans, English school-girls and boys, and urban working women. The juxtaposition of research crossing boundaries of time, race, gender, and culture makes this a par-ticularly fascinating volume. In the introduction, the editors examine atti-tudes toward research on the history of homosexuality, noting that many scholars still think of the subject as marginal, distasteful, and embarras-sing. Nevertheless, this is a rich volume in which previously published pieces were revised and nine completely new essays were commissioned. Because the history of lesbian and gay people has been suppressed, the hunger for knowledge of the past is strong. The editors write, "For many, gay history helps constitute the gay community by giving it a tradition, helps women and men validate and understand who they are by show-ing them who they have been" (p. 12). Extensive notes and information about the contributors are appended. *Topic*: History.

Due, Linnea. *Joining the Tribe: Growing Up Gay and Lesbian in the 90's.* Doubleday, 1995. Paper $12.95 (ISBN 0385475004). Ages 14 up.

This collection of poignant interviews with young lesbian and gay peo-ple explains why increased visibility does not immediately translate into improved quality of life. As one interviewee says, "Now they know we're here." In her excellent introduction, Due examines the complex issues and challenges young lesbians and gays face today. She writes, "A larger and more active gay community cannot ameliorate the isola-tion and loneliness of teens who are not part of it" (p. 43). She traveled around the country, interviewing urban, suburban, and rural kids from diverse geographic, ethnic, class, and philosophical backgrounds. The results are reported in depth and demonstrate the intelligence, courage, and sensitivity of the interviewees. They vividly recount the ostracism, harassment, condemnation, and violence they have experienced. Some speak about the ways in which they found support, love, pride, and self-acceptance. There are some heart-wrenching stories here, but Due never makes her subjects seem tragic. Victoria Edminster from Missouri came out to her mother when she was seven years old and had her first rela-tionship when she was in the ninth grade. Brandon Clark, a gay agitator at the University of Portland, was kicked out of his dorm a few weeks before the interview. Allyson Mount came out at her prep school because silence is a form of lying. John Swensen sits at home talking to other lonely gay teens on the Internet. Caroline Anchors received death threats at Xavier University in New Orleans. Her mother hid her acceptance letter to Bryn Mawr, so Caroline ended up at a community college. These and other stories make this a book that is impossible to put down. In the postscript, Due makes suggestions for ways concerned adults can help and provides an update on each of the interviewees. *Joining the Tribe* is both disturbing and hopeful. A compelling tribute to determination and resiliency, it reveals how much progress we have made and how much work there is yet to be done. *Topics*: Coming Out, Interviews.

Faderman, Lillian. *To Believe in Women: What Lesbians Have Done for America—A History.* Houghton Mifflin, 1999. Hardcover $30.00 (ISBN 039585010X). Ages 17 up.

Homophobia and heterosexism take many forms. One of them is era-sure, which is a serious problem in history books. Often histories of lesbian and gay men delete any information about their personal lives or go to great lengths to obscure their sexual identities. This is why *To Believe in Women* is such an important book. Lillian Faderman sets the record straight (or unstraight) about a number of late nineteenth- and early twentieth-century women whose lives can be described as lesbian and who were in the forefront of the battle to gain the rights and privi-leges that large numbers of American women enjoy today. A ground-breaking reappraisal of women who are known by history but whose personal stories have been incomplete, *To Believe in Women* examines how their lesbianism may have facilitated their accomplishments. This well-documented, fascinating, and accessible book preserves lesbian his-tory, and in so doing provides exciting possibilities for role models for young lesbians. Faderman, who wrote *Odd Girls and Twilight Lovers, Sur-passing the Love of Men: Romantic Friendship and Love Between Women from the Renaissance to the Present,* and *Chloe Plus Olivia: An Anthology of Lesbian Literature from the Seventeenth Century to the Present,* argues persuasively that many notable women had what would now be called lesbian rela-tionships, free from the constraints of traditional heterosexual arrange-ments, which would have impeded their pursuits in education, politics, professional life, and culture. Here at last are the reclaimed histories of Susan B. Anthony, Frances Willard, Jane Addams, Anna Howard Shaw, Carrie Chapman Catt, and many others. Faderman writes, "By emphasiz-ing what I call the "lesbian presence" in movements that have bettered America, I aim to bring to the forefront what has been unfairly neglected and for too long unspoken" (p. 12). Particularly affirming to lesbians who have been denied this information are excerpts from letters and diaries. For example, Faderman tells us that Jane Addams and Mary Rozet Smith were together for more than forty years. When Smith died, Addams was devastated, as she wrote in a letter to her nephew, "I suppose I could have willed my heart to stop beating, but the thought of what she had been to me for so long kept me from being cowardly" (p. 132). Addams survived Smith by only fourteen months. By writing this book, Faderman has given us a precious gift, one that will affirm young lesbians and give them hope for a future that includes love, acceptance, and dignity. Black-and-white photographs, extensive chapter notes, and an index are included. *Topics*: Activists, Lesbian History, Suffrage Leaders.

Ford, Michael Thomas. *100 Questions and Answers About AIDS: A Guide for Young People*. Macmillan, 1992. Paper $4.95 (ISBN 0688126979). Ages 11 up. *Awards*: ALA Best Book for Young Adults, New York Public Library Best Book for the Teen Age.

This frank, well-organized book combines comprehensive information with poignant personal stories. Direct answers to questions cover modes of transmission, stages of infection, myths, prevention, diagnosis, and treatment. Using a nonjudgmental tone, Ford successfully conveys the message that young people can take control of their own destinies and avoid infection. Explicit details include directions for how to use a condom, how to make and use a dental dam, and how to clean a syringe. The questions are first listed in the front of the book and then each one is printed in boldface type preceding the answer. In the introduction, Ford reminds readers that no one is immune to the AIDS virus. People of all ages, races, sexual orientations, and genders can be infected. The voices of the four young interviewees who are living with HIV say more about the reality of the epidemic than any statistics, facts, or numbers can. Dawn Marcel, a heterosexual woman whose daughter died when she was eighteen months old, talks about the advice she gives people: "You really have to be conscious of the choices you are making now, because if I had made different choices for myself, my daughter would be alive today, and that's something I have to live with every second of my life" (p. 50). A glossary, index, list of organizations, and hotline directory for every state are appended. William B. Rubenstein, Director of the ACLU National AIDS Project wrote: "This is one of the best books explaining HIV disease—to people of any age—that I have ever read. I hope it becomes required reading in high schools across America." *Topics*: AIDS, Health, HIV, Interviews.

Ford, Michael Thomas. *Outspoken: Role Models from the Lesbian and Gay Community*. Morrow, 1998. Hardcover $16.00 (ISBN 0688148964); Paper $4.95 (ISBN 0688148972). Ages 10 up. *Awards*: *Booklist* Editors' Choice "Top of the List" Selection for Young Adult Nonfiction, National Council of Social Studies–Children's Book Council Notable Children's Book, New York Public Library Best Book for the Teen Age, Lambda Literary Award Finalist, Voice of Youth Advocate Nonfiction Honor Award.

This excellent collection of interviews with eleven out lesbians and gay men is designed to provide young people with positive images of individuals who are leading happy, healthy, and productive lives. The interviewees include: Alison Bechdel, cartoonist; Dan Butler, actor; Lisa Edwards, rabbi; Nancy Garden, author; Tim Gill, business executive; Kevin Jennings, educator; Mark Leduc, boxer; Jenifer Levin, writer; Martin Palmer, doctor; Sarah Pettit, magazine editor; and Edgar Rodriguez, police officer. Ford's questions are individualized for each interviewee, and the engaging responses demonstrate the diversity within the lesbian/gay community. Each spokesperson offers heartfelt advice to young lesbians and gays. Nancy Garden says, "You have to hang on to the fact that you have every right to be here and to be exactly who you are. . . . You're a unique, special person, and you have a right to live your own life" (p. 66). Interspersed throughout the book are lists of films, books, organizations, support groups, and on-line resources. *Outspoken* also includes eleven "Lesbian and Gay Fast Facts" such as "How Do I Know If I'm Lesbian or Gay?," "What is Homophobia?," and "How Do I Find Other Gay Young People?" *Topics*: Interviews, Role Models.

Ford, Michael Thomas. *The Voices of AIDS*. Morrow, 1995. Hardcover $15.00 (ISBN 068805322X); Paper $4.95 (ISBN 0688053238). Ages 12 up. *Awards*: ALA Best Book for Young Adults, National Science Teachers Association–Children's Book Council Outstanding Science Trade Book for Children, *Booklist* Editors' Choice.

In this compassionate book, Michael Thomas Ford interviews twelve people whose lives have been touched by AIDS. The interviewees, who come from diverse cultural and social backgrounds, include young adults who are HIV positive, relatives and friends of AIDS patients, and AIDS educators and activists. Interspersed with the interviews are "AIDS Fast Facts," frank discussions about AIDS transmission, safer sex, the hows and whys of testing, and what young people can do to fight AIDS. *The Voices of AIDS* has been praised for its unflinching, succinct information, honest, moving interviews, and examination of themes of self-esteem, self-respect, and respect for others. It includes an index, a list of AIDS hotlines and organizations, and the addresses of each of the interviewees. One of the interviewees is Penny Raife Durant, who talks about why she wrote *When Heroes Die*, which is reviewed in Chapter 2 of this book. She says, "if this book keeps one kid safe or makes one kid think about it enough to ask the questions and get the information she or he needs not to get AIDS, then it's worth it" (p. 102). In the introduction, Ford writes, "Together, we can all work to encourage understanding of this frightening disease and the growing number of people who live with it every day of their lives" (p. xi). *Topics*: AIDS, HIV, Interviews.

Ford, Michael Thomas. *The World Out There: Becoming Part of the Lesbian and Gay Community*. The New Press, 1996. Hardcover $22.50 (ISBN 1565843339); Paper $14.95 (ISBN 1565842340). Ages 14 up. *Awards*: Lambda Literary Award Finalist, Firecracker Alternative Book Award Finalist.

Many adult lesbians and gay men will wish that a book like this had been available to them at a time when they were isolated and alone, desperately searching for information about how to find others like themselves. *The World Out There* provides basic information about what it means to be part of a lesbian and gay community. In a reassuring tone, Ford answers questions such as "What is a Gay Community?," "Why Should I Become Involved in the Gay Community?," and "How Can I Find the Gay Community?" Portraits of the communities in eight cities are included: Atlanta, Boston, New York City, San Francisco, Seattle, St. Louis, Toronto, and Washington, D.C. Brief biographical profiles of admirable lesbian and gay men such as Melissa Etheridge and Stephen Gendel are interspersed along with useful lists of books, magazines, songs, films, artists, and schools. This is a practical, affirming resource for young lesbians and gays. Ford writes, "If you are in a situation right now where you feel all alone or depressed, I hope that you will see that you are not really alone. . . . The gay community is filled with wonderful people doing exciting things with their lives, and you can be a part of that" (p. 189). *Topics*: Community, Role Models.

Fried, Scott. *If I Grow Up: Talking with Teens About AIDS, Love, and Staying Alive*. Scott Fried, 1997. Paper $12.00 (ISBN 0965904601). Ages 12 up.

This unique book is a collection of lectures, stories, and poems Scott Fried gathered over a period of five years as he traveled around the country meeting with tens of thousands of teenagers. Fried talks about how he became infected with HIV in 1987 and shares his message of hope, helping teens understand that in order to learn how to be safe, one must first learn *why* to stay safe. His inspirational book is filled with courage, love, and compassion. He writes, "When I was a teenager, very few people ever said to me, 'It's okay to love yourself exactly as you are. It's okay to love whomever you choose to love. It's okay to believe in yourself and all that you stand for, no matter how different you may feel from everyone else'" (Author's Note). He hopes to galvanize an "army of teenagers across this country and around the world, that [will change] the general perception of AIDS from ignorance to education, from fear to motivation, and from loss to love" (p. 8). This poignant book is divided into twelve sections: "My Story," "Love," "No," "Denial,"

"Abstinence," "Safer Sex," "Fear," "Testing," "Death," "Suicide," "Heroes," and "Activism." Powerful poems written by young people respond to three themes: "If I grow up," "If my friend had AIDS," and "This is my prayer as I race under the moon." The words appear in various sizes and fonts, with some messages printed in large bold letters. "That's why you say 'No.' Because you're worth it!" Fried has helped create HIV education programs around the country, encouraging teenagers to teach their own peer groups. His heartfelt message is one of self-respect and self-acceptance: if we love ourselves, we will do everything we can to protect ourselves and others. *Topic*: AIDS Prevention.

Gillespie, Peggy, editor. *Love Makes a Family: Portraits of Lesbian, Gay, Bisexual, and Transgender Parents and Their Families*. Photographs by Gigi Kaeser. University of Massachusetts Press, 1999. Hardcover $40.00 (ISBN 1558491800). Paper $19.95 (ISBN 1558491619). Photos: Ages 4 up, Text: Ages 14 up.

Foreword by Minnie Bruce Pratt; Introduction by Kath Weston; and Afterword by April Martin. Through beautiful black-and-white photographs and candid interviews, this exquisitely designed book challenges traditional definitions of family. Lively photographs show parents and children from diverse racial, economic, ethnic, and regional groups, family structures, and occupations. Adults and children talk about the joys, problems, concerns, and comforts of their family constellations. April Martin writes, "We must discard notions that attribute undue importance to family constellation, and instead recognize that love, resources, and commitment are the relevant variables. A parenting family is that grouping of people, bound together by affection and dedication, with a commitment to love, take care of, educate, and be responsible for a child" (p. 252). Martin estimates that there are between 3 million and 8 million lesbian, gay, bisexual, and transgender parents in the United States. When evaluating a family, she suggests that people consider "the maturity of the parents, their humanity, their constancy, their willingness to learn from their mistakes, their ability to let their actions be guided by both their hearts and their better judgment, their playfulness, and their capacity to find goodness across a wide range of diversity" (p. 252). Scholarly studies of parenthood overwhelmingly conclude that it is impossible to tell which children came from lesbian and gay households when examining their emotional, social, intellectual, gender role, and sexual orientation development. Twelve-year-old Sarah Zashin-Jacobson, who has two mothers, says it best: "My parents are there for me, and as far as I'm concerned, it doesn't matter what your family is like as long as they love you and you love them. And it doesn't matter what other people think because I know that my family is special no matter what" (p. 247). This oversized book ends with a resource guide to organizations, bibliographies, videos, curriculum guides, posters, and catalogues. *Love Makes a Family* is based on a traveling photo-text exhibit with the same name which has traveled nationwide since 1995 to public and private schools, universities, houses of worship, workplaces, corporate headquarters, conferences, pride events, galleries, and museums. More information is available through Family Diversity Projects, which distributes multiple copies of three additional exhibits: Of Many Colors: Portraits of Multiracial Families; Nothing to Hide: Mental Illness in the Family; and In Our Family: Portraits of All Kinds of Families. *Topics*: Lesbian, Gay, Bisexual, and Transgender Parents, Parenting, Photographs.

Gray, Mary L. *In Your Face: Stories from the Lives of Queer Youth*. Harrington Park Press, 1999. Hardcover $29.95 (ISBN 0789000768); Paper $17.95 (ISBN 1560238879). Ages 13 up.

Fifteen teens, ages 14–18, discuss their lives, personal backgrounds, and visions for the future in this valuable addition to the literature documenting the experiences of queer youth. Mary L. Gray, a queer rights advocate and activist, gathered these stories from transcriptions of taped sessions in which the participants interviewed each other. The topics discussed are apparent in the chapter titles: "You're WHAT? Coming Out to Family," "Do You Have to Let the Whole World Know?," "Condemned or Redeemed: What Does Your God Think of All This?," "Kids in the Hall: What Is It Like at School?," "CyberQueer: Finding Community on the Internet," "Community Views: The Lesbian/Bi/Gay World and Beyond," "Getting Involved: Extracurriculars in the Community," "First Kisses, Relationships, and Other Such Things," "The Future: Where Are We Going?," and "Listen Up! Messages to Others." After surviving ostracism, humiliation, substance abuse, self-mutilation, and suicide attempts, these courageous teens are all committed to making political change for the betterment of the queer community part of their life's work. Dawn, who is seventeen, says, "I really want to work in social change and activism and education, probably write some books" (p. 147). Eighteen-year-old Adam also wants to make a difference. "I hope that I can be a role model to other gay kids" (p. 146). Mary, who is eighteen, says, "I plan on making my queer identity a large part of my life. . . . I'm going to be a professional activist, and a lot of that's going to be stopping the existence of homophobia" (p. 153). In her summary, Gray notes, "Sharp criticisms are made of the adult queer community for the neglect of queer youth. Educators and others in positions of authority receive strong calls to action to intercede and support queer and questioning youth in school environments" (p. 144). *Topics*: Coming Out, Interviews.

Griffin, Pat. *Strong Women, Deep Closets: Lesbians and Homophobia in Sport.* Human Kinetics, 1998. Paper $19.95 (ISBN 088011729X). Ages 16 up.

This excellent book is important reading for everyone committed to social justice, even if they are not particularly interested in sports. What it has to say about homophobia and heterosexism is so well written it can be applied to any other field. *Strong Women, Deep Closets* examines the experiences of lesbians in sport, the effects of homophobia and heterosexism on all women athletes, and the connections between sexism, homophobia, and heterosexism. Pat Griffin, an athlete and coach, writes, "I hope to make the experiences of lesbians in sport visible, and in the process, discredit the corrosive stereotypes of lesbians that haunt all women in sport" (p. x). Engagingly written, the book combines interviews, research findings, historical accounts, personal narratives, photographs, cartoons, and tables. After her insightful preface and introduction, Griffin shares her own experiences growing up in a homophobic society. "Being an athlete and a lesbian have profoundly shaped who I am. Home for me is finally being able to embrace both proudly" (p. 2). She writes about the fear and shame she felt as a closeted lesbian athlete and coach and how she overcame them, going on to conduct workshops on homophobia, heterosexism, and other forms of social injustice. The psychological toll the closet exacts from its inhabitants echoes in the words of the interviewees. Griffin identifies the issues that must be addressed in order for sport to become more open and acceptable to lesbians. She recommends strategies for change in the areas of education, research, legislation, institutionalization, connection, agitation, and visibility. This remarkable book ends with an extensive list of references and an index. *Topic*: Sport.

Herdt, Gilbert and Andrew Boxer. *Children of Horizons: How Gay and Lesbian Teens Are Leading a New Way Out of the Closet.* Beacon, 1993. Hardcover $25.00 (ISBN 0807079286); 1996. Paper $14.00 (ISBN 0807079294). Ages 16 up.

At Horizons, a lesbian and gay community service founded in 1973 in Chicago, teens gather weekly to share experiences and get support as they begin the process of coming out. Gilbert Herdt, an anthropologist, and Andrew Boxer, a developmental psychologist, both of whom are gay, conducted a two-year study of over 200 of these ethnically diverse teenagers. In personal portraits and accounts of group meetings and activities, the authors follow the youth along the journey that takes them from isolation and secrecy to self-acceptance and active participation in lesbian and gay culture. *Children of Horizons* has been praised for its honest, thoughtful examination of the coming-out process, passionate analysis of the core of who these young people are, and groundbreaking work that confronts myths about lesbian and gay youth. The authors demonstrate that any confusion the teens may experience is not about their sexual identity but about how to express themselves in a homophobic, heterosexist society. When they feel free to come out of the closet, they emerge from this process both as psychologically healthy and as socially competent as their heterosexual peers. The authors write, "All things human built on respect and dignity for the individual, and equal rights for individuals as members of cultures in our society, will, in turn, create life-cherishing social relations" (p. 253). Index included. *Topics*: AIDS, Chicago, Coming Out, Pride Celebrations, Research.

Herman, Ellen. *Psychiatry, Psychology, and Homosexuality.* Chelsea House, 1995. Hardcover $24.95 (ISBN 0791026280); Paper $12.95 (ISBN 0791029778). Ages 14 up.

Series: Issues in Lesbian and Gay Life. Harvard professor Ellen Herman provides a comprehensive account of the ways in which psychiatry has shaped society's views of homosexuality and impacted lesbian and gay people's self-esteem. She demonstrates the power that mental health experts have in upholding or challenging the conventional belief that heterosexuality is normal and homosexuality is not. During World War II, psychiatrists gained influence by offering ways to diagnose and cure homosexuality, which they characterized as a disease. Arguing that lesbian and gay people were in need of help rather than punishment, psychiatrists employed such cruel methods of "cure" as shock treatments, genital surgeries, and institutionalization. They set themselves up as judges and gatekeepers, grouping homosexuality with schizophrenia, manic depression, and other serious disorders. The first edition of psychiatry's diagnostic bible, the *Diagnostic and Statistical Manual: Mental Disorders*, published in 1952, listed homosexuality as a "sociopathic personality disturbance." Until 1973, the American Psychiatric Association treated homosexuality as an illness rooted in arrested development and leading to a loveless life. The turning point is illustrated in the chapter titles: "Experts on Our Own Lives" and "Off the Couches, Into the Streets." Pressure from activists involved in the Lesbian/Gay Pride movement helped mental health professionals understand that homophobia, not homosexuality, is the problem. However, the profession as a whole still has problems. In 1991, the American Psychiatric Association's Committee on Lesbian and Gay Concerns released an alarming report: 58 percent of the experts polled had personal knowledge of biased, inadequate, and inappropriate practice. Herman ends her investigation with these words: "The current state of gay-friendly psychology is something to be proud of, and it certainly has been hard won. But the history of psychology and homosexuality shows that it is probably too soon to conclude that the war has been won. Relying too heavily on the kindness of strangers has been an error in the past, and it is still an error today. Whether the future will hold psychological well-being or misery for gay and lesbian Americans has not been permanently decided" (p. 145). Black-and-white photographs, a bibliography, and an index are included. *Topic*: Psychology.

Heron, Ann, editor. *Two Teenagers in Twenty: Writings by Gay and Lesbian Youth.* Alyson Publications, 1995. Paper $10.95 (ISBN 1555832822). Ages 10 up.

Personal narratives written by forty-three teenagers describe how they realized that they were lesbian or gay, what happened when they came out to family and friends, and how their lives have been affected by their sexual identity. Absorbing and moving, this valuable collection is important reading not only for teens but for everyone who works with them and cares about them. In this updated version of *One Teenager in Ten* (Alyson Publications, 1983), Heron interspersed nineteen new stories among twenty-four of the original pieces. When she conducted the research for the second book, she was hoping that things had gotten better for lesbian and gay teens. She writes, "Sadly, that was not the case. In 1993, *more* of the kids with whom I corresponded were talking about suicide than had done so a decade earlier. . . . These stories make it clear: the isolation and self-hatred that our society imposes on gay teenagers can kill them" (p. 177). Teens write about parents who screen their calls, go through their drawers, and read their letters; coaches who tell them they are just nervous about the opposite sex; police officers who crack offensive jokes; and friends who betray them and tell everyone at school. Along with grim stories of beatings, vandalized lockers, and restraining orders are reassuring tales of journal writing, youth groups, and supportive relatives. Twelve-year-old Nicole, who came out to her sister and her mother when she was ten, called a family meeting to discuss her lesbianism. Later, her older brother surprised her by telling her he was also gay. Christopher writes, "I am seventeen years old, a senior in high school, and openly gay. . . . I was never ashamed" (p. 23). Elizabeth, a sixteen-year-old from a small town in Kansas, committed suicide before publication of her story. She wrote about a librarian who hassled and embarrassed her when she requested a copy of *One Teenager in Ten*, parents who sent her to a psychiatric hospital, and classmates who beat her and vandalized her locker. Even though some of these stories are depressing, on balance the collection rings with determination to thrive in a hostile environment. Heron ends this courageous book with advice for people who work with teenagers, an annotated reading list, and information about a pen pal service. *Topic*: Personal Narratives.

Hogan, Steve and Lee Hudson. *Completely Queer: The Gay and Lesbian Encyclopedia*. Henry Holt, 1998. Hardcover $50.00 (ISBN 0805036296); Paper $25.00 (ISBN 0805060316). Ages 14 up.

Dedicated "To those who first took the risk of remembering: the grassroots lesbian and gay archives and oral history projects," this informative encyclopedia offers more than 500 succinct entries. Entries featuring lesbian and gay people, places, history, and ideas are arranged alphabetically and supplemented by 200 black-and-white illustrations. New York–based writers and researchers Lee Hudson and Steve Hogan list their objectives for this ambitious volume: balance between lesbian and gay interests; comprehensive coverage of the most influential early movement leaders and organizations; extensive coverage of both pre- and post-Stonewall groups and notables; global coverage (with separate entries on twenty-five major countries); selective coverage of issues, concepts, and historical periods important to an understanding of lesbian and gay subcultures; and complete coverage on all large and several small religious groups and their positions on same-sex relationships. Features of interest to book lovers include essays on lesbian and gay bookstores, detective fiction, literary awards, archives and libraries, and publishing houses, as well as biographical information about numerous writers. Remarkably entertaining, the essays, quotes, facts, lists, and tables cover a wide range of topics such as lesbian and gay slogans, a list of slang terms that originated in England, the publishing history of *The Well of Loneliness*, and a list of famous homophobes. Sources for further information, references to related entries, a seventy-five-page chronology from c. 12,000 B.C. to November 1996, and an extensive index add to the usefulness of this accessible volume. *Topic*: Encyclopedia.

Jacobs, Sue-Ellen, Wesley Thomas, and Sabine Lang, editors. *Two-Spirit People: Native American Gender Identity, Sexuality, and Spirituality*. Harrington Park Press, 1997. Hardcover $29.95 (ISBN 0789000032); University of Illinois Press, 1997. Paper $19.95 (ISBN 0252066456). Ages 16 up.

Combining the voices of Native Americans and non-Indians, anthropologists, and others, this volume explores sexual identity issues as they relate to lesbian, gay, bisexual, and transgendered Native Americans. The first two sections deal with questions of terminology and rebuilding anthropological narratives concerning two-spirit people. The third section corrects the stereotyped images of the past with an intimate array of voices from contemporary two-spirit people and how they feel about themselves and their communities, how other Native people treat them, and how anthropologists and other scholars interpret them and their cultures. This volume documents the diversity of two-spirit people and exposes the inadequacies of anthropological theories to capture their essence. Beverly Little Thunder, Standing Rock Lakota, writes, "The words I would like to see written about me and read fifty years from now should be words that reflect who I am as an individual" (p. 204). Doyle V. Robertson, Sisseton/Wahpeton Dakota, writes about his experiences in a compelling article titled "I Ask You to Listen to Who I Am." He writes, "Every time that homophobia, racism, and ignorance are confronted head-on, there is a battle, and I am in the trenches of that war by standing on the Main Street of a small town as an openly 'queer' Indian. But those words are only an identifier others place on me, they are not the essence of who I am" (p. 233). *Topics*: Native Americans, Two-Spirit People.

Jennings, Kevin, editor. *Becoming Visible: A Reader in Gay and Lesbian History for High School and College Students*. Alyson Publications, 1994. Paper $11.95 (ISBN 1555832547). Ages 14 up.

Drawing from both primary and secondary sources, this reader is filled with powerful human stories and a wealth of important information. It covers over 2,000 years of history and is inclusive of a diverse range of cultures. The reader is divided into three sections: "Gay People in Premodern Societies," "The Emergence of the Modern Gay Movement," and "The Ongoing Struggle: Gays and Lesbians in the Eighties and Nineties." Topics addressed include the Holocaust, McCarthyism, the Homophile Movement, Stonewall, court cases, a collection of manifestoes and platforms, and much more. Each selection is followed by thought-provoking questions, helpful suggestions for classroom activities, and a list of related resources for further study. This engrossing history book vividly brings to life the individual and collective challenges and triumphs lesbians and gays have experienced. In the introduction, Jennings writes, "we, as teachers, must teach gay history because it is intellectually dishonest not to do so. . . . teaching such history may help our students to create a better society" (p. 16). Indeed, this book gives hope for a future in which people will be able to follow the advice of young lesbians and gays such as Stephanie Johnson, a first-generation American from Jamaica, who says, "Take risks. Be proud of who you are, every part of you. Dare to be different, dare to be who you are" (p. 270). *Topics*: Civil Rights, History.

Kuklin, Susan. *Speaking Out: Teenagers Take on Race, Sex, and Identity*. Putnam, 1993. Hardcover $15.95 (ISBN 0399223436). Ages 12 up.

Susan Kuklin spent a year with the students and staff at Bayard Rustin High School for the Humanities in New York City, which reflects the social, racial, religious, economic, and sexual diversity of the larger culture. In candid and thought-provoking interviews, teens grapple with difficult questions, reflect on their own lives, and share their views about contemporary issues. In "Loving a Woman," Rachel, who knew she was a lesbian when she was nine, talks about coming out to her parents when she was fourteen. She discusses her fear of physical violence if people find out that she is a lesbian. She says, "Luckily, the threats didn't make me question who I am. For me, the issue has never been, 'Am I? Is it okay? Is it not okay?' I always felt that whatever my choice, it would be okay" (p. 84). Rachel talks about how she overcame her own internalized homophobic stereotypes of lesbians. When her first lover left her for a man, all her self-critical homophobia returned. Her new lover embraces her lesbianism, saying that her title is Lesbian. In "I'm an Illusion," Tracy calls himself a "loud, flamboyant homo" (p. 88). He realized that he was gay when he was twelve. He talks about some of the misconceptions of gay people. "My strict parents didn't make me gay. Actually, what made me gay is me. I felt gay. I thought gay" (p. 90). He enjoys wearing dresses and he has never had a fight in his life. Bayard Rustin, for whom the school was named, was gay, a political activist, socialist, pacifist, and an advisor to Martin Luther King, Jr. Dedicated to the women and men who devote their lives to the teaching profession, this interesting book includes photographs along with the words of the teenagers. *Topic*: Interpersonal Relationships.

Manahan, Nancy, editor. *On My Honor: Lesbians Reflect on Their Scouting Experience*. Madwoman Press, 1997. Paper $18.95 (ISBN 1886231028). Ages 14 up.

This interesting book documents the contributions lesbians have made to the Girl Scouts, the impact scouting has had on lesbians, and some of the problems undermining the relationship between lesbians and scouting. *On My Honor* features diverse pieces by thirty-three Girl Scouts who break the taboo against speaking out about their lesbianism. The fundamental stance of the Girl Scouts organization is that sexual orientation is not an issue; appropriate behavior is. Nancy Manahan states, "The Girl Scout position, in a nutshell, is 'don't ask, don't tell' " (p. 5). She continues, "It is time for Girl Scouts everywhere to try, on their honor, to do their duty to end overt- and covert-discrimination against what is probably the organization's largest minority. It is time for Girl Scouts in the U.S.A. to affirm its lesbian members, openly and proudly" (p. 12). She suggests that they build on their present position of nondiscrimination by implementing a plan similar to the one she outlines in "A Letter of Reconciliation I Wish Girl Scouts of the U.S.A. Would Write." The book is divided into four sections. Part I, "Empowerment," contains stories about girls discovering nature, independence, female strength, and lesbian role models. For many girls, scouting is their first and possibly only experience of women making all the decisions, doing all the important, creative jobs, and modeling leadership qualities. Part II, "Fulfillment," documents how scouting shaped lesbians' lives, not only in the past, but in the present as leaders, innovators, and activists. Manahan notes that 64 percent of women listed in *Who's Who in American Women* were once Girl Scouts. Part III, "Disillusionment," features stories by lesbians who encountered homophobia, racism, dishonesty, and fear within the organization. In "Testimony," Kristen Renn writes about the heartbreak of losing her job with the Girl Scouts, and how she testified before the Rhode Island state legislature, helping that body pass a bill banning discrimination on the basis of sexual orientation for the whole state. Part IV, "Integration and Acceptance," celebrates stories by Girl Scouts who have experienced various levels of acceptance by the organization. Manahan writes, "hiding reinforces homophobia. . . . It deprives members of the community and of the organization—gay and straight—of opportunities to unlearn stereotypes and accept genuine diversity. The organization is already committed to ethnic diversity. It's time for the Girl Scouts to openly accept and integrate its lesbian members as well" (p. 195). This courageous book includes black-and-white photographs, biographical profiles of the contributors, a glossary, and an index. *Topic*: Girl Scouts.

Marcus, Eric. *Is It a Choice? Answers to 300 of the Most Frequently Asked Questions About Gays and Lesbians*. Harper, 1999. Paper $13.00 (ISBN 006251623X). Ages 10 up.

In this comprehensive resource, Eric Marcus answers a wide variety of questions such as: "What is a homosexual?," "Are you born gay?," "What's it like to be a gay or lesbian teenager?," "Do gay people raise gay children?," "Why do people discriminate against, harass, and attack gay men and lesbians?," and "What does the rainbow flag stand for?" Marcus' answers are honest, clear, concise, and humorous. To the title question, "Is it a choice?" he responds, "Just as heterosexual people don't choose their feelings of sexual attraction, gay and lesbian people don't choose theirs. All of us become aware of our feelings of sexual attraction as we grow, whether those feelings are for someone of the same sex, the opposite sex, or both sexes. For gay and lesbian people, the only real choice is between suppressing these feelings of same-sex attraction—and pretending to be asexual or heterosexual—and living the full emotional and physical life of a gay man or lesbian" (p. 9). The questions are printed in large bold type, followed by answers that vary in length from one to five paragraphs, often including anecdotes, opinions, and quotes from books, magazine and newspaper articles, and friends. The book is divided into chapters that address the following issues: self-discovery, coming out, family and children, dating, relationships and marriage, work, the military, demographics, friends, religion, discrimination and violence, sex, media, sports, education, activism, AIDS, and aging. Marcus writes, "The answers I offer here are not the only possible answers to these questions. Other gay and lesbian people would likely answer these questions differently because gay men and lesbians are a diverse population with different values and different ways of looking at our world" (p. xiv). The book includes a list of resources, a bibliography, and an index. *Topics*: Coming Out, Self-Help.

Nava, Michael and Robert Dawidoff. *Created Equal: Why Gay Rights Matter to America*. St. Martin's Press, 1994. Hardcover $17.95 (ISBN 031210443X). Ages 14 up.

Created Equal is a compelling and galvanizing book that calls for Americans to affirm the Bill of Rights and the Constitution of the United States and give lesbian and gay people what should already be theirs: first-class citizenship. Anything less denies the guarantee of equality for all American citizens and widens the chasm between what our country promises and what it delivers. The authors answer crucial questions, debunk debilitating myths, and analyze the current campaign against lesbian and gay equality. They provide accurate information about the real lesbian and gay agenda, which is *not* to have special privileges but to have the ordinary rights that all Americans enjoy. They explain that heterosexual Americans should care about the rights of lesbians and gay men because equality for all people is central to the continuing defense of individual liberty. The struggle is about privacy, civil equality, and the right of all citizens to be free. The authors write, "The traditional American doctrine that governments are instituted for the purpose of protecting the fundamental rights of individuals, and the historical process by which these rights have been extended to groups who were enslaved, oppressed, and otherwise unacknowledged at the time of the founding, are the twin pillars of the gay rights movement, as they have been of every struggle to extend the promise of individual liberty to Americans" (p. 8). *Topics*: Civil Rights, Court Cases.

Nelson, Richard E. and Judith C. Galas. *The Power to Prevent Suicide: A Guide for Teens Helping Teens*. Free Spirit Publishing, 1994. Paper $11.95 (ISBN 0915793709). Ages 12 up. *Award*: New York Public Library Best Book for the Teen Age.

When teenagers were asked, "Who would you tell about wanting to commit suicide?" 90 percent said that they would tell a friend first. This practical manual, written in a language and style teenagers will understand, is based on the premise that teenagers are in an important position to help prevent suicide because many young people feel that their friends understand them better than adults do. This lifesaving book is divided into three parts: "Why, What, and Who," "How to Be a Suicide Preventer," and "Resources." The authors quote research that estimates that each day more than 1,000 American teenagers attempt suicide, and 18 of them die. Suicide is the number two killer of young people between the ages of 15 and 24 in the United States and Canada. The section titled "Teens Who Are Gay, Lesbian, or Questioning Their Sexual Orientation" states that lesbian and gay teens make up an unusually high number of youth suicides. "The teenage years are difficult for all young people, but for gay youth the problems are compounded by isolation, rejection, fear, and often self-hatred. If you have a gay friend, then remember that just being gay in a society where homosexuality isn't accepted can add to your friend's overall stress level" (p. 46). The authors wrote the book because they believe that teenagers are capable of noticing when a friend might be suicidal and caring enough to want to do something about it. Helpful charts and lists include: Problems and Situations That Have Pushed Teens to Attempt or Complete Suicide, Verbal Warnings, Warning Signs, Active Listening Do's and Don't's, How to Help a Friend Through a Suicidal Crisis, and a Crisis Checklist. Also included is information about Natural Helpers, a peer helping program that operates in hundreds of schools in the United States and Canada. A bibliography and index are included. *Topic*: Suicide Prevention.

Oliver, Marilyn Tower. *Gay and Lesbian Rights: A Struggle*. Enslow, 1998. Hardcover $19.95 (ISBN 0894909584). Ages 12 up.

This concise volume introduces the issues confronting lesbian and gay people in their quest for equal rights. Beginning with a brief history of homosexuality, Oliver provides examples of hate crimes and gives quick overviews of the Mattachine Society, Daughters of Bilitis, the Kinsey report, Stonewall, and the assassination of Harvey Milk. Chapters focus on job discrimination, lesbian and gay issues in schools, gays and lesbians in the military, same-sex marriage and adoption, and health care issues. The author includes dissenting opinions, juxtaposing arguments for and against each of the issues presented. Case laws, current statistics, research results, and quotes from both sides of the issues are woven into the chapters. Black-and-white photographs, maps, banners, posters, and photographs are also liberally sprinkled through out the book. Although the author uses the misleading term *sexual preference* in place of the more accurate term *sexual identity*, this is a good resource. Extensive chapter notes, a bibliography, and a list of organizations both for and against lesbian and gay rights are appended along with an index. *Topics*: Civil Rights, Court Cases, Laws and Legislation.

Plant, Richard. *The Pink Triangle: The Nazi War Against Homosexuals.* Holt, 1995. Paper $11.95 (ISBN 0805006001). Ages 14 up.

This chilling history of the Nazi attempt to exterminate gay men is framed against the poignant story of the author's own flight from Germany and his return more than thirty years later. Richard Plant, a gay Jewish linguist who escaped Germany in 1933, writes about his painful journey back to his homeland to research materials on homosexuals during the war and to seek information about friends who disappeared. Plant examines the climate and conditions that gave rise to the vicious campaign against gay men, which resulted in tens of thousands of arrests and thousands of deaths. The lives of two of the Nazi leaders, Ernst Roehm, who was gay, and Heinrich Himmler, a vicious homophobe, are examined in detail. Plant analyzes the widespread omission of information about the persecution of gay men after the war, writing, "This book seeks to end the silence toward the fate of homosexuals under the Third Reich" (p. 19). Because the anti-homosexual laws of 1935 remained in effect until 1969, gay survivors did not have a platform to air their undeniable grievances. In addition, researchers found that "the mortality rate for homosexuals incarcerated by the Nazis was . . . relatively higher, in the camps and after their release, than that for other persecuted groups" (p. 14). The few who survived were hesitant to publicize their sexual identity. Only a few pages of this book provide information about lesbians in Germany during World War II. More research is needed in this area. Appendices include the text of Paragraph 175, the antihomosexual law; a detailed chronology from 1871 to 1945; extensive notes; and a selected bibliography of books, articles, letters, and interviews. *Topics*: Holocaust, World War II.

Pollack, Rachel and Cheryl Schwartz. *The Journey Out: A Guide for and About Lesbian, Gay, and Bisexual Teens.* Viking Penguin, 1995. Hardcover $14.99 (ISBN 0670858455); Puffin, 1995. Paper $6.99 (ISBN 0140372547). Ages 11 up.

Compassionate and reassuring, this guide provides practical information about health, terminology, substance abuse, harassment, religion, politics, and legal issues. It offers helpful suggestions for building self-esteem; whether, how, and when to come out to relatives and friends; and combatting myths and stereotypes. A succinct history of the lesbian/gay civil rights movement is included, along with the names of famous lesbian and gay people. The tone is gentle, kind, and hopeful, and the information is organized in an easy-to-use format. Quotes from teenagers are interspersed throughout, and an extensive glossary is provided. Appendices include an extensive list of community centers organized by state, organizations, crisis hotlines, and an annotated bibliography of suggested reading materials. The book ends with quotes from teens about their ideas of a perfect world. Jody says, "A Utopia for me would be . . . where today's youth can feel comfortable expressing themselves without fear of persecution. It would be a place where they can freely embrace their true selves and live with the serenity of knowing that they are just as important as everyone else" (p. 113). *Topics*: Coming Out, Community, Health, Religion.

Ratti, Rakesh, editor. *A Lotus of Another Color: An Unfolding of the South Asian Gay and Lesbian Experience.* Alyson Publications, 1993. Paper $9.95 (ISBN 1555831710). Ages 16 up.

South Asian lesbians and gay men fill these pages with stories of their pain and exhilaration, challenges and victories, and losses and loves. The term *South Asian* refers to an individual who is an inhabitant of or is descended from the inhabitants of Bangladesh, Bhutan, India, the Maldives, Nepal, Pakistan, or Sri Lanka. In the introduction, Rakesh Ratti, who was born in India and grew up in California, discusses his hopes that this book will increase their visibility in both the South Asian and the lesbian and gay communities. Black-and-white photographs of temple carvings, statues, and paintings accompany more than forty powerful essays, poems, and interviews. Issues and themes addressed include sexism and misogyny manifested by many gay men, friction between lesbian and gay male communities, racist attitudes that are rooted in both color and caste consciousness, and relating to and networking with non–South Asian lesbians and gays. Among the contributors is Pratibha Parmar, who is best known for her groundbreaking work as a filmmaker.

In a piece titled "Fighting Back," she says, "We are lesbians and gays
and it's not a problem for us. If it's a problem for others, they need to
look at or read our work on our terms; we don't have to be apologetic
about who we are or try to explain it" (p. 39). Other contributors include
Raj Ayyar, Kaushalya Bannerji, Zariamma Harat, Ashok Jethanandani,
Arvind Kumar, and Urvashi Vaid. Glossaries of South Asian terms and
of lesbian and gay terms are appended. Strong language. *Topic*: South
Asians.

Robson, Ruthann. *Gay Men, Lesbians and the Law*. Chelsea House,
1995. Hardcover $24.95 (ISBN 0791026124); Paper $12.95 (ISBN
0791029638). Ages 14 up.

Series: Issues in Lesbian and Gay Life. A clear, well-organized account
of the law as it applies to lesbian and gay people, this title examines
both high-profile and lesser-known cases. The book is divided into seven
chapters: "The Legal Regulation of Sexual Expression," "Discrimination
Against Sexual Minorities," "Educational Issues," "Families," "Criminal
Justice," "Health," and "The Legal Profession." Topics covered include
the military, Boy Scouts, employment, curriculum, sports, marriage,
child custody, hate crimes, adoption, domestic violence, and sex statutes.
A list of the twenty-nine cases cited in the book follows the introduction.
Besides noting the law's symbolic effects, Robson probes the practical
consequences wrought by the legal system's stance toward homosexuality—from health insurance to senior proms to psychiatric abuse. For
example, she discusses a case in which a psychiatrist prescribed and
personally administered "fornication therapy" to cure a patient's lesbianism. "Such forced heterosexual encounters—some might term them
rape—have a long history in the treatment of lesbian, gay, bisexual, and
transgendered persons" (pp. 66–67). Robson raises other alarming issues,
such as the estimate that "approximately 40 percent of the women on
death row in the United States may be lesbians" (pp. 94–95). In the last
chapter, Robson discusses the challenges facing lesbian and gay people
who work in the legal profession as judges, attorneys, paralegals, and
legal secretaries. Using understandable language, she deftly navigates
the murky waters of the constantly changing legal system. The text is
supported by well-captioned archival photographs, one of which shows
members of the Gay and Lesbian Alliance Against Defamation petition-
ing the California School Board to include information about lesbian and
gay people in textbooks and other curriculum materials. A picketer's sign
reads, "School Textbooks Have Been Set a Little Too Straight" (p. 57).
Robson includes a short bibliography and an index . *Topics*: Court Cases,
Law and Legislation.

Romesburg, Don, editor. *Young, Gay, and Proud.* Alyson Publications, 1995. Paper $5.95 (ISBN 1555832792). Ages 12 up.

A helpful guide to all aspects of being a lesbian or gay teenager, this book addresses questions related to coming out, health, sexuality, stereotypes, and self-image. Short biographical sketches of lesbian and gay people from the past are provided. Letters asking for advice are followed by supportive suggestions, offering ideas for ways to cope with the many challenges facing lesbian and gay youth. This useful resource includes an annotated list of books for further reading. *Topics*: Coming Out, Health, Self-Help.

Signorile, Michelangelo. *Outing Yourself: How to Come Out as Lesbian or Gay to Your Family, Friends, and Coworkers.* Random House, 1995. Hardcover $20.00 (ISBN 0679438386); Paper $4.99 (ISBN 0517193523). Ages 16 up.

Although this book may have been intended for adults, it has some important features not included in other coming-out guides that will be extremely helpful for young people. The practical fourteen-step self-help program includes writing, self-talk, meditation, anger checks, researching, reading, networking, and envisioning exercises designed to ease the lifelong coming-out process. Signorile writes, "Coming out of the closet is a process that gets you in touch with the real you, the person you were meant to be before you were forced to wear the mask of heterosexuality" (p. xxiii). He decided to write this guide after his first book, *Queer in America* (which is a study of the closet and how it harms people), hit the stores and he was flooded with hundreds of letters from people who were either sharing their coming-out stories or asking his advice on the best way to come out. Signorile interviewed letter-writers who were at different stages of coming out and filled his book with their heartfelt stories. He developed a program that begins with self-identification and self-acceptance and moves to coming out to other lesbian and gay people, next to straight friends, then family, and then coworkers. The author writes, "The stress of coming out will never be as hard on you as the stress of staying in was" (p. xi). Written in a gentle, supportive tone, this strong, sensible book is easy to read and absorb. The message throughout is that homosexuality is not a disease, but homophobia is. In the foreword, Betty Berzon writes about the potency of self-affirmation for healing body, mind, and spirit. "The freedom to be your natural self is elementary to your mental and emotional health" (p. xvii). *Topics*: Coming-Out Guide, Self-Help.

Silver, Diane. *The New Civil War: The Lesbian and Gay Struggle for Civil Rights.* Franklin Watts, 1997. Hardcover $24.00 (ISBN 053111290X). Ages 12 up.

This carefully researched book addresses numerous debates surrounding lesbian and gay civil rights. A brief history of the movement for equality is followed by chapters devoted to specific issues such as religion, employment and housing, military service, AIDS, domestic partnerships, and adoption. Each chapter opens with a statement that defines the issue, followed by clearly presented pro and con arguments and discussion. Silver draws parallels between the lesbian and gay struggle for equal rights with other civil rights movements in the United States. In the introduction she writes, "The purpose of this book is to give you the information you need to understand the fight and to make up your own mind about the issues" (p. 14). In "A Day in the Life of Lesbian and Gay Kansas," she shows ordinary lesbian and gay people going to work, attending classes, taking care of patients, attending a school fundraiser, viewing a movie, and enjoying a potluck. In "A World Without Homosexuality," she demonstrates how our lives would be impoverished without the contributions of specific musicians, writers, artists, actors, and others. "Portrait of a Child Molester" shows that most child molesters are heterosexual males who are acquainted with their victims. This well-organized book ends with extensive chapter notes, a directory of organizations that support and oppose civil rights for lesbian and gay people, a list of books and Internet sites, and an index. *Topic*: Civil Rights.

Sutton, Roger. *Hearing Us Out: Voices from the Gay and Lesbian Community.* Photographs by Lisa Ebright. Little, Brown, 1994. Hardcover $16.95 (ISBN 0316823260); Paper $8.70 (ISBN 0316823139). Ages 12 up. *Award*: ALA Best Book for Young Adults.

In moving first-person interviews and clear black-and-white photographs, this important book is filled with a wide range of lesbian and gay voices, lighthearted and wise, funny and sad, and proud and heartening. A lesbian police officer, a gay Presbyterian minister, a lesbian lawyer, the AIDS commissioner for the city of Chicago, and three teenagers are among the nineteen people profiled here. In stories that touch on coming out, building community, self-acceptance, and homophobia, the interviewees share their thoughts and feelings with honesty, passion, and humor. *Hearing Us Out* provides a compelling portrait of the lesbian and gay community as a diverse and proud group of individuals with their own stories, history, and future. It reassures lesbian and gay teens that "life goes on past junior-high humiliation and high-school ostracism" (p. xiv). In the eloquent foreword, young adult author M. E. Kerr writes, "One of my great blessings is being part of this community that refuses to be diminished by the prejudice and rigidity of others" (p. x). A list of books for further reading and a list of organizations are appended. *Topics*: Interviews, Role Models.

Witt, Lynn, Sherry Thomas and Eric Marcus, editors. *Out in All Directions: A Treasury of Gay and Lesbian America*. Time Warner, 1995. Paper $16.99 (ISBN 0446672378). Ages 14 up.

This valuable resource features hundreds of lively articles and interesting facts covering every aspect of lesbian and gay life, culture, community, and history. Over 600 pages are devoted to facts, figures, anecdotes, essays, trivia, photographs, cartoons, and quotes. "Did You Know?" sidebars list such interesting topics as " 'Mainstream' Queer Authors Who Got Their Start with the Gay and Feminist Press." Another reads, "Did you know the Minneapolis-based Womyn's Braille Press, founded in 1980, is the only organization in the United States dedicated to making feminist and lesbian literature available on tape and in Braille. The volunteer-run organization currently offers more than 800 book titles, periodicals, and pamphlets to its readership" (p. 146). Quotes are printed in large bold type. For example, one reads, "In the beginning, it required small presses, gay newspapers and magazines, and mainstream houses all working together to launch gay and lesbian literature" (p. 148). Photographs of Michael Nava, Marlon Riggs, Vito Russo, Pratibha Parmar, Mariana Romo-Carmona, June Chen, and many others are included. The ten chapters cover more than 175 different topics; fifty-five contributors wrote over ninety original pieces, and 125 writers granted permission to reprint previously published works. Entertaining and informative, this book is hard to put down. *Topics*: Community, Culture, History, Trivia.

Woog, Dan. *Jocks: True Stories of America's Gay Male Athletes*. Alyson Publications, 1998. Paper $12.95 (ISBN 1555833993). Ages 16 up.

Journalist Dan Woog, a openly gay soccer coach, interviewed dozens of gay high school and college athletes and coaches in the fields of wrestling, tennis, running, gymnastics, swimming, basketball, and other athletics. The resulting collection of over twenty-five inspiring stories disputes the contention that the term *gay athlete* is an oxymoron and shatters stereotypes still held by millions of Americans. These candid stories expose the ridicule that keeps numerous youngsters off of teams and the harassment and violence that threaten many players. However, many of those interviewed report increasing tolerance and understanding among teammates, coaches, and fans. Among those profiled are high school track coach Eric Anderson, who came out in conservative Orange County, California; Jay, a wrestler from New England; Jon Arterton, a track star at all-male St. Albans School in Washington, D.C.; and Brett Parson, a National Hockey League referee. Woog, in a chapter titled "Time-Out: The Author's Story," traces his own coming-out process and discusses a workshop he presented titled "Homophobia and Soccer" at a National Soccer Coaches Association Convention. He writes, "As an openly gay soccer coach, I am happier, healthier, even more successful than ever before. I have the respect of my athletes and colleagues, and more important, of myself" (p. 143). Woog ends his engaging book with helpful suggestions for coaches and physical educators. He writes, "Do not assume that everyone on a team is straight . . . deal decisively with antigay slurs and actions . . . and speak out against injustice and prejudice wherever it occurs" (p. 233). *Topic*: Sports.

Young, Perry Deane. *Lesbians and Gays in Sports*. Chelsea House, 1995. Hardcover $24.95 (ISBN 0791026116); Paper $12.95 (ISBN 0791029514). Ages 14 up. *Award*: New York Public Library Best Book for the Teen Age.

Series: Issues in Lesbian and Gay Life. The sports world is notorious for its hostility toward lesbian and gay people. This title discusses the forms homophobia takes in athletics from cruel school pranks to corporate withdrawal of sponsorship. Illustrated with black-and white photographs, chapters discuss both women and men in a variety of sports including football, baseball, and tennis. Although homophobia keeps most athletes in the closet, a few have been open about their sexual identity. The contributions of notable athletes such as Martina Navratilova, David Kopay, Billie Jean King, Bill Tilden, Tom Waddell, Bruce Hayes, and Greg Louganis are examined. In response to the bigotry, lesbian and gay athletes have created leagues and organizations that proudly celebrate both their athleticism and their sexuality. The last two chapters of the book celebrate the Gay Games, launched in 1982 by Dr. Tom Waddell, a U.S. decathlate at the 1968 Olympics. Denied use of the Olympic name by the United States Olympic Committee, the Gay Games have nonetheless become enormously successful, with more than 500,000 in attendance at the 1994 competition in New York City. Young writes, "What is clearly a new day in the history of gay people will perhaps mark a new beginning for sports" (p. 139). Bibliography and index included. *Topics*: Gay Games, Sports.

5

Biography and Autobiography

Anzaldúa, Gloria. "La Prieta." (The Dark One). In *This Bridge Called My Back: Writings by Radical Women of Color*, edited by Cherríe Moraga and Gloria Anzaldúa. Persephone, 1981. Paper $8.95 (ISBN 0930436105). Ages 14 up.

"The whole time growing up I felt like I was not of this earth. An alien from another planet" (p. 199). In this powerful piece, Gloria Anzaldúa, the renowned Chicana lesbian writer and cultural theorist, writes about her childhood growing up in the Rio Grande Valley in South Texas. When she was born, her grandmother inspected her dark skin color. But Mamágrande Locha loved her anyway, because "What I lacked in whiteness, I had in smartness" (p. 198). Early in her childhood she refused her estate, challenged the status quo, and resisted the constricting definitions surrounding her. She wore boots, exchanged her sunbonnet for a sombrero, and was unafraid of knives and snakes. Anzaldúa writes about her contempt for traditional women's roles, her refusal to settle down and get married, and the way her mother criticized and yet secretly admired her refusal to act like a nice little girl. When her father gave her a pocket western, the only book he could find at the local drugstore, her life was transformed. "The act of reading changed me forever" (p. 200). Today, Anzaldúa is known for her groundbreaking work in tackling the difficult and immense task of changing culture and all its interlocking machinations. Her prophetic analysis of the intersections of race, gender, class, language, and sexual identity has made her one of the most original and hopeful voices in feminist literature. *Topics:* Chicana Literature, Mother-Daughter Relationship.

Arruda, Tiana. "How Can I Live a Life of Lies?" In *Compañeras: Latina Lesbians*, edited by Juanita Ramos. Routledge, 1994. Paper $14.95 (ISBN 0415909260). Ages 14 up.

First published in 1987 by the Latina Lesbian History Project, *Compañeras: Latina Lesbians* is a collection of oral histories, essays, poems, short stories, letters, and artwork by forty-seven women born in ten different countries. Tiana Arruda was born and raised in Río de Janeiro, Brazil, and now lives in the United States. In her oral history, "How Can I Live a Life of Lies?" she talks about her desire to go back home because she misses her culture, family, and first language, but she is concerned about having to conform to the standards of family and friends. "I always feel like I'm a person split into segments" (p. 184). Arruda says that since the second grade, she has always fallen in love with women. As a child, she didn't know that lesbianism existed, she just knew that she was drawn to women. She talks about her introduction to the lesbian/gay world, her first lover, and her involvement with the San Francisco Coalition for Human Rights. When she came out to her mother, she offered to pay for Arruda to go to therapy. Arruda, who was part of the bookstore collective of Old Wives Tales in San Francisco, says that moving away from her family "gave me freedom to explore who I was and to direct my life without the pressure of other people telling me what I should be doing and choosing friends for me" (p. 184). *Topics*: Brazil, Immigrants, Latina Literature, Oral History.

Bernstein, Samuel, editor. *Uncommon Heroes: A Celebration of Heroes and Role Models for Gay and Lesbian Americans*. Fletcher, 1994. Paper $25.00 (ISBN 0964177900). Ages 12 up.

This wonderful book features over 145 courageous lesbian and gay people who choose to live their lives outside the closet and who challenge society's beliefs and stereotypes. Full-page black-and-white photographs, biographical profiles, inspirational quotes, and sidebar tributes introduce the reader to artists, athletes, politicians, activists, philosophers, poets, journalists, musicians, novelists, entertainers, comedians, spiritual leaders, philanthropists, and more. Writers include Luis Alfaro, Dorothy Allison, Malcolm Boyd, Rita Mae Brown, Charles Busch, Chrystos, Rob Eichberg, Harvey Fierstein, Katherine V. Forrest, Jewelle Gomez, Larry Kramer, Tony Kushner, Audre Lorde, Eric Marcus, Armistead Maupin, Paul Monette, Ann Northrop, Ron Nyswaner, Juan R. Paloma, Troy Perry, Mary Renault, Ned Rorem, Richard Rouilard, Paul Rudnick,

Vito Russo, Randy Shilts, Michelangelo Signorile, Andrew Sullivan, Terry Sweeney, Mark Thompson, and Merle Woo. Lyn Duff, a youth activist, devotes much of her time to working to ensure that other young lesbian and gay people do not get locked up the way she did. When she was fifteen, "her mother committed her to a locked psychiatric institution where she was forced to undergo 'therapy,' including hypnosis, isolation, physical restraints, and powerful drugs—all intended to 'cure' her lesbianism" (p. 150). She finally escaped and got a court order giving guardianship to a lesbian couple. The tribute Sonia Sanchez wrote to Audre Lorde reads, "Audre Lorde's poetry summons us to our ancestral beauty. Terrible and sweet. Tough and soft. Ancient and modern. As she weaves a legacy of imagery, her words become constant awakenings, making us walk and talk a mile of truths. A season change. A life of honor" (p. 4). Dorothy Allison, author of *Bastard Out of Carolina*, writes, "I write to save my own life, and so that young people will have hope" (p. 135). Indeed, these pages are filled with hope. These heroes have contributed to their communities and to society as a whole and their lives are transforming public perceptions of who lesbian and gay people are. This important book makes it clear: We are everywhere! *Topics*: Heroes, Photographs, Role Models, Writers.

Bruchac, Joseph. "I Climb the Mesas in My Dreams: An Interview with Paula Gunn Allen." In *Survival This Way: Interviews with American Indian Poets*. University of Arizona Press, 1990. Hardcover $25.00 (ISBN 0816511780). Ages 14 up.

Paula Gunn Allen, who is of Laguna Pueblo and Lebanese ancestry, is a prominent lesbian feminist theorist, writer, and critic. In this interview she talks about her life, the major influences on her writing, and the forces that have shaped contemporary Native poetry. Her mother taught her the importance of treating people of all ages with respect, acknowledging their intelligence and individuality. Indeed, one of the most interesting parts of the interview is Allen's perceptions about age. She talks about the beauty and power of old women and how they have been ignored, trivialized, and degraded by mainstream society. "I think of old women not as grotesque and ugly, but as singular with vibrancy, alive just as the leaves get before they fall" (p. 13). Writers who have influenced Allen's writing include Gertrude Stein, Judy Grahn, Adrienne Rich, Audre Lorde, Denise Levertov, and N. Scott Momaday. Bruchac and Allen discuss the imagery in her poetry—the searching, loss, movement, and mountains. Allen examines the ways in which music, psychic phenomena, and her mixed-blood heritage have impacted her work. Although the interview does not directly address the lesbian content in Allen's work, the biographical sketch mentions that Allen was living with poet Judy Grahn in Berkeley at the time of the interview. Works by Paula Gunn Allen include *The Woman Who Owned the Shadows*, *Shadow Country*, and *Skin and Bones*. *Topics*: Paula Gunn Allen, Native American Literature, Poets.

Cammermeyer, Margarethe with Chris Fisher. *Serving in Silence*. Viking, 1994. Hardcover $22.95 (ISBN 0670851671); Paper $11.95 (ISBN 0140231595). Ages 16 up.

Margarethe Cammermeyer, a much-decorated colonel in the United States Army and a Vietnam veteran, was discharged after she came out as a lesbian in 1989. With the same personal strength and integrity that won her one leadership position after another, she writes about her decision to challenge the military's anti-gay policy. In 1994, a federal court in Seattle ruled that policy unconstitutional and ordered her reinstated. Born in 1942 in Norway, Cammermeyer spent her early childhood under the Nazi occupation while her parents participated in the Resistance. After the family moved to the United States in the early 1950s, she entered medical school even though her father refused to pay her tuition. She describes growing up in a family with a subservient mother and a misogynistic father who recognized only his sons as his offspring. At school, where she felt "too tall, too shy, too Norwegian" (p. 30), she developed crushes on her gym teachers. Later in college, she was similarly drawn to a teacher who "was brilliant, very strict, yet there was something that was very compelling to me" (p. 26). Cammermeyer describes her early melancholia and self-mutilation and how she ignored her feelings that she might be a lesbian and agreed to a marriage that was plagued from the beginning. Several years after the marriage ended, Cammermeyer fell in love with Diane, an artist and university professor. "Meeting Diane and realizing the rightness of being with her made me realize I am a lesbian" (p. 218). By refusing to hide her sexual identity, she lost her career but found the most important mission of her life as an outspoken advocate for lesbian and gay rights. Written with clarity and courage, this important memoir is dedicated "To those who have served, and those who will continue to serve, in silence." Cammermeyer's story is the subject of the movie, "Serving in Silence," starring Glenn Close (available at 1–800–438–9653). *Topics*: Court Cases, Military, Nurses, Vietnam War.

Chase, Clifford, editor. *Queer 13: Lesbian and Gay Writers Recall Seventh Grade*. Morrow, 1998. Hardcover $24.00 (ISBN 0688158110). Ages 13 up.

"School had become unbearable. Junior high was an obstacle course of rude boys, or of girls with hair, or both" (p. 29), writes Regina Gillis in "The Number Line." Twenty-five lesbian and gay writers reminisce about the hallways and locker rooms of their youth in this collection of diverse and compelling memoirs. In "Mudpies and Medusa," Marcus Mabry remembers monitoring "my every gesture, every change of timbre in my voice, to make sure I didn't betray sissiness" (p. 82). Several contributors recall their experiences at summer camp. "It took two weeks before I heard the word *fag*. . . . It was odd how this word had followed me, all the way across the continent" (p. 73), writes Robert Marshall in "Notes on Camp." Rebecca Brown writes about one of her camp counselors in "Nancy Booth, Wherever You Are." "She didn't tell me everything. . . . She didn't want to frighten me, just to tell enough to let me know that there were other, different, still mysterious, ways that I could live" (p. 186). When he started sixth grade, Clifford Chase writes in "Outtakes," he "entered a realm of humiliation" (p. 57). He figured out what homosexuality was by looking it up in the encyclopedia. Most of the adults in these stories are at best, indifferent and at worst, cruel and oppressive. However, in "A Close Escape," David Bergman writes about a supportive teacher who encouraged him to write poetry. "He gave me the sense for the first time that I might actually become a writer" (p. 132). One of the most beautifully written pieces is by Etel Adnan, an Arab-American poet and writer from California. She writes, "I discovered within my heart a kind of secret space that Helen inhabited. . . . In the course of my life I have thought about love over and over again. . . . Love is the most important matter we have to deal with, but it is always the hardest" (pp. 240, 245). Bia Lowe, in "Waiting for Blastoff," captures the essence of these stories best when she writes about the "mortifications of adolescence" and the decades it took for her to learn to rewrite her bitterness and gain an understanding of what it all meant (pp. 141–142). In "The Wind in the Louvers," Andrew Holleran writes about how he withdrew into the world of books, forced there by the "strict and alert guardians of heterosexuality (p. 255), whose heterosexism schooled him in loneliness. "How We Get That Way," by Mariana Romo-Carmona, is reviewed in detail elsewhere in this chapter. Although many of these stories are heartrending, they ultimately offer hope. Somehow, these writers survived those difficult years and went on to embrace their sexual identities and become successful writers. Explicit language. *Topics*: Coming Out, Education, Schools, Writers.

Chiu, Christina. *Lives of Notable Asian Americans: Literature and Education.* Chelsea House, 1996. Hardcover $18.95 (ISBN 0791021823). Ages 10 up.

Part of the twelve-volume series "The Asian American Experience," this book presents short biographies of fourteen established and emerging Asian-American writers, poets, and playwrights. Two of these writers, Willyce Kim and Dwight Okita, are of interest to readers searching for lesbian and gay literature. Willyce Kim, a Korean-American poet and novelist, was one of the first Asian-American lesbians to be published in the United States. Born in Honolulu, Kim grew up in Hawaii and California. When she thinks back about her childhood, she describes herself as a tomboy. She enjoyed sports and often joined the neighborhood boys in games of basketball, football, and baseball. She knew from an early age that she was a lesbian and she met her first woman lover while attending college in San Francisco, where she majored in English Literature. Kim, who loved reading from an early age, won a writing contest when she was nine years old. Her work has been published in numerous journals and anthologies and her novels, *Dancer Dawkins and the California Kid* and its sequel, *Dead Heat*, have been praised for their humor, complexity, and unique writing style. The second gay writer, Dwight Okita, is a Japanese-American poet, playwright, and musician. He started writing poetry when he was in the second grade. Okita's friends called him Words because he possessed an impressively large vocabulary. Always interested in the arts, he came out to his parents when he was sixteen by drawing a picture with the words "gay love," "gay pride," and "gay is good." He majored in creative writing in college and has since written several plays, including *The Rainy Season, The Salad Bowl Dance,* and *Richard Speck*. He says, "I'm happy to see myself moving every day, as a writer, closer and closer to where I want to be" (p. 113). The biographies of these creative writers are written with enthusiasm, insight, and intelligence. Chiu wisely chooses to include the challenges they have faced as Asian Americans and as lesbian and gay people along with their joys and successes. *Topics*: Asian-American Literature, Japanese-American Writers, Korean-American Writers.

Cowan, Tom. *Gay Men and Women Who Enriched the World.* Alyson Publications, 1996. Paper $10.95 (ISBN 1555833918). Ages 12 up.

Forty-seven lesbian and gay people (thirty-four men and thirteen women) who enriched the world are profiled in this useful book. In his introduction, Cowan writes about the impact growing up as an outsider has on an individual. As outsiders, lesbian and gay people learn "early in life to trust the unique sources of creativity within them[selves and to] survive and even prevail against the enormous cultural odds arrayed against them. Forced to enrich their own world without many of the social, legal, economic, and spiritual benefits available to those who fit the heterosexual model more completely, they can emerge as strong, self-confident personalities capable of enriching the world at large" (p. xv). Cowan argues that it may be the struggle itself, the lifelong grappling with being an outsider, that enables many lesbian and gay people to emerge with the strength, sensitivity, and creativity to enrich the world. In deciding who to include, Cowan notes that he not only felt that it was important to span the centuries with people from the ancient world, but that he also wanted to include gay and lesbian people from non-English-speaking countries whose impact has been significant in the United States. The fields represented include mathematics, science, literature, theater, art, music, philosophy, economics, politics, and military strategy. Subjects profiled in the order featured in the book are Alexander the Great, Plato, Sappho, Leonardo da Vinci, Desiderius Erasmus, Michelangelo, Francis Bacon, Christopher Marlowe, Frederick the Great, Madame de Stael, Lord Byron, Herman Melville, Walt Whitman, Horatio Alger, Jr., Oscar Wilde, Peter Ilyich Tchaikovsky, Marcel Proust, Willa Cather, Colette, Amy Lowell, Gertrude Stein, E. M. Forster, Virginia Woolf, John Maynard Keynes, T. E. Lawrence, Ludwig Wittgenstein, Jean Cocteau, Janet Flanner, Bessie Smith, Charles Laughton, Noel Coward, Marguerite Yourcenar, Christopher Isherwood, Laurence Olivier, Elizabeth Bishop, Tennessee Williams, May Sarton, Alan Turing, Benjamin Britten, Leonard Bernstein, Pier Paola Pasolini, James Baldwin, Yukio Mishima, Andy Warhol, Barbara Jordan, Rudolf Nureyev, and Michael Bennett. The illustrations that accompany each chapter were drawn by Michael Willholte. No index. *Topics*: Artists, Mathematicians, Musicians, Politicians, Role Models, Scientists, Writers.

DeCaro, Frank. *A Boy Called Phyllis: A Suburban Memoir.* Addison-Wesley, 1996. Hardcover $22.95 (ISBN 0201409674); Viking, 1997. Paper $11.95 (ISBN 0140255370). Ages 16 up.

Salted with one-liners and pop-cultural references, this is a hilarious and moving memoir about growing up gay in an Italian Catholic family in Little Falls, New Jersey in the 1960s and 1970s. DeCaro, a writer for the *New York Observer* and a contributing editor to *Martha Stewart Living*, spent much of his childhood being taunted by bullies. He survived by excelling academically, watching television, reading, and later becoming involved in theater. The teachers at his school did nothing to protect gay and lesbian kids from their tormentors; in fact, one sex education teacher said, "Personally, I think they should shoot the bastards" (p. 100). Kicked, spat upon, and ostracized, DeCaro found role models in Elton John and Paul Lynde. "Elton John . . . made it clear to me that I could reinvent myself, as he had done, taking my natural flamboyance and running with it" (p. 124). Although he was brought up to believe that being gay was the worst thing he could possibly be, he writes, "I never really wished I were straight, even though it would have made my life a lot easier" (p. 111). When he came out to his father, he said, "if I had known you were going to be like this, I would have killed you at birth"

(p. 199). Using deadpan wit and ironic turns of phrase, DeCaro writes about how he survived all this devastating homophobia to go on to embrace his sexual identity and become a successful writer. His laudable memoir is as whimsical as it is poignant, as heartfelt as it is uproarious. Explicit sex. *Topics*: Italian-American Literature, New Jersey, Theater, Writers.

Duplechan, Larry. "She's My Mother." In *A Member of the Family: Gay Men Write About Their Families*, edited by John Preston. Dutton, 1994. Paper $12.95 (ISBN 0452270324). Ages 14 up.

Larry Duplechan is the author of several critically acclaimed novels for adults including *Eight Days a Week, Blackbird*, and *Tangled Up in Blue*. A native of Los Angeles, his work has been widely anthologized in journals and collections. In this autobiographical piece he mixes laughter and tears with his hard-edged, wisecracking description of his mother. Duplechan writes, "As I grew up, Mom remained my champion, my harshest task master, and my biggest fan" (pp. 45–46). When he came out to her, she "stared directly at me, her glare hard and accusatory. 'It's like hearing you'd been killed in a car crash' " (p. 48). Duplechan despaired of ever having a cordial connection with her again but gradually through the years they have found ways to begin mending their relationship. Even though she refuses invitations to his house, she "greets my white male lover–friend–life partner at her door with hugs and kisses" (p. 51). The autobiographical essays by twenty-seven gay writers in this poignant collection chronicle similar paradoxes, betrayals, reconciliations, and unresolved conflicts. John Preston, editor of the collection, wrote, "Examining our families and understanding what they have done to us and what we have done to them is a crucial part of our learning about how we are gay in our society" (p. 13). Duplechan settles for what his mother can give him. "Seems we're stuck with each other. I'm her baby. She's my mother" (p. 52). *Topics*: African-American Literature, Autobiographical Short Stories, Mother/Son Relationship, Writers.

Freedman, Russell. *Babe Didrickson Zaharias: The Making of a Champion*. Clarion Bocks, 1999. Hardcover $18.00 (ISBN 0395633672). Ages 10 up.

Animated by the reminiscences of Babe's friends, family, and competitors, and illustrated with rare archival photographs, this exemplary biography by Newbery Medalist Russell Freedman brings to life one of the most remarkable figures in the history of sport—Babe Didrickson Zaharias (1911–1956). Among the greatest athletes of the twentieth century, Babe excelled at golf, basketball, tennis, track and field, and every other sport she tackled. Freedman's attractive, oversized biography has been described as engaging, lively, sparkling, vibrant, superbly crafted, and impeccably documented. The biographer not only celebrates Babe's phenomenal athletic ability and extraordinary determination but captures her exuberant energy, love of life, and irrepressible enthusiasm. Regarding her long-term relationship with Betty Dodd, another golfer, Freedman writes, "They developed an intimate friendship, a close and lasting bond that would sustain Babe for the rest of her life" (p. 144). He refers to them as "constant companions" and "partners in everything" (p. 144). Later, in the detailed bibliography, Freedman cites a biography written by Susan E. Cayleff titled *Babe: The Life and Legend of Babe Didrickson Zaharias* in which she examines "rumors that [Babe] was a lesbian" (p. 181). According to *Completely Queer*, she was "one of the first famous female athletes to have her 'femininity,' gender identity, and even her estrogen level called into question" (p. 186). Freedman pays tribute to a charismatic athlete who defied gender and socioeconomic restrictions, redefined how women athletes were expected to act, and inspired generations of females. Detailed notes, a bibliography, and an index are included. *Topics*: Appearance, Basketball, Golf, Olympics, Track and Field.

Fricke, Aaron. *Reflections of a Rock Lobster: A Story About Growing Up Gay.* Alyson Publications, 1995. Paper $5.95 (ISBN 1555836070). Ages 13 up.

In 1980 Aaron Fricke successfully sued the principal of his high school in Cumberland, Rhode Island for the right to attend his senior prom with his male date. A year later he wrote this moving memoir about his experiences as a person who knew that he was gay from his earliest memories. This book is as remarkable almost twenty years later as it was when it was first published in 1981. Fricke articulates beautifully his feelings as he gradually realized that his love for other boys was something that was despised by society. As he internalized this homophobia, he changed from a confident little boy to an anxious, isolated teenager. He describes the verbal and physical abuse he experienced in the locker room from which the principal refused to protect him; the graffiti painted on the door of his house; the "fruit cocktail" jokes told by some of the teachers in his school; and the prejudice and hatred the principal instilled in the students. The mental anguish forced Fricke to withdraw into a shell that resembled a rock lobster. How did he emerge from that shell and develop the pride and courage to challenge his school's homophobic policy? Significantly, it started with finding one ally. Fricke writes, "Helping a gay person develop a positive self-identity is an opportunity that any gay (or well-informed straight person) should cherish" (p. 48).

Reflections of a Rock Lobster has been described as an unassuming, remarkable book and a triumphant tale of courage, told with wit and humor but without self-pity. Sexual activities are named but not described. Strong language. Sequel: *Sudden Strangers*. *Topics*: Court Cases: *Fricke v. Lynch*.

Fricke, Aaron and Walter Fricke. *Sudden Strangers: The Story of a Gay Son and His Father.* St. Martin's Press, 1992. Paper $8.95 (ISBN 0312078552). Ages 13 up.

In this long-anticipated sequel to *Reflections of a Rock Lobster*, Aaron Fricke and his father, Walter, share the ups and downs of their relationship, from early companionship to estrangement to reconciliation. It was their collaboration on the book that helped them bridge the communication gap that threatened to tear their relationship apart. Although the language doesn't flow as smoothly as it did in the earlier book, it is characterized by the same good humor, earnestness, and integrity. Aaron notes that his father "was not a wealth of inspiration regarding homosexuality" (p. 111). Indeed, the reconciliation was made possible in large part because Aaron was determined to tolerate his father's homophobic remarks, focussing instead on small signs of growth. In a chapter titled "Accepting Your Heterosexual Parents," Aaron writes, "give your parents the benefit of the doubt. Don't judge them by what you wish they could or would be like" (p. 74). Walter is at his worst when he says that it is a "thousand times harder" (p. 66) for the parents than it is for the gay child. He is at his best when he advises parents to "keep in mind that this person is the same one you have always loved and nurtured" (p. 82). Aaron chose to write this book with his father because he didn't have any major conflicts with his mother. Black-and-white photographs are scattered throughout this painfully honest account of a father and son learning how to overcome the homophobia that separates them. In the epilogue, Aaron writes about his father's unexpected death from cancer after the book was written but before it was published and his relief that he did the right thing before it was too late. *Topic*: Father/Son Relationship.

Giard, Robert. *Particular Voices: Portraits of Gay and Lesbian Writers.* Massachusetts Institute of Technology Press, 1997. Hardcover $45.00 (ISBN 0262071800); 1998. Paper $25.00 (ISBN 0262571250). Ages 12 up. *Award*: Lambda Literary Award.

This extraordinary collection of black-and-white photographs and excerpts captures the vitality, diversity, and beauty of lesbian and gay writers in the United States. In 1985, photographer Robert Giard set out to create an archive of what was to become the most extensive photographic record of the gay and lesbian literary community ever undertaken. This beautiful book contains 182 of the more than 500 portraits Giard has made, honoring the centrality of literature as a validating force in the lives of a people so long denied a history. With his camera, Giard provides confirmation: We are here. We exist. This is who we are. His stirring book features a foreword by Julia VanHaaften, Curator of Photographs at the New York Public Library; an introduction by Giard, titled "Self-Portrait of a Gay Reader"; an essay by Joan Nestle on lesbian writing; and an essay by Christopher Bram on gay writing. The images and text are organized by theme: the idea of the book, the word, the archive; early pioneering figures, forms of oppression, Stonewall; family, community, and identity; illness, death, and grieving; and finally, the writer alone, reaffirming language and story. Each portrait is accompanied by a well-chosen excerpt from the work of the writer shown. Subjects include: Francisco X. Alarcón, Paula Gunn Allen, Dorothy Allison, Gloria Anzaldúa, Becky Birtha, Beth Brant, Chrystos, Forman Brown, Terri de la Peña, Martin Duberman, Allen Ginsberg, Jewelle Gomez, Barbara Grier, Essex Hemphill, Larry Kramer, Audre Lorde, Phyllis Lyon, Del Martin, Paul Monette, Michael Nava, Pat Parker, Adrienne Rich, Vito Russo, Randy Shilts, Barbara Smith, Kitty Tsui, and Norman Wong. Giard writes about his experiences while he was traveling around the country, photographing these remarkable writers. "When I first undertook this work, I did not realize just how extensive a task lay ahead of me. Nor did a lot of other people, gay or straight. When I'd inform them that I had so far photographed thirty writers for the series, they'd regard me with surprise and query, "You mean there are more?" (p. xiv). Indeed, Giard tells us that his work is not finished. By giving us the faces behind the words, Giard has documented the very essence of who lesbian and gay people are as writers and as a community. No index. *Topics:* Authorship, Photographs, Writers.

Greene, Harlan. "What She Gave Me: My Mother Regina and History." In *A Member of the Family: Gay Men Write About Their Families*, edited by John Preston. Dutton, 1994. Paper $12.95 (ISBN 0452270324). Ages 14 up.

Harlan Greene is the author of the novels *Why We Never Danced the Charleston* and *What the Dead Remember*, and the nonfiction book *Charleston, City of Memory*. In this beautifully written autobiographical piece he pays tribute to his beloved mother, Regina. Born in Warsaw, Poland in 1920, she rarely talked about her experiences as a Jew during World War II. Greene felt cut off from history and grew up feeling different, outside the mainstream. "From Momma, I had gotten the message to believe in myself and to do what I thought right no matter what others said or thought of me" (p. 80). When he came out to his mother, they talked, "and she threw her stereotypes away and started reading" (p. 81). Greene shares his "twilight world of horror (p. 82) when his lover was hospitalized with what they feared might be AIDS. He painfully draws parallels between his lover's illness and the Holocaust his mother had survived. "No, no, we were both screaming to ourselves as the world tilted and the hole in history yawned open" (p. 82). Greene's memories of his mother—her honor, honesty, and liberality of spirit—contrast sharply with the experiences of many lesbians and gay men. Her capacity to comprehend the connections between anti-Semitism and homophobia provides hope to all who are suffering from stereotypes, hate, and bigotry. *Topics:* Holocaust, Jews, Mother/Son Relationship, Writers.

Haskins, James. *Bayard Rustin: Behind the Scenes of the Civil Rights Movement.* Hyperion, 1997. Hardcover $14.45 (ISBN 0786801689). Ages 10 up. *Award:* Coretta Scott King Honor Award.

Bayard (pronounced Buyard) Rustin (1912–1987) worked tirelessly behind the scenes of the Civil Rights Movement for decades, organizing conferences, demonstrations, and marches. His proudest moment was the 1963 March on Washington, of which he wrote, "it was one of my most beautiful periods of work in my life" (p. 99). In this well-documented biography, James Haskins paints a vivid portrait of Rustin's life and work against the backdrop of the twentieth-century Civil Rights Movement in the United States. Rustin was born and raised in Pennsylvania, where his grandmother passed on her Quaker beliefs to her children and grandchildren. He was valedictorian of his senior class and earned a music scholarship to Wilberforce University in Ohio. Rustin realized that he was gay during his first year of college, and his family accepted his sexual identity. "I never felt it necessary to do a great deal of pretending. And I never had feelings of guilt" (p. 15). Haskins describes how opponents of the Civil Rights Movement tried to use Rustin's homosexuality to discredit the movement and how he consistently triumphed over these homophobic tactics. A passionate believer in non-violent resistance, Rustin also organized actions in Northern Rhodesia, England, and Germany and was active in the International Rescue Committee's efforts in Cambodia, Vietnam, and Thailand. Haskins details his unparalleled genius for organizing and unwavering commitment to civil and human rights, but does not mention whether or not he was involved in the lesbian and gay movement. Rustin received eighteen honorary doctorates in recognition of his contributions to peace and justice around the world. The only sour note in this well-written biography is the following sentence about Hall Johnson, leader of the Hall Johnson Choir and one of the most important African-American musicians of his time: "Because Johnson was a homosexual who did not flaunt his sexual preferences, Rustin looked to him also as a role model" (p. 16). Black-and-white photographs, extensive chapter notes, a bibliography, and an index are included. *Topics*: African Americans, Civil Rights Movement, Nonviolence, Organizers, Quakers.

Holmlund, Mona. *Women Together: Portraits of Love, Commitment, and Life*. Photographs by Cyndy Warwick. Running Press, 1999. Hardcover $27.50 (ISBN 0762400641). Ages 12 up.

This attractive book features beautiful black-and-white photographs of twenty-nine lesbian couples. Essayist Mona Holmlund and photographer Cyndy Warwick spent three years traveling from the Canadian prairies to America's heartland, from New York to Los Angeles, from Alaska to Hawaii, from Miami Beach to Puget Sound, searching for couples of different races, ages, class backgrounds, and philosophies. "It is our hope that taken as a whole *Women Together* will provide insight, understanding, and celebration of the love between women" (p. 15). Some of the subjects are well-known lesbians such as activists Phyllis Lyon and Del Martin, professional golfer Muffin Spencer-Devlin and her lover Lynda Roth, and the former Chief Nurse of the Washington National Guard, Margarethe Cammermeyer, and her partner Diane Divelbess. Among the youngest are Kelli Peterson and Erin Wiser, who founded a Gay/Straight Alliance at their high school in Salt Lake City, Utah. In response, the local school board banned all extracurricular clubs from the school. Linda Velasques and Stella Guillan, who became friends in the sixth grade, have been lovers for more than twenty years. Tammy Rodrigues and Antoinette Pregil, who met at a high school dance, are among several couples in Hawaii who are trying to get married legally. In the foreword to this striking book Candace Gingrich writes, "Because the relationships you will read about have been fought for, and have endured, in the face of such adversity, they should be cherished even more. *Women Together* is a positive representation of what lesbians can achieve. This perhaps is truly the ultimate goal: that all of us should have the right to have love in our lives in an open, honest, fulfilling, and joyful way" (p. 12). *Topics*: Lesbian Relationships, Photographs.

Jackson-Paris, Rod and Bob Jackson-Paris. *Straight from the Heart: A Love Story*. Warner, 1994. Hardcover $21.95 (ISBN 0446517488); 1995. Paper $11.99 (ISBN 0446670669). Ages 14 up.

Dedicated to "gay, lesbian, and bisexual youth who must struggle so hard to find their place in this world, and to those who never made it due to emotional, spiritual, and physical abuse," this inspiring dual memoir chronicles how two gay men met, fell in love, got married, and achieved their dreams. When they met, Rod Jackson was a successful model and Bob Paris was a renowned bodybuilder, soon to be crowned "Mr. Universe." Now gay rights activists, they speak on the high school and college lecture circuits, appear on television talk shows, and have launched the "Be True to Yourself" foundation along with a self-help video (with the same title) for young people. Written in alternating paragraphs from each man's perspective, this book has been described as disarmingly honest, appealingly candid, and ultimately charming. They each write movingly about growing up gay in a homophobic society. Both were raised by abusive alcoholic fathers in midwestern, working-class families; both experienced fear and loneliness while struggling to accept their sexual identity; and both found the inner resources to come out with dignity. After finding each other, they decided to share their story "to show that it's possible to find someone you can love and who loves you in return. . . . Through our example we hope you'll see that it's possible . . . to overcome the odds, to live life with pride, to stand up and have dignity, and still succeed—and thrive" (p. xi). With admirable candor they share the ups and downs of their relationship; how they cope with the pressure of societal intolerance, including denial and rejection from relatives; and how the entire experience has transformed them from closeted physical fitness icons to courageous, outspoken advocates for gay and lesbian rights. "We think it's key for us to take responsibility for raising a new generation. None of us wants yet another generation to go through the kinds of anguish we did growing up. . . . [We] have an obligation to those who will face the same challenges" (p. 299). *Straight from the Heart* was written to counteract the negative images that bombard young gay and lesbian people. The authors encourage other lesbian and gay adults to take an active role in empowering young people. Black-and-white photographs. *Topics:* Bodybuilding, Marriage, Modeling.

Jennings, Kevin, editor. *Telling Tales Out of School: Gays, Lesbians, and Bisexuals Revisit Their School Days*. Alyson Publications, 1998. Paper $13.95 (ISBN 1555834183). Ages 14 up. *Award:* Lambda Literary Award.

"You must be very fierce to save your heart for the people worthy of your love" (p. 53), writes John Di Carlo in his inspiring piece in this extraordinary book. Thirty-seven gay, lesbian, and bisexual people write about their experiences in school, exposing an alarming campaign of ridicule, harassment, and violence. The personal memoirs collected here are sharp and varied, detailing small acts of rebellion, valiant struggles, unexpected allies, and survival strategies. Written with humor, pain, and love, these tales show how the writers unlearned the self-hatred they were taught in school and survived to speak out for future generations. Jennings writes, "For nongay readers, I hope you'll emerge from these stories with a deeper sense of exactly how horrible it is for most people to grow up gay in this country, and a strong enough sense of outrage that you actually try to do something about it" (p. xiv). Sally Gearhart writes about the "occasional angels" who provided her with hope that her "pain was temporary" and gave her room "to imagine the unspeakable" (p. 11). Ed Brock discusses the similarities and differences between the oppression he experienced as a gay person and as an African American. He writes about how he "learned to wear the masks of docility, assimilation, fear, and silence" (p. 67), and how later, as a teacher, he realized that the work of self-affirmation is an ongoing struggle. Loraine Hutchins acknowledges the pain of a friend who "can't face going back to the school even to this day. . . . Entering those halls still makes him physically ill" (p. 74). Michael Kozuch feels that the school system failed him because it didn't challenge homophobia and racism. "I can't go back and change what happened to me or any of my gay brothers and sisters. I can do something now to stop the violence and indifference" (p. 91). Many write about the hell of recesses and the horrors of physical education classes and locker rooms. Others remember kisses in cloakrooms, embraces at slumber parties, hiding in libraries, and writing flowery poems. Like John Di Carlo, they learned to fight hard for the life they wanted and deserved (p. 51). Somehow hope radiates through this collection, even though it is filled with heartrending stories of degradation, sorrow, and isolation. This is an important book, one that will hopefully galvanize readers to do whatever they can to "teach respect for all in our schools" (Motto of the Gay, Lesbian, Straight Education Network, of which Kevin Jennings is the executive director). *Topics*: Anthology, Education, Schools.

Kenan, Randall. *James Baldwin*. Chelsea House, 1994. Hardcover $19.95 (ISBN 079102301X); Paper $9.95 (ISBN 0791028763). Ages 14 up.

Series: Lives of Notable Gay Men and Lesbians. James Baldwin, one of America's most acclaimed writers, used his prophetic literary voice to decry the fears and hypocrisies that deny African Americans and gay people individual identities. This compelling biography charts Baldwin's remarkable journey from Harlem, where he was born in 1924, to the small apartments and gay bars of Greenwich Village in the 1940s; from literary exile in postwar Paris to activism on the front lines of the Civil Rights Movement in the United States; from devastating poverty to fame and wealth at the top of the best-seller lists; from an adolescence as a teenage preacher in Harlem's storefront churches to adulthood as a literary prophet, both honored and neglected in his own country; and from an America torn by racial hatred and violence to the peaceful Provence farmhouse where he died of cancer of the esophagus in 1987. Baldwin was internationally renowned for his eloquent, complex literary explorations of the tangled racial and sexual prejudices and illusions plaguing the United States. His reputation as a fearless and perceptive critic of injustice grew with the publication of each of his novels, memoirs, plays, and collections of essays and short stories. This biography has many strengths, including the sensitive portrayal of Baldwin's childhood, the thought-provoking analysis of his writing, and the careful examination of the impact his racial and sexual identities had on his life, writing, and his role in the Civil Rights Movement. Kenan pays tribute to a writer who spent his life "in passionate, honest, and intelligent search for the truth" (p. 136). Several years before his death Baldwin told an interviewer, "I know we can be better than we are . . . That's the sum total of my wisdom after all these years" (p. 134). Photographs, bibliographies, a chronology, and an index are included. *Topics*: African-American Literature, Authorship, Civil Rights Movement, Writers.

Kopay, David and Perry Deane Young. *The David Kopay Story: An Extraordinary Self-Revelation*. Donald I. Fine Books, 1988. Paper $9.95 (ISBN 1558110804). Ages 16 up.

First published in 1977, this book tells the poignant story of a well-known football player who courageously decided to publicly reveal his sexual identity. One of the first professional athletes to come out, David Kopay was a ten-year veteran running back for the San Francisco Forty-Niners, the Detroit Lions, the Washington Redskins, the New Orleans Saints, and the Green Bay Packers. With the skilled collaboration of gay writer Perry Deane Young, Kopay traces his search for his sexual identity from adolescence to maturity. This moving account includes his years growing up in a Catholic family with a silent, abusive father; his early education at a Catholic seminary; his distinguished football career in high school, college, and the National Football League; his sexual experiences with both men and women; his psychotherapy that, while under hypnosis, helped induce him to marry a female flight attendant; his heartbreaking confrontations with his parents and older brother; and the unpredictable support from other relatives and former teammates. In December 1975, Kopay came out in an article published in the *Washington Star*. He subsequently appeared on several television programs, including *The David Susskind Show* and the *Tomorrow* show. Kopay says, "It has been a long and difficult journey for me. Sometimes I feel cheated for all the long years I wasted in hiding. . . . There was a time when I felt that it would be the end of the world if people found out about my homosexuality. What I have found out is that it is the beginning of a new world for me" (p. 19). Kopay's story is told through first-person narratives, third-person accounts, clippings from sports pages of newspapers, letters from people responding to the television shows, and photographs. One of the most alarming things about this book is that the oppression experienced by the subject has not changed significantly in over twenty-five years. The use of the term *preference* is one of the few clues that this book isn't a recent release. *The David Kopay Story* is of interest to everyone, although sports enthusiasts will especially enjoy the football action. Explicit Sex. *Topic*: Football.

Krull, Kathleen. *Lives of the Musicians: Good Times, Bad Times (And What the Neighbors Thought)*. Illustrated by Kathryn Hewitt. Harcourt Brace Jovanovich, 1993. Hardcover $18.95 (ISBN 0152480102). Ages 8–12.

Here are the fascinating and often humorous stories of twenty famous musicians from various countries and historical periods. Only two women are included: Clara Schumann and Nadia Boulanger. (Interested readers will find more information in *Women Composers: The Lost Tradition Found* by Diane Peacock Jezic and *Woman Composers* by Carol Planta Mura.) In her unusual approach to biography, Kathleen Krull writes as much about the eccentricities of her subjects as she does about their music. Providing the stories behind the famous names, she answers intriguing questions such as: "What were these musicians like as children?," "What were their favorite foods?," "What did they wear?," "What were their phobias, quirks, and bad habits?," "What did their neighbors think of them?" "And who were their significant others?" In her profile of Peter Ilich Tchaikovsky (1840–1893), Krull tells readers that he burned all the volumes of his diary because he knew people would know all his secrets after he died. One theory about his death held that he took poison because he was being blackmailed. "Tchaikovsky was homosexual at a time when this was considered completely unacceptable socially, and members of the aristocracy were said to be threatening to expose him unless he killed himself" (p. 57). Even though many of the other musicians lived tormented lives, the opening line of Tchailovsky's profile reads, "Was there anyone ever so unhappy as Peter Tchalkovsky?" ... Writing music, he felt, was the only thing that redeemed him from worthlessness" (p. 55). This is a mostly sympathetic portrait of the popular nineteenth-century Russian composer who is famous for ballets, symphonies, the 1812 Overture, and the First Piano Concerto. The only two relationships mentioned are those he had with women. "Tchaikovsky married a woman who said she would kill herself if he didn't marry her. . . . After nine weeks of marriage, he tried to commit suicide by diving into an icy river" (pp. 56–57). Tchaikovsky survived and soon began a long friendship with a rich woman who sent him money on the condition that they never meet. When she abruptly broke off communication without explanation, Tchaikovsky was distraught and died three years later. The illustrations in *Lives of the Musicians* are colorful caricatures of these temperamental geniuses. Although many will undoubtedly find them amusing, others will wish for at least one realistic photograph or drawing of each subject. Appendices include a glossary of musical terms, an index of composers, and a bibliography of materials for further reading and listening. *Topics*: Composers, Musicians, Peter Tchaikovsky.

Lafferty, Peter. *Leonardo da Vinci*. Bookwright Press, 1990. Hardcover $12.40 (ISBN 0531183483). Ages 7–12.

Series: Pioneers of Science. Leonardo da Vinci (1452–1519) is best known as the painter of the "Mona Lisa." Yet art was only one of his many interests—he was also skilled as an architect, musician, engineer, inventor, designer, mechanic, and scientist. Peter's Lafferty's biographies examine the work of individual scientists and show how their findings have contributed to our knowledge and understanding of the world. He traces da Vinci's life from his birth in a small village near Florence, Italy to his death in France at the age of sixty-seven. He writes, "In 1476, misfortune overtook Leonardo. For the whole of his life, he had never seemed interested in women, except as mother figures. This suggested to some people that he was a homosexual. A charge was brought against him and others by an unknown person who wrote an unsigned letter to the city governors. The charge was dismissed, but it caused Leonardo much distress. . . . His life was scarred by the accusation of homosexuality" (p. 10). Lafferty does not comment further on the homophobia that created this situation. Many biographers choose to erase the sexual identity of their lesbian and gay subjects, but they often go into great detail about the love lives of their heterosexual subjects. The field of children's literature is waiting for a biographer who will provide a more critical analysis of homophobia and the ways in which it may have impacted Da Vinci's life. Nevertheless, Lafferty's admiration for his subject's achievements is apparent throughout the book. He includes da Vinci's drawings, diagrams, paintings, and quotes along with a date chart, bibliography, glossary, and index. (According to *The Alyson Almanac*, da Vinci had two long-term relationships with men. He and Andrea Salaino were inseparable for twenty-five years. Salaino was succeeded by Francesco Melzia, who remained with da Vinci until the painter's death and inherited many of his drawings and paintings.) *Topics*: Artists, Italy, Scientists.

Lannin, Joanne. *Billie Jean King: Tennis Trailblazer*. Lerner Publishing Group, 1999. Hardcover $25.95 (ISBN 082254959X). Ages 10 up.

Joanne Lannin based this engaging biography on interviews with Billie Jean King and some of her contemporaries, along with information from King's autobiographies and other books and articles. One of the greatest tennis players in history, King won twenty titles at Wimbledon—including six singles titles—and numerous other championships. In 1987 she was elected to the Tennis Hall of Fame. As a rising tennis star King wanted everyone to have an opportunity to enjoy tennis, which had traditionally been a game for the wealthy. She also worked hard to change society's view of women in sports. She championed equal opportunity for girls and lobbied tirelessly for the right of women tennis players to earn as much money on the court as men. And after years of hiding in the closet, King finally came out to her parents in 1995. In an interview with Lannin she talked about her early years, her marriage, and her struggle to come out. "I was so unclear about everything . . . was totally overwhelmed with my sexuality, my homophobia" (p. 65). Born in 1943, King, like many others, internalized the homophobic attitudes of the society in which she found herself. Now, she lives with her longtime partner in Chicago and feels more at peace with herself than she ever has. *Billie Jean King: Tennis Trailblazer* is a well-written book that includes an examination of the lawsuit that outed King in 1981 when she was sued by her former assistant, Marilyn Barnett; an intriguing account of King's defeat of Bobby Riggs in the much-publicized "Battle of the Sexes"; and an appraisal of King's later work as a coach. Also included are full-color and black-and-white photographs, a note about scoring in tennis, a bibliography, and an index. *Topic*: Tennis.

Louganis, Greg with Eric Marcus. *Breaking the Surface*. NAL/Dutton, 1996. Paper $12.95 (ISBN 0452275903). Ages 16 up.

Four-time Olympic gold medal diving champion Greg Louganis breaks years of silence and isolation by coming out as a gay man. Born to a young Samoan father and Northern European mother and adopted at nine months, Louganis began performing at age three in local dance and acrobatic competitions. He started diving lessons at age nine, and at sixteen he won a silver medal at the 1976 Montreal Olympics. But despite his athletic skill, he struggled with late-detected dyslexia, prejudice toward his dark skin coloring, and ostracism because of his sexual identity. In addition to being beaten up and called names at school, his father and some of his coaches constantly pressured him, criticizing his mistakes and minimizing his successes. Louganis writes about how he internalized all of this to the point of feeling that he let everyone down

when he won the silver instead of the gold. *Breaking the Surface* is the
unflinchingly honest story of how an adored, gifted athlete could become
so depressed that he tried to kill himself three times. He writes about
substance abuse, domestic violence, AIDS prevention, and homophobia.
Louganis, who had tested positive for HIV a few months before the 1988
Olympics, writes, "I hope my story will help anyone who has to face
adversity. . . . I also hope to dispel myths about gay people, some of
which I have struggled with for most of my life. Maybe I can prevent
one teenager from being infected with HIV. And maybe I can give hope
to people who are in abusive relationships: You can get out and start
over again" (p. xiii). Determined to finally live his life openly and honestly, he writes, "Fear has ruled my life for too long. . . . I want never
again to feel compelled to . . . edit what I say and lie about my life" (p.
xiii). (*Breaking the Surface* is available on video at 1–800–438–9653.) *Topics*:
Divers, Family Violence, Olympics, Pacific Islander Americans, Suicide
(attempted).

Luck, Joyce. *Melissa Etheridge: Our Little Secret.* ECW Press, 1997. Paper $16.95 (ISBN 1550222988). Ages 14 up.

"I'm just really proud to say that I've been a lesbian all my life" (p.
136). With these words, singer Melissa Etheridge came out publicly in
1993 although her family, friends, and many of her fans had known for
years. This engaging biography follows her life and career from her birth
in 1961 in Leavenworth, Kansas to the years she spent performing in
lesbian bars in southern California to her recent international acclaim as
the "First Lady of Rock-and-Roll." Etheridge, who has been compared
with Janis Joplin, is known for her crowd-pleasing antics, performance
innovations, and genuine openness. Critics have described her as energetic, vibrant, gritty, spirited, raw, dynamic, charismatic, and intense.
Etheridge, whose interest in music started early, received her first guitar
when she was eight years old, composed her first song at ten, and enjoyed her first public appearance at eleven. She fell in love with her best
friend when she was seventeen. Although she never hid her lesbianism,
she waited fifteen years to come out publicly for fear that the news
would destroy her career. Surprisingly, the dreaded backlash never ma-
terialized. (Etheridge's friend, k. d. lang, another popular singer, had
come out the year before with no damage to her career.) *Our Little Secret*
details each of Etheridge's songs, explaining why she wrote them, describing where and how they were performed, and analyzing the responses to them. It also chronicles Etheridge's political work, including
the controversial People for the Ethical Treatment of Animals ad "I'd
rather go naked than wear fur," which featured Etheridge and her lover,
Julie Cypher. This compelling tribute to a talented singer includes nu-

merous full-color and black-and-white photographs, an extensive discography, and a bibliography, but alas, no index. *Topics*: Musicians, Singers.

Martin, W. K. *Marlene Dietrich*. Chelsea House, 1995. Hardcover $19.95 (ISBN 0791028623); Paper $9.95 (ISBN 079102881X). Ages 14 up.

Series: Lives of Notable Gay Men and Lesbians. Many readers will undoubtedly wonder why Chelsea House chose Marlene Dietrich, a bisexual, as one of ten people for their notable biography series, when there are dozens of lesbian and gay candidates whose lives offer inspiration and hope for young readers. Series editor Martin Duberman writes, "Dietrich did not exclusively or centrally devote herself to or sleep with other women; nor did she either publicly or privately characterize herself as 'a lesbian' " (p. 11). However, biographer W. K. Martin argues that Dietrich's "attractions to women were definitely special, more far-reaching, intense" (p. 32). Martin describes Dietrich as "unstraight" and writes about her as an icon: the Marlene who publicly kissed other women on the mouth, who danced cheek-to-cheek with her female lovers, who frequented gay and transvestite clubs, and who dressed as she pleased, often subverting traditional images of femininity. At the age of sixteen, Dietrich was in love with the Countess Christine Gersdorf, writing, "I am dying of love for her. . . . I would like to hold her hand and kiss it wildly until I die. . . . She does not know how great my love for her is . . . it's really passion, deep, deep love" (p. 27). On the screen, Dietrich projected a blasé demeanor and often insinuated lesbian references into her strong performances. Offscreen, she scandalized the public with her nontraditional choice of clothing, her relationships with women, and her circle of well-known "unstraight" friends. She decried Hollywood hypocrisy, denounced Nazism and became a citizen of the United States, joined the USO and entertained thousands of Allied soldiers—for which she became the first woman to be awarded the U.S. Medal of Freedom—and enjoyed a twenty-year career as one of the world's most popular cabaret entertainers. Famous for her trademark tuxedo and top hat and nicknamed "The Best Dressed Man in Hollywood," Dietrich defied conventional notions of womanhood. This is an interesting book about a glamorous actress who playfully tweaked traditional mores in her acclaimed films and unconventional social life. Black-and-white photographs, a bibliography, a chronology, and an index are included. *Topics*: Actors, Bisexuals, Germany, Hollywood.

Martinac, Paula. *k. d. lang*. Chelsea House, 1997. Hardcover $19.95 (ISBN 0791028720); Paper $9.95 (ISBN 0791028992) Ages 14 up. *Award*: New York Public Library Best Book for the Teen Age.

Series: Lives of Notable Gay Men and Lesbians. In this exceptionally well-written biography of k. d. lang, Paula Martinac has captured the captivating charm of a musician often heralded as the best singing voice of her generation. Martinac's analysis of the ways in which homophobia and heterosexism have impacted lang's personal and public lives is woven into this spirited and engaging volume. The biographer examines lang's childhood as Kathryn Dawn Lang in Alberta, Canada, her early career as an eccentric country singer, and her meteoric rise to fame as one of Canada's most popular performers. Lang, who knew that she was a lesbian long before she'd heard the word, came out to her mother when she was seventeen. Then in 1992, she became the first major female recording artist to publicly acknowledge her sexual identity, although she had never denied it. She had always refused to conform to traditional notions concerning female appearance and behavior. Indeed, lang has been known not only for her unique approach to music but also her refreshingly short hair, comfortable clothes, and natural face (she refuses to wear makeup). Details about her movie, "Salmonberries," the dozens of awards and honors that she has received, and the way in which she weathered the controversy surrounding her "Meat Stinks" public service announcement for animal rights are included. Filled with black-and-white photographs, this empathic biography ends with a discography of lang's albums, compilations, collaborations, and music videos, a chronology of the majors events in lang's life, a bibliography, and an index. *Topics*: Canada, Musicians, Singers.

Mastoon, Adam. *The Shared Heart: Portraits and Stories Celebrating Lesbian, Gay, and Bisexual Young People*. Morrow, 1997. Hardcover $25.00 (ISBN 0688149316). Ages 10 up. *Award*: ALA Gay, Lesbian, and Bisexual Task Force Award for Nonfiction.

An extraordinary combination of photography and narrative, *The Shared Heart* joins exquisite portraits of forty young lesbian, gay, and bisexual people with eloquent personal statements about their lives. With pride, strength, and dignity, these young people describe coming out, escaping the loneliness and isolation of keeping their sexuality a secret, and embracing their identity. Musicians, athletes, artists, actors, and class presidents eloquently speak about the challenges and victories of coming out to themselves, family, friends, and community. Each person is presented in a personal essay, a handwritten note, and a striking full-page photograph. Those portrayed are from diverse ethnic groups and are in their late teens and early twenties. Twenty-two-year-old Salva writes, "I have always been queer since the second I was born. It just took me a while to realize it, then to accept it" (p. 62). Nineteen-year-old Adam writes that coming out "was like breathing for the first time" (p. 27).

Eighteen-year-old Liz writes, "You can put a label on me—call me big dyke, call me damned, call me whatever you want—and you will not come close to the truth of what I am. I'm a woman, I'm a poet, I'm a daughter, a sister, a friend, I'm an activist, I'm a Jew, I'm a leader, a scholar, a fighter. I'm a lesbian. I am not afraid. And I am happy" (p. 81). She remembers hiding in the library, searching for information, absorbing lesbian culture, whispering to the characters in the books, "I'm gay. I'm gay" (p. 80). Photographer Adam Mastoon created this book because "I wanted to make visible the images I longed for when I was young" (p. vii). The Shared Heart Initiatives is a nonprofit organization, the mission of which is to promote awareness, understanding, and acceptance of sexual orientations, particularly of lesbian, gay, and bisexual youth. An exhibition of the photographs presented in this book is touring high schools, colleges, and workplaces. For more information, write: The Shared Heart Initiatives, P.O. Box 562, Brookline, MA 02146. *Topics*: Coming Out, Photographs.

McKissack, Patricia and Frederick L. McKissack. *Young, Black, and Determined: A Biography of Lorraine Hansberry.* Holiday, 1998. Hardcover $18.95 (ISBN 0823413004). Ages 12 up.

In this carefully researched biography, the McKissacks explore the life and times of gifted playwright Lorraine Hansberry (1930–1964). In her short thirty-four years, she was not only one of the most successful playwrights of a generation but a brilliant essayist, a spirited activist, and a social critic. Through engaging prose, black-and white photographs, excerpts from Hansberry's journals, and interviews with her sister, the authors have created a significant tribute to this gifted writer, who is best known for her play *A Raisin in the Sun*. This noteworthy biography is made even more special by the way it is framed within the context of the events, people, and literature of the times. Although Hansberry's parents were wealthy, she identified with those of her race who suffered from poverty. Throughout her short life she was dedicated to the cause of civil rights. Regarding her sexual identity, the biographers state,

Although Hansberry's views about homosexuality were not a primary part of her activism, she stated in an unsigned article in *The Ladder*, a lesbian publication, that "homosexual persecution" had at its roots not only social ignorance, but sexism as well. Lorraine Hansberry's sexuality has been the topic of much debate. Was she a lesbian? During her lifetime, she chose not to discuss her sexuality publicly, and until more of Hansberry's writings are made public and the research about her life more carefully and thoughtfully researched, it is impossible to say much more about that subject. (p. 121)

The text of Hansberry letters, which were printed in *The Ladder*, are available in *Gay American History: Lesbians and Gay Men in the U.S.A.* by Jonathan Katz. She wrote, "Considering Mattachine, Bilitis, ONE, all seem to be cropping up on the West Coast rather than here where a vigorous and active gay set almost bump one another off the streets— what is it in the air out there?" (p. 639). The McKissacks include a time-line, a bibliography, and an index in this moving biography of an extraordinary woman whose writings and vision changed the American theater and continue to inspire people of all ages and backgrounds. *Topics*: African Americans, Playwrights, Theatre.

Min, Anchee. *Red Azalea: A Memoir*. Berkley, 1999. Paper $13.00 (ISBN 0425166872). Ages 17 up.

This riveting memoir covers the years from 1957, when the narrator was born in Shanghai, until 1984, when she left China for the United States. The oldest of four children, Min's responsibilities made her feel like an adult by the age of five. A devoted revolutionary, she became the head of her school's Little Red Guard at the age of thirteen and was sent to Red Fire Farm to work as a peasant when she was seventeen. There she fell in love with Yan, the Party secretary and commander of the squad. Shadowed by the constant threat of discovery and possible execution, they entered into a passionate relationship that brought joy into their lives. They spent grueling days cultivating the salty soil and toiling in the rice fields, where they were preyed upon by leeches and spied upon by suspicious coworkers. Then Min's life took an unexpected turn when she was chosen to compete for the starring role in comrade Jiang Ching's movie, *Red Azalea*. Separated from Yan and driven by ambition, Min became involved with a man identified only as the Supervisor, a cultural advisor to Jiang Ching. Production of the film ended with Mao's death, and six years later Min emigrated to the United States. This evocative memoir is not just another book about the Cultural Revolution. It is the beautifully written story of the love between two women. After Min and Yan tell each other their life stories, "We were still talking when we reached the barracks. We stood in the dark, filled with incredible delight. . . . [Later], Yan did not speak to me in the room, but there was life and fresh air. I felt spring" (p. 90). Min's love for Yan survives, even though circumstances divide them. Wherever she goes, Yan is with her. "I felt Yan under my skin" (p. 281). As she is preparing to leave China, she is missing Yan. Some reviewers felt that the two women fell in love only because they were forbidden contact with the opposite sex. That might have been true for Yan, but certainly not for Min. She makes it clear that it was love she felt for Yan and ambition that she shared with the Supervisor. *Topics*: China, Cultural Revolution, Filmmaking.

Mungo, Ray. *Liberace*. Chelsea House, 1995. Hardcover $19.95 (ISBN 079102850X); Paper $9.95 (ISBN 0791028852). Ages 14 up.

Series: Lives of Notable Gay Men and Lesbians. A musical prodigy at the age of four, Wladziu Valentino Liberace (1919–1987) defied convention to become one of the most popular pianists in American history. Flamboyant, outspoken, and controversial, he built his career on calculated outrageousness. His trademark mixture of classical and popular music thrilled audiences and dismayed music critics. Liberace's costumes, candalabras, wealth, and signature songs earned him the title "Mr. Showmanship." Meanwhile, Liberace led a double life, privately pursuing a number of gay relationships while publicly claiming to be heterosexual. The more successful he became in his career, the more he felt compelled to hide his sexual identity. "For an entertainer like Liberace, with a large, adoring female following, the revelation of homosexuality would have seriously threatened and possibly destroyed his career" (p. 12). Ray Mungo makes it clear that Liberace lived a double life not because of some personal flaw, but rather because of the homophobic society in which he lived. Although he became more public about his homosexuality during his last years—especially in his four year relationship with Scott Thorson—he was still terrified of being exposed "as the world's biggest liar." His fear of discovery continued until his death from AIDS in 1987. Mungo compassionately examines Liberace's life in the closet, his innovative and whimsical musical style, and his obsessive accumulation of wealth, fame, and possessions. Series editor Martin Duberman writes, "Liberace's life tells us much about what traits our culture will or will not reward, and also much about the distortions of personality that follow the quest for public notoriety. . . . It could be argued that Liberace's character, relationships, and integrity were seriously flawed—but then so was the world that formed him" (p. 12). Liberace was shaping his career at a time when the psychiatric profession was all but unanimous in declaring homosexuality an illness. Black-and-white photographs, a bibliography, a chronology, and an index are included. *Topics*: Musicians, Pianists.

Nava, Michael. "Abuelo: My Grandfather, Raymond Acuña." In *A Member of the Family: Gay Men Write About Their Families*, edited by John Preston. Dutton, 1992. Paper $12.95 (ISBN 0452270324). Ages 12 up.

"Childhood had been a form of imprisonment for me," (p. 19), writes Michael Nava in this compelling autobiographical short story about his life growing up in a semi-rural barrio in Sacramento, California. Now an acclaimed writer whose work is set apart by its insight, compassion, and sense of social justice, Nava reflects on a childhood spent buried in books, searching for a way to make sense of life. He pays tribute to his grandfather, who "represented a kind of masculinity from which I was not excluded by reason of my intelligence or, later, my homosexuality. . . . Fat, myopic, and brainy, I escaped sissyhood only because of the aggressive gloominess I shared with my grandfather" (p. 17). Raymond Acuña, a Yaqui Indian, was an intelligent, solitary person who spent much of his life working in a monotonous job in a large cannery. One of the most liberating lessons he taught his grandson was that masculinity and self-denial are not the same thing. Nava writes unflinchingly about the pain and isolation of his early years, of waiting for his life to begin, of being moody, withdrawn, precocious, and "fiercely unhappy" (p. 17). He describes his feelings of being cast off completely when, at eleven, he was sexually molested by an adult family member. The complexity of this powerful piece is difficult to capture; short quotes and paraphrases do not convey the poignancy of Nava's writing. He finally escaped the desperation of his childhood to graduate from Stanford Law School and embark on a successful career as a lawyer. He is the highly acclaimed writer of an award-winning mystery series featuring a gay Latino lawyer. (More information about Michael Nava is available in Chapter 7 of this book.) *Topics*: Autobiographical Short Stories, Grandfathers, Mexican-American Literature.

Nava, Michael. "The Marriage of Michael and Bill." In *Friends and Lovers: Gay Men Write About the Families They Create*, edited by John Preston. Dutton, 1995. Paper $12.95 (ISBN 0452272548). Ages 14 up.

Michael Nava writes unflinchingly about the despair of his early years, when he blamed himself for his family's poverty and his stepfather's irresponsibility. When he realized that he was gay, it was "the final, crushing blow" (p. 112). He tried to compensate by being the model child: smart, well-behaved, and respectful of elders. After a suicide attempt when he was fourteen, he cut himself off from his feelings and became "driven to make up in outside achievement the inner deficiency I felt" (p. 114). Years later, at Stanford Law School, he met Bill, a fellow student who would become his lover. After years of tortured boyhoods, the two set out to build a life together. Nava writes, "Bill was not the first family I had, but he was the first family I chose" (p. 124). Nava beautifully describes the ways in which love "softened the harshness with which I viewed myself and . . . opened up to me a possibility of happiness I had never even considered" (p. 112). *Topics*: Marriage, Mexican-American Literature, Non-Traditional Families.

O'Brien, Sharon. *Willa Cather*. Chelsea House, 1995. Hardcover $19.95 (ISBN 0791023028); Paper $9.95 (ISBN 079102887X). Ages 14 up. *Award*: New York Public Library Best Book for the Teen Age.

Series: Lives of Notable Gay Men and Lesbians. Willa Cather (1873–1947) defied the "hateful distinction" between masculine and feminine roles, which attributed self-expression and individual achievement to males and domestic tranquillity and delicate emotions to females. As a young adult she cut her hair short, wore tailored suits and a derby hat, and renamed herself William. "As a teenager, the stage of life when most of us are most vulnerable to outside opinion, Cather was willing to risk criticism and perhaps ostracism because she did not want to silence herself" (p. 26). During her years at the University of Nebraska she fell in love with Louise Pound, another student. O'Brien is one of the first biographers to deal openly with Willa's Cather's lesbian identity, examining her strong connections with women, including Edith Lewis, her partner of forty years. This is an engaging portrait of a writer who declared that the power and quality of art arise from "the inexplicable presence of the thing not named" (p. 47). The recognition of Cather's lesbianism, a fact of her life long ignored or obscured, has created an exciting new context for understanding her life and work. O'Brien examines each of Cather's works, including her classic novels *O Pioneers!*, *My Antonia*, and *One of Ours*, which won the 1923 Pulitzer Prize, along with an analysis of the critical reception each received. The only sour note in this excellent book is the use of the offensive term *mannish*. O'Brien spent fifteen years researching and writing her full-length biography, *Willa Cather: The Emerging Voice*. Black-and-white photographs, bibliographies, a chronology, and an index are included. *Topics*: Authorship, Nebraska, Writers.

Reed, Rita. *Growing Up Gay: The Sorrows and Joys of Gay and Lesbian Adolescence.* W. W. Norton, 1997. Hardcover $35.00 (ISBN 0393040925); Paper $19.95 (ISBN 0393316599). Ages 12 up.

This extraordinary book follows the lives of two teenagers, Amy Grahn and Jamie Nabozny, over a period of several years. A series of black-and-white photographs accompanied by the teenagers' own words capture the sorrows and joys of growing up lesbian and gay in a homophobic and heterosexist society. In the beautifully written introduction to this volume, *Minneapolis Star Tribune* staff photographer Rita Reed writes about the need for books like this to support young lesbians and gays in their search for self-acceptance and validation. Her photographs are sensitive, moving, and intimate, and they establish a level of understanding difficult to achieve with words alone. Amy and Jamie generously share excruciatingly painful experiences and all the courageous steps along the way toward self-acceptance. Their heartrending stories include rejection, isolation, self-mutilation, harassment, beatings, humiliations, running away, dropping out of school, suicide attempts, and hospitalizations as well as the joys of first love, finding community, and developing a strong sense of self. This compelling book is a tribute to these courageous young people, and hopefully it will help others feel supported and less isolated. The epilogue includes information about Jamie's case, *Nabozny v. Podlesny*, in which he successfully sued his school, claiming a violation of his constitutional rights of equal protection and due process. The ruling has been heralded as a victory for gay and lesbian students nationwide because it puts school officials on notice that not only the district but they personally may be held liable if they fall to address anti-gay harassment and abuse in their schools. *Topics*: Coming Out, Court Cases, Amy Grahn, Hate Crimes, Jamie Nabozny, *Nabozny v. Podlesny*, Photographs, Suicide (attempted).

Reef, Catherine. *Walt Whitman*. Houghton Mifflin, 1995. Hardcover $16.95 (ISBN 0395687055). Ages 10–14.

How Walt Whitman (1819–1892), a self-described loafer who left school at the age of eleven, could have created verse that radically altered the form and content of American poetry has puzzled scholars for decades. Catherine Reef chronicles significant events in his life, from his childhood in New York's Long Island when his mother said, "He was a very good, but very strange boy" (p. 10) to his declining years in Camden, New Jersey, emphasizing the Civil War years when he served as a battlefield nurse and wrote some of his most powerful poems. She traces the thirty-five-year history of his collected poems, *Leaves of Grass*, from the self-published first edition in 1855, which included twelve poems, to the 1892 edition, which included over 400 poems. Integrated into the narrative are carefully selected poems, along with an analysis of the admiration and anger they elicited from his contemporaries, the impact they have had on American literature, and Reef's own thoughtful interpretations. Over seventy black-and-white photographs, paintings, etchings, and engravings enhance this biography of a self-educated poet who believed he could use words to reach across time and great distance to connect with people. Although many biographers have avoided claiming that Whitman was a homosexual, Reef addresses his sexual identity openly, though too briefly. She writes, "Some of the poems added to the book in 1860 make it apparent that Whitman was homosexual. They celebrate 'manly attachment' and 'athletic love' " (p. 69). She quotes lines from his poem "A Glimpse" in which two men sit quietly holding hands, enjoying each other's company. She adds, "Homosexuality was poorly understood in Whitman's time. Many people had no idea that it was possible for someone to feel attracted to members of his or her own sex" (p. 69). A bibliography and an index are included. *Topic*: Poets.

Reid, Catherine and Holly Iglesias, editors. *Every Woman I've Ever Loved: Lesbian Writers on Their Mothers.* Cleis, 1997. Paper $16.95 (ISBN 1573440302). Ages 15 up.

Twenty-eight lesbian authors write about their relationships with their mothers in this poignant anthology. The stories told here—tender and disturbing, eloquent and startling—pay tribute, struggle for understanding, and bare the truths of mothers who did and did not protect, support, and sustain their lesbian daughters. Contributors include Dorothy Allison, Gloria Anzaldúa, Claudia Bepko, Lisa Colbert, Meg Daly, Shoshona T. Daniel, Christine Downing, Jyl Lynn Felman, Terry Galloway, Marilyn Hacker, Ellen Hawley, Holly Hughes, Helena Lipstadt, Audre Lorde, Laura Markowitz, Jane Miller, Cherríe Moraga, Linda Grant Niemann, Mattie Richardson, Maureen Seaton, Mab Segrest, Lu Vickers, and Shay Youngblood. Several write about mothers who were distant, reserved, or unavailable. In "In My Mother's Eyes," Claudia Bepko writes, "It's hard to describe how much I loved my mother and how much she wouldn't let me. . . . She gave me books so I read books. She wanted to be a writer, so I became a writer" (p. 146). In "Clay," Shoshona T. Daniel writes, "It's true that we hold each other to impossible standards, measures invented to push away and pull" (p. 2). One of the themes that runs throughout this collection is loss. "When you're a lesbian with a dead mother," writes Laura Markowitz in "Mom, Elvis and Me," "people immediately assume that's the cause, as if you're compelled to spend your life searching for your mother over and over" (p. 84). For Jyl Lynn Felman, in "Private Rituals," the grief of her mother's death "lives in my body whole. . . . Only the memories live in my body, until all I am is one giant memory of mother loss" (p. 92). In "The Moon, My Mother and Me," Helena Lipstadt writes about living the horror of the Holocaust as an infant, knowing it intimately through a "cellular knowledge" of her mother's suffering. Thus, she received her themes: "Dislocation, Grief, Fear, Hiding, Depression, Silence, Rage, Activism, Connection, Compassion, Voice, Elusive Joy" (p. 177). Her mother was "silent about the sources of her pain. . . . It was this silence that finally, in my thirties, squeezed my writing out of me" (pp. 178–179). The role mothers play in attempting to force heterosexuality on their lesbian daughters is apparent in several pieces including "She Breaks My Heart" by Holly Iglesias, who writes about the fighting that began the year she turned twelve. "A battery of restraints: girdles, bras, Kotex belts. . . . No bikes or roller skates or horseback riding. Hair styled with curlers. Nail polish, lipstick, deodorant" (p. 44). Each of these writers squeezed out their stories, focusing on their personal connections with their mothers, with all the love, pain, loss, grief, and paradoxes that those relationships entail in a society that reveres mothers, denigrates women, and ignores lesbians. *Topic*: Mother/Daughter Relationships.

Romo-Carmona, Mariana. "How We Get That Way." In *Queer 13: Lesbian and Gay Writers Recall Seventh Grade*, edited by Clifford Chase. Morrow, 1998. Hardcover $24.00 (ISBN 0688158110). Ages 13 up.

Mariana Romo-Carmona writes about the loneliness she experienced the year she moved from Chile to Connecticut and how, as she walked to school alone each day, she fell in love with a little dogwood tree that "saved my soul when it bloomed" (p. 5). Soothed by the "inexpressibly, superbly pink, pink" blossoms, she realized later that the tree evoked feelings that had already been stirring in her heart. She reminisces about her close bonds with her schoolmates back at the all-girls school in Calama, Chile, recalling with pleasure a game she played with Maria Eugenia, where she would try to find the gold chain hidden inside her friend's shirt collar. Later, when she moved to Connecticut in the middle of seventh grade, she was faced with a new country, a different culture, and a strange language. "The junior high experience was fiercely heterosexual" (p. 9). Almost everyone was dating and going steady with someone of the opposite sex. One day Romo-Carmona made the mistake of wearing a new green jumper, only to learn about a strange custom called Queer Thursday. "It didn't take long for the whispers—she's queer, she's queer!—to register" (p. 11). A new friend tried to reassure her that it wasn't that she was queer, it was just that she was a foreigner. But "in Spanish I thought, no, this is true; I am queer. This is me" (p. 12). Mariana Romo-Carmona is the co-founder of the Latina Lesbian History Project. "How We Get That Way" is one of twenty-five poignant autobiographical pieces in *Queer 13*, which is reviewed elsewhere in this chapter. *Topics*: Chile, Immigrants, Latina Literature, Schools.

Scholinski, Daphne with Jane Meredith Adams. *The Last Time I Wore a Dress*. Putnam, 1997. Hardcover $23.95 (ISBN 1573220779); Berkeley Publishing, 1998. Paper $13.00 (ISBN 1573226963). Ages 14 up.

In her profoundly moving memoir, Daphne Scholinski writes about the three years she spent in mental hospitals where she was committed by her parents when she was fifteen. Written with intelligence and verve, this shocking book is an indictment of the mental health system and the inexcusable psychiatric abuse suffered by untold numbers of people, Scholinski writes about a childhood filled with problems—neglected by her mother, physically abused by her father, sexually abused by neighbors, involved in fighting, stealing, and drugs—she was depressed, suicidal, and "out of control." But once she was institutionalized, her doctors diagnosed her with gender identity disorder (GID). Instead of helping her deal with being betrayed and abandoned by her parents, they decided that her problems stemmed from being an "inappropriate female." Her treatment plan? To wear makeup, curl her hair, dress like a girl, and explore her feelings toward the opposite sex. "The staff was under orders to scrutinize my femininity: the way I walked, the way I sat with my ankle on my knee, the clothes I wore, the way I kept my hair" (p. x). The fact that she had grown up a tomboy who liked to ride her bicycle, wear comfortable clothes, and play softball was held against her. "I knew I walked tough and sat with my legs apart and did not defer to men and boys, but I was a girl in the only way I knew how to be one" (p. 16). The doctors encouraged Scholinski to engage in hetero-sexual activities and prohibited her from spending time with Valerie, a young woman with whom she developed a close friendship. Scholinski writes about her attempts to deflect attention from her so-called disorder by pretending to be anorexic and addicted to drugs. The years that should have been spent enjoying a typical high school experience were replaced by periods of seclusion and physical restraint, frequent doses of sedatives, meaningless counseling sessions, and abuse by other pa-tients. Scholinski's childhood memories, hospital experiences, diagnostic evaluations, and art are woven together in this extraordinary memoir. Her incarceration occurred in the early 1980s, but GID is still listed in the psychiatric bible *Diagnostic and Statistical Manual of Mental Disorders* (fourth edition). Scholinski appends the text of this cruel and heterosexist diagnosis, along with a resource list of agencies where young people can find support and services. In the last chapter, Scholinski writes about the years following her hospitalization. She came out as a lesbian in college and now lives in San Francisco, where she is a successful artist. Although she still has nightmares, she has found solace in her drawings and paint-ings. "[Art] saved my life" (p. 199). In her acknowledgments she pays tribute to her third grade teacher, who "proved what a difference an individual can make in the life of a young person" (p. 201). *Topics*: Ap-pearance, Parenting, Psychiatric Abuse.

Seel, Pierre. *Liberation Was for Others: Memoirs of a Gay Survivor of the Nazi Holocaust.* Translated from the French by Joachim Neugroschel. De Capo Press, 1997. Paper $13.95 (ISBN 0306807564). Ages 14 up.

First published under the title *Moi, Pierre Seel, déporté homosexual (I, Pierre Seel, Deported Homosexual)*, this is the deeply moving memoir of one gay man's horrifyingly cruel treatment by the Nazis and the tragic aftermath of a life ravaged by suffering buried under denial, secrets, and shame. In one of the few firsthand accounts of the Nazi persecution of gay men, Seel writes about his decision to bear witness after decades of silence in order to protect the future and overcome the amnesia of his contemporaries. Haunted by memories of the horrors of the Schirmeck-Vorbruch concentration camp where he was tortured, starved, and forced to witness the brutal murder of his lover, he realized, "If I do not speak, I will become the accomplice of my torturers" (p. 188). For decades he kept the pact of silence imposed by his father, anti-homosexual laws, and a bigoted, homophobic society. He got married and raised three children, feeling that "liberation was only for others" (p. 88). Despondent and suicidal, he finally realized that his secret was devouring him. The last chapter of the book, titled "Out of the Closet: A Painful Testimony," details Seel's efforts to expose the Nazi persecution of homosexuals and to demand restitution for the past. Dedicated "To my friend, Jo, Murdered in 1941, And all the victims of the Nazi barbarity," this is a powerful and heartbreaking memoir, extraordinary for its frankness and courage. The appended chapter notes are not referenced within the text. *Topics*: Concentration Camps, Hate Crimes, Holocaust, World War II.

Shyer, Marlene Fanta and Christopher Shyer. *Not Like Other Boys: Growing Up Gay: A Mother and Son Look Back*. Houghton Mifflin, 1996. Hardcover $21.95 (ISBN 0395709393); Alyson Publications, 1997. Paper $11.95 (ISBN 1555834493). Ages 16 up.

In alternating voices, this compelling memoir chronicles the painful journey a mother and son took from denial, concealment, and shame to acceptance, respect, and hope. Christopher writes about his early fears that he was somehow wrong, vile, heinous. "The sense of having a tainted soul, of being in some way sordid, deviant and dirty, is the deepest and most tearing shame possible" (p. 13). Marlene, who worried obsessively from the time Chris was in kindergarten, took him to a series of psychologists, seeking assurances that he was heterosexual. Now, filled with remorse that she swallowed the homophobic attitudes of society, she realizes that she could have "saved my son fifteen years of desolation, assuaged a childhood and adolescence of torment and freed him from the pathology of self-hatred" (p. viii). By sharing their most painful, intimate experiences, Christopher and Marlene, who are now close friends, have given readers a generous gift. The pages of this powerful book cry out with the sorrow of unnecessary pain, the anguish of isolation and humiliation, the loss of loving words unspoken. The concomitant need for eradicating our society of heterosexism and homophobia flows through every chapter. Finally, after years of internalized homophobia, Chris is able to write, "It's not us in the homosexual community who are deficient. It's those who condemn and deride us, those who are ignorant and misinformed who should be scorned and ridiculed" (p. 238). *Not Like Other Boys* should be required reading for every prospective parent. *Topics*: Mother/Son Relationship, Socioeconomic Class.

Snyder, Jane McIntosh. *Sappho*. Chelsea, House, 1995. Hardcover $19.95 (ISBN 0791023087); Paper $9.95 (ISBN 0791028836). Ages 14 up.

Series: Lives of Notable Gay Men and Lesbians. Jane McIntosh Snyder presents the life and poetry of Sappho of Lesbos, whose work has been deliberately mistranslated and censored through the ages. Born at the end of the seventh century B.C., Sappho has proved to be one of the most enduring and influential poets of all time. A woman whose passionate voice moves readers as much as it disturbs homophobic moralists, Sappho is known for her unapologetic representation of lesbian desire, combined with her skillful use of imagery and her power of expression. Snyder exposes the ways in which scholars have delesbianized and co-opted her work, even deliberately destroying it. This is just one example of the erasure of the existence of lesbians and their ideas and works throughout time. Snyder and others are working to reclaim the excised past and celebrate an identity excluded by patriarchal norms. Sappho's poem, "Hymn to Aphrodite," and her poetic fragments are included, along with Snyder's insightful interpretations. In one fragment, Sappho answers her own question concerning the most beautiful thing on earth: "Her lovely walk and the bright sparkle of her face/I would rather look upon than/all the Lydian chariots/and full-armed infantry" (p. 77). Despite the quandary Sappho has posed to homophobic critics, she has inspired generations of lesbian authors. Indeed, her words continue to influence lesbian writers today. In one of her most poetic lines, Snyder writes, "Sappho floats across the centuries as an island in the sea of writers of the past, a solitary example of a woman writer attempting to define woman's desire for women" (p. 101). What Snyder doesn't mention is that countless other lesbian writers from the past undoubtedly have been obscured, erased, and heterosexualized. The last chapter of this inspiring book examines Sappho's legacy and the specific influence she has had on lesbian poets including Amy Lowell, Renée Vivien, Hilda Doolittle (H. D.), May Sarton, and Olga Broumas. Photographs of funerary sculptures, statues, vase paintings, drawings, maps, and an index are included, along with bibliographies of books about Sappho and works by and about modern women poets influenced by Sappho. *Topics*: Greece, Poetry, Poets.

Souhami, Diana. *Gertrude and Alice*. Parmer Books, 1991. Hardcover $25.00 (ISBN 0614230012); Pandora, 1993. Paper $14.00 (ISBN 004440848X). Ages 16 up. *Award*: Lambda Literary Award Nominee.

This fascinating dual biography focuses on the thirty-nine-year relationship between Gertrude Stein and Alice B. Toklas. The book is dedicated to these remarkable women: "Gertrude Stein and Alice Babette Toklas first met on Sunday 8 September 1907, in Paris. From that day on they were together, until Gertrude's death on Saturday 27 July 1946." The biography is balanced, providing information about both women's lives before they met as well as Toklas' twenty-one years after the death of her companion. Distinguished by Souhami's respect and admiration for her subjects, along with her nonjudgmental and at times witty reporting, this is a commendable book. Souhami writes, "they were so emphatically and uncompromisingly themselves, that the world could do nothing less than accept them as they were" (p. 15). She acknowledges the role Toklas played in furthering Stein's career, as her manager, editor, publisher, amanuensis, and secretary. But what makes this biography so special is the way it celebrates their relationship. "They fell in love, saw life from the same point of view, and lived as a couple, with much emphasis on domestic harmony, until parted by death. They were happy, and they said so" (p. 13). Indeed, they had much in common. Both were daughters of European Jews who were first-generation immigrants to the United States, and both grew up in the San Francisco Bay area of California. "For Gertrude and Alice love budded and flowered" (p. 114). They married, vowed commitment, and devoted themselves to each other. Inseparable, they called each other Lovey and Pussy, and wrote notes to each other inscribed YD (Your Darling) and DD (Darling Darling). During World War I they distributed supplies to hospitals in France, and during World War II they were protected by friends while supporting resistance fighters. After Stein's death, Toklas wrote, "could such perfection such happiness and such beauty have been here and now be gone away" (p. 253). In spite of resistance from the Stein family, Toklas dedicated herself to furthering Gertrude's reputation. "Alice carried on for Gertrude, guarding Gertrude's privacy, promoting her genius, encouraging publication and translation of all that she had written" (p. 260). Toklas also wrote two cookbooks and her memoir, *What Is Remembered*, before she died in 1967, two months before her ninetieth birthday. Black-and-white photographs, a bibliography, and an index are included. *Topics*: Authorship, France, Jews, Writers.

Steffan, Joseph. *Honor Bound: A Gay American Fights for the Right to Serve His Country*. Villard, 1992. Hardcover $22.50 (ISBN 0679416609); Avon, 1993. $10.00 (ISBN 0380715015). Ages 16 up.

Discharged from the United States Naval Academy in 1987 for being gay, Joseph Steffan filed suit a year later to overturn the military's restriction on gay and lesbian service members. His memoir is an engaging story of his battle against discrimination at the highest levels of our country's military establishment. Born and raised in a small town in Minnesota, Steffan excelled academically and enjoyed running on the track team and singing in the school choir. Salutatorian of his high school class, he was voted most likely to succeed by his classmates. He flourished at Annapolis, rising to a top leadership position, with direct responsibility for 800 of his classmates. But weeks short of graduation, Steffan was stripped of his rank, denied his degree, and told to resign or be kicked out. In stirring personal terms, Steffan tells the story of his early years, his career at the Naval Academy, his public humiliation, and his fight for justice. Most memorable is his moving account of coming out to himself. He describes the anguish of self-denial and the process he went through to accept his identity. "I had finally stopped fighting who I knew I was and began accepting myself" (p. 105). After his discharge he contacted the Lambda Legal Defense and Education Fund, who helped him launch a courtroom challenge of the anti-gay policy. Steffan charts the case: the Navy's desperate attempts to uncover new, irrelevant evidence to shore up its case; a federal judge who calls Steffan a "homo"; and the discovery of suppressed studies that conclude that having a same-gender or an opposite-gender orientation is unrelated to job performance in the same way as being left- or right-handed. Steffan ended his book before the case was decided, since it would likely take years for a decision to be reached. Meanwhile, he has become an active public speaker and is one of the nation's leading advocates against the military ban. In his closing remarks he analyzes the roots of bigotry, hypocrisy, and suppression of diversity. He asks, "How come I was never taught anything about homosexuality when I was growing up?" Steffan's courageous story is important reading, especially for young lesbian and gay people who are considering a career in the military. Black-and-white photographs are included. *Topics*: Court Cases, Military, Navy.

Stendhal, Renate, editor. *Gertrude Stein: In Words and Pictures*. Algonquin, 1994. Paper $19.95 (ISBN 0945575998). Ages 16 up. *Award*: Lambda Literary Award.

Who was Gertrude Stein? Editor Renate Stendhal answers this question by matching over 350 black-and-white photographs with quotes from Stein's work and from letters and memoirs of those who knew her. "I like to cry not in real life but in books in real life there was nothing much to cry about but in books oh dear me, it was wonderful there was so much to cry about" (from *Wars I Have Seen*, p. 1). In her fascinating introduction Stendhal traces her own understanding of Stein's writing, sharing interesting theories about the way the writer expressed her femaleness, Jewishness, and lesbianism through word games, sound associations, false abstractions, maskings, and masquerades. Stendhal discusses the ways in which Stein's writing and theories about writing liberated language, freeing it from its grammatical traditions. "Stein took the same freedom with her appearance as she took with her writing. Shortly after her arrival in Paris ... she removed her stays, literally stepping out of the corset of convention" (p. xi), rejecting the confining traditions of the fathers. Alice B. Toklas, Stein's lifetime companion, is also in many of the pictures taken after they met in 1907. They secretly married in 1908, when Stein was thirty-four and Toklas was thirty-one. In 1930, Toklas created her own publishing company, Plain Edition, to further Stein's work. Toklas was "for years the only person who understood Stein's work, who validated and discussed it with her" (p. xv). In fact, Stein's first public recognition didn't come until she was fifty-nine years old. She produced over 600 titles and played with every possible literary genre, from nursery rhymes to opera libretti. Stendhal's brilliant juxtaposition of words and images pays tribute to an intriguing writer who has been called the Mother of Modernism. The book includes a bibliography and an index. *Topics*: Authorship, France, Jews, Photographs, Writers.

Taylor, Shella Ortiz. *Imaginary Parents: A Family Autobiography.* Artwork by Sandra Ortiz Taylor. University of New Mexico Press, 1996. Paper $18.95 (ISBN 0826317634). Ages 16 up.

In this innovative memoir, one sister uses words, the other installations to refract memories of their early years growing up in Los Angeles during the 1940s and 1950s. What emerges is an inventive collage of vignettes, reminiscences invoked by photographs, and miniature worlds contained within intriguing little boxes (*cajitas*). By examining and arranging small objects—food, toys, flowers, photographs, candles, *recuerdos*—the Ortiz Taylor sisters try to understand their glamorous parents, their extended family, and how their past "continues to influence the present tense" (p. xv) of their lives. From her earliest memories, Sheila, the observer, is tuned in to the members of her family, remembering decades later in detail the images, tastes, sounds, and nuances of their everyday lives. These pages are filled with jacaranda trees, handmade tortillas, arched eyebrows, vaccination scabs, khaki jodhpurs, and shiny black Cadillac ambulances. Their Anglo lawyer-musician father, who felt one should always be learning something new, never let them take an easy breath with his plans to sail around the world after selling the large house he built for them. Their beautiful Latina mother, the twelfth child of thirteen, quit high school in tenth grade and went to work in a yo-yo factory. Sheila and Sandra negotiate their busy lives, often escaping to scale crumbling cliffs of sandstone, ride their bicycles at breakneck speed, climb through skeletal new houses, and jump out of upstairs windows. They prefer cap pistols to dolls and wear T-shirts and pants instead of the pinafores, sundresses, and velvet jumpers their mother sews for them. In kindergarten Sheila falls in love with her classmate, Hazel Medina, with "her dark, dark eyes smoldering" (p. 103). In high school she falls in love with Miss Highsmith, her physical education teacher, takes to writing poetry in a secret notebook, and dreams of becoming a famous writer. Sandra Ortiz Taylor is a visual artist from San Francisco and Sheila Ortiz Taylor, a professor of English at Florida State University, Tallahassee, is the author of several books including *Coachella*. (More information about Sheila is available in Chapter 7 of this book.) *Topics*: Art, Latina Authors and Artists, Family Relationships.

Turner, Robyn Montana. *Rosa Bonheur: Portraits of Women Artists for Children*. Little, Brown, 1991. Hardcover $15.95 (ISBN 0316856487). Ages 7 up.

The beautiful book is filled with full-color reproductions of Rosa Bonheur's original paintings, including "The Horse Fair," "Sheep by the Sea," "Plowing in the Nivernais," and "Rabbits Nibbling Carrots." Turner wrote this book and others because she discovered that there are very few biographies of women artists written for young readers. This is a carefully researched, engaging book and it will bring Bonheur's fascinating life and work to a wider audience. Born in France in 1822, Bonheur's artistic talent was encouraged from an early age. She grew up painting, drawing, and sculpting in her father's studio. She is known primarily for her realistic paintings of animals, especially horses, cattle, sheep, dogs, deer, and lions. Turner describes the obstacles Bonheur overcame during a time when women were not allowed to attend the best art schools and were discouraged from pursuing their interests in art. She tells readers that Bonheur had to obtain a police permit to wear trousers while she drew in the slaughterhouses. "She also chose to wear her hair cropped short. And she rode her horse astride, rather than side-saddle" (p. 18). What she doesn't say is that Bonheur wore trousers most of the time and was greatly criticized for it. Turner mentions Bonheur's lifetime companion twice. When they first met as adolescents, Turner writes, "During this time Rosa and Nathalie developed a friendship that would last the rest of their lives" (p. 13). Later she writes, "Rosa, with her lifetime friend Nathalie, followed the artwork across the English Channel to visit the queen at Buckingham Palace" (p. 20). Dore Ashton provides more information about their relationship in *Rosa Bonheur: A Life and a Legend* (Viking, 1981, out of print). Before traveling to the Pyrenees, Rosa and Nathalie applied for authorization to wear what was then described as masculine clothing so that they could travel comfortably. When Nathalie's father was on his deathbed, he called the two young women together and admonished them to stay together, giving them his blessing as if they were about to marry. Years later, when Nathalie died, Bonheur found life almost unendurable. She wrote, "She alone knew me." The issue of how much information to include in biographies of lesbian and gay people for young readers is the subject of much debate. Many biographers (and publishers) are unfortunately afraid to broach the subject, especially in books for this age group. *Topics:* Artists, France.

Zwerman, Gilda. *Martina Navratilova*. Chelsea House, 1995. Hardcover $19.95 (ISBN 0791023036); Paper $9.95 (ISBN 079102878X). Ages 14 up.

Series: Lives of Notable Gay Men and Lesbians. In this carefully researched biography, Gilda Zwerman examines the life of Martina Navratilova, widely heralded as the greatest woman tennis player of all time. As a child in communist Czechoslovakia Navratilova demonstrated natural athleticism and strong determination. By the time she was seventeen she was competing professionally, and in 1975 she made the difficult decision to defect to the United States. As she rose to the top of the international circuit, winning the first of a record nine Wimbledon championships in 1978, Navratilova became known for her powerful, athletic style as well as her wit and candor. She retired in 1994 after twenty-two years of professional competition. Zwerman provides information about Czechoslovakian history, traces the changes in the field of women's tennis, and examines the ways in which Navratilova suffered from homophobia and heterosexism. "The impact of homophobia on a gay individual is not something that is readily perceptible or easily measured . . . prejudice and discrimination can and do have chronic and cumulative effects on the self-worth of the individual who experiences them, even on an individual as resilient as Navratilova" (pp. 94–95). Navratilova realized she was a lesbian several months before she left her homeland. Adjusting to a new country, language, and customs, she steadfastly refused to hide her sexual identity. "She did not hate herself or wish that she was straight" (p. 85). In 1991, during a nationally televised interview with Barbara Walters, she announced to the world that she was a lesbian. She became involved with the lesbian/gay rights movement, campaigning against Amendment Two in Colorado and speaking before a crowd of 500,000 at the Lesbian and Gay Rights March on Washington in 1993. Zwerman provides a complex study of Navratilova, portraying her as a generous, tenacious, funny, and gracious person. Details about her relationships with Rita Mae Brown, Nancy

Lieberman, and Judy Nelson are woven into the book. The only sour note is the choice of titles for one of the chapters: "Sex as Sublimation for Tennis" (p. 91). Includes black-and-white photographs, a bibliography, and a chronology. *Topics*: Czechoslovakia, Tennis.

6

Books for Librarians, Educators, Parents, and Other Adults

Aarons, Leroy. *Prayers for Bobby: A Mother's Coming to Terms with the Suicide of Her Gay Son*. HarperSanFrancisco, 1995. Hardcover $22.00 (ISBN 006251122X); Paper $13.00 (ISBN 0062511238).

In 1983, after years of shame, degradation, and self-hatred drummed into him by a family and church that believed he was evil in the eyes of their God, twenty-year-old Bobby Griffith killed himself by jumping off a freeway overpass into the path of a large tractor trailer. *Prayers for Bobby* is the story of how his mother, Mary Griffith, changed from a "religious hard-nosed Bible thumper" (her words) into a tireless, outspoken advocate for gay and lesbian teens. Through Bobby's journal entries, his mother's reminiscences, and interviews with family, friends, and church members, gay journalist Leroy Aarons recreates the emotional turmoil that eventually led Bobby to end his life. This is the heartrending story of a mother who prayed that her son would be "healed," her anguish over his suicide, and the drama of her remarkable metamorphosis. As a child Bobby was eager to please, artistic, and interested in drawing and writing. Here was a child who said "good morning" to the trees, who won a prize for an essay he wrote about John Muir, and who organized carnivals in his backyard for the neighborhood kids. The story of how his self-esteem was gradually and relentlessly eroded by family, church, and society is important reading for everyone who cares about young people. He repeatedly contemplated suicide through agonizing years filled with Bible study and prayer meetings designed to "cure" him of his homosexuality. "Bobby, you're not praying hard enough," his mother would say. She blasted Christian radio into his room, left biblical messages about Sodom on his mirror, and prayed over him as he slept. Bobby wrote in his diary, "Why did you do this to me, God? . . . I'm rotten inside . . . I make myself sick. I'm a joke" (p. 125). After Bobby's death his mother embarked on a journey that enabled her to comprehend the enormity of her mistake and compelled her to proclaim an anguished message to parents everywhere: "Don't let this happen to your child" (p. 178). Written with clarity and poignancy, *Prayers for Bobby* is a powerful story of tragedy and transformation. It asks urgent questions: How many children must die in the name of rigid tradition or so-called family values? What can we each do to combat the sea of neglect, fear, and bigotry that continues to threaten the lives of young lesbian and gay people? In the afterword, Aarons provides information about some of the programs available to help lesbian and gay youth such as Project 10, Hetrick-Martin Institute, OutYouth, and Gay, Lesbian, and Straight Teachers Network. Black-and-white photographs and a directory of Help Organizations are included. *Topics*: Mother-Son Relationship, Parenting, PFLAG (Parents, Families, and Friends of Lesbians and Gays), Religious Fundamentalism, Suicide.

Baker, Jean M. *Family Secrets: Gay Sons—A Mother's Story*. Haworth Press, 1998. Hardcover $39.95 (ISBN 0789002485); Paper $14.95 (ISBN 1560239158).

Writing in her capacities as a devoted mother and a clinical psychologist, Jean M. Baker shares her heartbreaking experience of losing a beloved son to AIDS, along with solid suggestions for ways to eliminate the bigotry that is so destructive to lesbian and gay people. Baker writes extensively about her son, Gary Thomas Baker (1962–1989), and her own process of coming to terms with the homosexuality of both her sons. She is ashamed of her reaction when Gary first came out to her. "Being a psychologist didn't seem to help me at all" (p. 76). And in all the parenting books she had studied so carefully, there was not one word about the possibility that a child might be lesbian or gay, not one word of advice for parents. As she educated herself, she realized that "being gay is not the tragedy; what is tragic is that any parent can reject a child simply because that child is gay" (p. 181). Grief-stricken, Baker calls on other parents to help change social attitudes. "We must stir the consciousness of a nation and awaken empathy for our children and for all who have suffered from this disease" (p. 191). In the last chapter, "Homosexuality: Facts, Fallacies, Feelings," Baker debunks myths and makes a number of excellent recommendations for change. She intersperses excerpts from her son's journal and letters and comments made by his friends, colleagues, and relatives into this poignant book. *Family Secrets* has been described as a brave personal exposé, helpful, honest, encouraging, timely, and well-written. It is important reading for librarians, school counselors, psychologists, teachers, administrators, policymakers, and parents. Family photographs, an extensive bibliography, and an index are included. *Topics*: AIDS, Dying and Death, Mother-Son Relationship.

Bernstein, Robert A. *Straight Parents Gay Children: Keeping Families Together.* Thunder's Mouth Press, 1995. Hardcover $24.95 (ISBN 1560250852); Paper $13.95 (ISBN 1560252294).

In this engaging book, Bernstein describes his experiences as the father of a lesbian and as an activist with Parents, Families, and Friends of Lesbians and Gays (PFLAG). Weaving the personal stories of dozens of parents who discovered that their lives were not diminished, as they had originally feared, but enriched by their lesbian and gay children, Bernstein issues a call to action to parents not to just love their children, but to speak out on their behalf. He includes a survival guide designed to help parents move through the early stages of denial, shock, grief, and guilt through self-education to acceptance and beyond. Also included is information about the history and growth of PFLAG, anti-gay ballot initiatives in Arizona, Colorado, Idaho, and Oregon, religious issues, the Nazi persecution of gay and lesbian people, public figures who have lesbian and gay relatives, and much more. Bernstein encourages parents to spare their children years of inner turmoil, isolation, and self-doubt by enlisting in the fight against homophobia. By remaining silent they help perpetuate the oppression of those they love. "They do not realize they themselves have the power to end that injustice by speaking out against it" (p. 6). Bernstein believes that because parents, family, and friends of lesbian and gay people wield the clout of sheer numbers and are able to speak to the mainstream *from* the mainstream, they will be in the vanguard of the breakthrough to liberation. "The prejudice of centuries won't be eliminated overnight, but it cannot long survive a concerted challenge by those of us with gay loved ones" (p. 194). Index included. *Topics*: Parenting, PFLAG.

Berzon, Betty. *Positively Gay: New Approaches to Gay and Lesbian Life.* Celestial Arts, 1995. Paper $12.95 (ISBN 0890876762).

This recently updated and expanded resource examines many issues of importance to lesbian and gay people, including coming out, building relationships, reconciling religious beliefs, job security, voting power, parenting, aging, the cultural scene, AIDS, the experiences of people of color, and much more. One of the many interesting articles is "Latino Issues: Gay and Lesbian Latinos Claiming *La Raza*" by Eric-Steven Gutierrez, in which he encourages Latino/a lesbian and gay people to reject silence and shame and to integrate their cultural, ethnic, sexual, and geographic communities. He writes, "By living as a queer among Latinos and a Latino among queers, there is the hope of establishing those relationships based on courage and honesty instead of fear and shame" (p. 243). In her hopeful article, "The Brave New World of Gay and Lesbian Youth," Teresa DeCrescenzo showcases youth groups such as Project 10, Boston Alliance of Gay and Lesbian Youth (BAGLY), the Lavender Youth Recreation and Information Center (LYRIC) in San Francisco, and the Sexual Minority Youth Assistance League (SMYAL) in Washington, D.C. She provides suggestions for ways lesbian and gay adults can help lesbian and gay youth. She writes, "the gift we gay and lesbian adults have to offer our youngsters, [is] to open our lives to them in any way we can, to tell them our stories, to share our successes, to impart hope for a life that is viable and productive, free of injunctions to hide and pretend about something that is natural and understandable" (p. 287). The foreword was written by Congress person Barney Frank (D-Mass.); other contributors include Betty Fairchild, Ayofemi Folayan, Phyllis Lyon, Del Martin, Brian McNaught, Robin Podolsky, John Preston, Nancy Todor, and Terry Tofoya. Some articles are followed by lists of resources and organizations; the book ends with a helpful discussion guide for use in educational, training, and personal growth programs. Author and columnist Michelango Signorile wrote, "*Positively Gay* was the first gay book I ever read. It scared me. It challenged me. It excited me. And it eventually made me feel good about myself as it cleverly lurched me from the closet. In that sense, I suppose *Positively Gay* outed me—and I'm glad it did." *Topics*: Aging, AIDS, Coming Out, Lesbian and Gay People of Color, Parenting, Self-Help, Youth Groups.

Cantwell, Mary Ann. *Homosexuality: The Secret a Child Dare Not Tell.* Rafael Press, 1996. Paper $12.00 (ISBN 0964982994).

When Mary Ann Cantwell's forty-six-year-old gay son told her that he had known he was different from the age of five or six, she felt compelled to write a book to help other young lesbian and gay people and their families. She feels that much suffering could be avoided if parents acknowledged the fact that their children might be lesbian or gay and were prepared to give them support during their early years. Determined to educate herself, Cantwell formulated two sets of surveys: one for lesbian and gay people and one for their parents. She searched her memories of her son's early years and reread the newspaper columns she had written during his childhood titled "Family Growing Pains" for

The Indiana Catholic and Record. She attended PFLAG meetings, marched in Lesbian and Gay Pride parades, and talked with lesbians and gay men and their parents, including Mary Griffith, whose gay son had committed suicide. Cantwell concludes that the damaging messages given to lesbian and gay children are implicit as well as explicit. Without words, often without knowing it, parents teach their children that there is something wrong with them. They teach them so well that their children hide themselves to protect their parents from discovering that they are something unacceptable to them. Cantwell writes, "It should be the birthright of everyone to be accepted onto the planet where they are born" (p. 42). One of the respondents to the parent survey wrote, "As parents we owe it to our children and ourselves to learn all we can about any bias we hold, whether that is race, religion, cultural or homophobia, etc. Only by working on our own unfounded internal fears, views, and intolerances can we possibly offer unconditional acceptance to our children" (p. 75). Cantwell's heartfelt thoughts, unique style of writing, and message of hope make this book a welcome contribution to the literature meant to open the hearts and minds of parents and other adults. *Topics*: Parenting, Surveys.

Casper, Virginia and Steven Schultz. *Gay Parents, Straight Schools: Building Communication and Trust*. Teachers College Press, 1999. Hardcover $44.00 (ISBN 0807738255); Paper $20.95 (ISBN 0807738247).

Written for both educators and parents, this timely volume addresses the specific educational realities and needs of lesbian- and gay-headed families. It explores why lesbianism and gayness are perceived as threats, especially to the education of young children, when they actually have such potential to enrich the worldviews of both children and adults. Based on interviews with educators, lesbian parents, and gay parents, this book examines communication issues, homophobia at school and at home, gender roles, curriculum planning, and ways to connect children's family experiences with school experiences. One of the special features of this book is a section titled "Guidelines for Action," in which the authors offer practical suggestions to help educators and parents open channels of communication. For example, an idea for teachers suggests that they search for natural ways to welcome lesbian and gay parents into the life of their classrooms. Another idea involves a children's literature search in which books are evaluated in terms of age and maturity level. The authors ask, "How can you use some of the classic children's literature in a creative way to include more diverse family configurations?" (p. 174). Another section of the book offers a sample policy statement on families and the school that reads, in part, "We welcome all of our families: single-parent families, two-parent families of both the same and opposite sex, extended families, parents who live with their children, and those who do not" (p. 185). Another section touches on the New York City Rainbow Curriculum and other school board controversies, in which picture books like *Heather Has Two Mommies* by Lesléa Newman and *Daddy's Roommate* by Michael Willhoite played a role. *Gay Parents, Straight Schools* also features direct quotes from children, parents, teachers, and administrators, cartoons, a resource list of organizations, journals, magazines, and films, a bibliography, and an index. *Topic*: Education of Children of Gay Parents and Lesbian Parents.

Clark, Don. *Loving Someone Gay*. Celestial Arts, 1997. Paper $14.95 (ISBN 0890878374).

This third edition of a classic offers compassionate guidance to lesbians and gay men, their friends, their families, and the people who work with them and counsel them. Don Clark's sensitive approach and humorous wisdom have made this a popular guide for nearly three decades. Mixing anecdotes, advice, and philosophy, Clark answers the questions that family, friends, and colleagues are uncomfortable asking. In 1977, the first edition of *Loving Someone Gay* brought one of the first positive portrayals of lesbian and gay identity to a general audience. Now this completely rewritten edition speaks clearly and directly to individuals and to the global community, calling for practical, spiritual, and political awareness on personal, local, national, and international levels. The book is presented in four comprehensive parts: Being Gay, Gay and Growing, Loving Someone Gay, and Professional Help. The last section is written for librarians and educators, nurses and doctors, counselors and psychotherapists, clergy and police, and judges and lawmakers. Clark writes,

Teachers and librarians have thousands of opportunities to teach youngsters to appreciate their unique selves and to appreciate differences among people in general. . . . Casual remarks can reinforce the notion that being gay, like other natural human differences, is honorable and worthy of respect. There is no shortage of past heroes who were gay. . . . [They] are not presented as whole people if there is no mention of their gay identity. . . . Their gay identity must not be hidden or ignored. Such omissions are dishonest and defeat the understanding that feeds education. (pp. 351–352)

Throughout the book Clark touches on the important role books play in helping people understand themselves and others. "Reading is both stimulating and informative . . . books and articles coming out of the worldwide gay movement and the *alternative press* are sure to make you think and re-evaluate" (p. 87). In the last section, "Me and the Third Edition," Clark discusses his reasons for writing this book. He shares his own coming out story and traces his career as a licensed clinical psychologist who has worked in the gay and lesbian community for almost thirty years. Index included. *Topics*: Coming Out, Identity, Psychology.

DeCrescenzo, Teresa, editor. *Helping Gay and Lesbian Youth: New Policies, New Programs, New Practice*. Harrington Park Press, 1994. Hardcover $39.95 (ISBN 1560246782); Paper $14.95 (ISBN 1560230576).

This scholarly volume is written for social workers, educators, counselors, and policymakers. Eight well-researched and carefully documented essays discuss how homophobia interferes with adolescent development, offer specific counseling strategies, address medical concerns, clinical issues, and legal challenges, and analyze the influences shaping public policy. Topics include adoption, abuse, foster care, guardianship, health care, homelessness, identity, peer counseling, prostitution, role models, service organizations, substance abuse, suicide, violence, and much more. In "Service Organizations for Gay and Lesbian Youth," Greg Greeley profiles Boston Alliance of Gay and Lesbian Youth, Gay and Lesbian Adolescent Social Services (Los Angeles), Hetrick-Martin Institute (New York City), Los Angeles Gay and Lesbian Community Services Center, Project 10 (Los Angeles), and Sexual Minority Youth Assistance League (Washington, D.C.). The role literature plays in supporting youth is touched on in several essays; editor DeCrescenzo, who writes a book review column in *Lesbian News*, notes, "Books are being written by and for gay youth that can break through the isolation of the worried youngster with no one to talk to, no one with whom to identify" (p. xx). The Founding Executive Director of Gay and Lesbian Adolescent Social Services (GLASS) in California, DeCrescenzo adds, "what happens to the gay and lesbian people in this country happens to every person who cherishes citizenship in a democracy. . . . The challenge . . . must be met by . . . you, and me, and by everyone who cares about the well-being of young people, including those who happen to be gay or lesbian" (p. xxii). Index included. *Topics*: Counseling, Policy, Social Work.

Dew, Robb Forman. *The Family Heart: A Memoir of When Our Son Came Out*. Addison-Wesley, 1994. Hardcover $22.00 (ISBN 0201624508); Ballantine, 1995. Paper $11.00 (ISBN 0345394089).

When their nineteen-year-old son, Stephen, comes out to them, Robb and Charles Dew embark on a journey that takes them from a "paralysis of politeness" and "feigned heartiness" through guilt and grief to acceptance and activism. Along the way, Dew perceptively chronicles the nuances of her emotions, sharing her self-pity, mood swings, and excruciating mistakes. She writes compellingly about her struggle to re-orient herself in the wake of prejudices she didn't know she had. Even though she is an award-winning novelist who is familiar with fine con-temporary fiction by lesbian and gay writers, she "latched on to tabloid stereotypes." Her breakthrough finally comes one evening when she skims through her old Dr. Spock and Dr. Brazelton books on parenting and finds nothing on homosexuality. Enraged, she realizes that these specialists, along with pediatricians, teachers, and others, were cowards. "Their silence on the subject is tantamount to neglect and abuse" (p. 139). At last she understands "that parents' assumptions of the heterosexuality of their sons and daughters begins at birth and are a threat to their children's lives. . . . We unknowingly let our children grow up in a so-ciety that reflects back at them utter scorn for their legitimate emotions" (pp. 138–139). Sick of the closet, her sorrow and grief turn to outrage. She and her husband become official PFLAG representatives, write let-ters to columnists and congresspeople, and speak at local schools and churches. *The Family Heart* has been praised for its absorbing and in-spiring story, articulate outrage at entrenched homophobia, and extraor-dinarily honest examination of maternal, family, community, and societal attitudes toward homosexuality. Stephen emerges as a remarkably resil-ient, compassionate young man who patiently helps his parents under-stand who he is. This beautifully written memoir is a tremendous source of insight and strength to everyone who cares about real family values. *Topic*: Mother-Son Relationship.

Eng, David L. and Alice Y. Hom, editors. *Q & A: Queer in Asian America*. Temple University Press, 1998. Hardcover $69.95 (ISBN 1566396395); Paper $27.95 (ISBN 1566396409). *Award*: Lambda Literary Gay and Les-bian Anthologies/Non-Fiction Award.

Series: Asian American History and Culture. This spirited collection of twenty-six essays, thirteen black-and-white photographs, and seven cartoons approaches matters of identity from a variety of perspectives and academic disciplines in order to explore the multiple crossings of race and ethnicity with sexuality and gender. Drawing together the work of scholars, fiction writers, visual artists, community organizers, and par-ticipants in roundtable discussions, the volume gathers an array of voices and experiences that represent the emerging communities of queer Asian America. Collectively, the contributors contend that Asian-American studies needs to be more attentive to issues of sexuality and that queer studies needs to be more inclusive of other aspects of difference, espe-cially race and ethnicity. The book vigorously rejects the idea that a sym-metrical relationship between race and homosexuality would weaken lesbian/gay and queer movements. Jeff Yang, publisher and founder of

A. Magazine: Inside Asian America, wrote, "*Q & A* presents a compelling challenge to those who cling to the notion that race and sexual identities can be considered separate identities, rather than interwoven, interdependent aspects of one's singular social/political self." Other critics described the book as astute, spectacular, compelling, timely, thorough, brilliant, and exemplary. In the introduction the editors write, "We can no longer believe that a desirably queer world is one in which we remain perpetual aliens—queer houseguests—in a queer nation" (p. 14). This scholarly resource closes with a reference section consisting of an extensive bibliography and a resource guide of queer Asian-American organizations in the United States. *Topic*: Asian-American Studies.

Fairchild, Betty and Nancy Hayward. *Now That You Know: A Parents' Guide to Understanding Their Gay and Lesbian Children*. Harcourt Brace, 1998. Paper $13.00 (ISBN 0156006057). *Award*: ALA Gay Task Force Gay Book Award.

First published in 1979, this book offers support and information for parents who are trying to understand and accept their children's sexual identity. Written by two mothers of gay and lesbian children, the third edition of this book discusses the nature of homosexuality, counsels parents to respond supportively to their children, and suggests ways to maintain family bonds of acceptance and affirmation. Firsthand stories in the words that lesbian and gay people and their parents have written or spoken to each other or to the authors are woven into each chapter. Much of the text, including source notes, is from the 1970s, and the outdated term *lifestyle* has not been edited. Topics include coming out, job equality, religion, the history of PFLAG, and much more. A new postscript has been added to the chapter on AIDS and a new, annotated bibliography is divided into the following sections: "Coming Out," "About Homosexuality," "About AIDS," and "Grief and Dying." The authors encourage parents to listen to their children with love and empathy, sparing everyone unnecessary heartache and unproductive guilt. One of the many parents featured, Sarah Montgomery, responded to her son with these words, "Charlie, you've been through an awful lot without me beside you, and since you're out in the open now, I'll never be a closet mother" (p. 44). This last phrase, printed on a sign that Montgomery has carried in Lesbian Gay Pride Marches, has become a legend. Betty Fairchild is a founding member of the Washington, D.C. and Denver PFLAG chapters. Nancy Hayward was also an activist in the early years of PFLAG. *Topics*: Family Relationships, Parenting, PFLAG.

Fumia, Molly. *Honor Thy Children: One Family's Journey to Wholeness*. Conari, 1997. Hardcover $21.95 (ISBN 157432077X).

This is a heartbreaking, profound story of incalculable loss, regret, and transformation. Jane and Alexander Nakatani's three children died before age 30: one son was killed in a senseless shooting, and two died of AIDS. Written with compassion and insight, the book begins and ends with the youngest son's story. Guy Nakatani, a charismatic young gay man infected with the AIDS virus, spent the last years of his life as an AIDS educator, passionately speaking to over 40,000 people in schools, churches, and businesses. He asked Molly Fumia, the author of two previous books on bereavement, to tell the story of his family and himself. Guy tells her, "death doesn't seem so bad when you go through a whole lifetime of conflict. . . . Sometimes, leaving seemed like my only option. . . . If only I had been told, it's . . . okay to be gay, you'll still succeed. That's all I needed to hear" (pp. 220–221). Later he adds, "How can gay kids go through what they go through internally and not want to die? . . . When you're gay, you can live totally undercover, or you can live in opposition to society. Nice choices" (p. 269). Al Nakatani, who assisted his son during his lectures and continued the work after Guy died, says, "Ultimately, my family's story is not about AIDS or homosexuality, but about what happens to all of us when a child is denigrated, whether it be because of race, gender, sexual orientation, size, or shape. . . . Anything that wounds the self-esteem of a child is the enemy we should be fighting" (p. 313). The Nakatani family decided to share their ordeal publicly, hoping others will learn from their mistakes. They encourage parents to nurture their children in an environment of love, trust, and communication. "Their legacy is that ignorance can no longer be our excuse. If we lose a son or daughter to self-hatred, we are making a choice. We are sending them out into a world we have not made safe for them" (p. 312). This powerful book includes photographs of the Nakatani family. *Topics*: AIDS, Dying and Death, Japanese-American Families, Parenting.

Griffin, Carolyn Welch, Marian J. Wirth and Arthur G. Wirth. *Beyond Acceptance: Parents of Lesbians and Gays Talk About Their Experiences.* St. Martin's Press, 1996. Hardcover $21.95 (ISBN 0312145500); 1997. Paper $11.95 (ISBN 0312167814).

Beyond Acceptance offers support and guidance to parents who need help in accepting and understanding their lesbian and gay children. Based on the experiences of twenty-three white, middle-class parents who worked together over a period of years in a self-help organization called Parents, Families, and Friends of Lesbians and Gays (PFLAG), this readable book lets parents know that they are not alone and gently helps them through the emotional stages leading to reconciliation with their children. The authors encourage parents to go beyond acceptance and to join the struggle for safety and equity for lesbian and gay people. The first section of the book addresses the emotional, spiritual, biological, and social loss many parents experience when they first find out their child is lesbian or gay. Interviewees talk about the initial fear, hurt, denial, anger, alienation, shame, and isolation they experienced. The remainder of the book details the process parents go through to accept their children including unlearning myths, educating oneself, sharing feelings, changing inner perceptions, confronting ingrained prejudice, and coming out to others. One parent said, "Each step I took . . . left me stronger" (p. 116). Many parents reported that their journey toward acceptance taught them important lessons about life. "I found that prejudice, though hard to give up, was an enormous burden" (p. 174). "Accepting differences in others helps me to be kinder to myself, to accept my own differences" (p. 175). "I have come to understand that my son's being gay has been a major source of personal liberation for me. . . . [Gay and lesbian children] can help us expand our lives by widening the range of differences that we can embrace and enjoy" (p. 171). This highly acclaimed book also includes chapters titled "Religious Thinking in Transition" and "About AIDS," as well as a bibliography of recommended books and an index. *Topics*: Parenting, PFLAG.

Harbeck, Karen M. *Coming Out of the Classroom Closet: Gay and Lesbian Students, Teachers, and Curricula.* Harrington Park Press, 1992. Hardcover $49.95 (ISBN 1560242167); Paper $19.95 (ISBN 1560230134).

This collection of recent research on homosexuality and education was simultaneously issued under the same title as a series of special issues of the *Journal of Homosexuality*. Written for classroom teachers, administrators, librarians, curriculum specialists, counselors, social workers, nurses, physical education teachers, and university professors, this well-researched book is for everyone dedicated to ensuring that our educational institutions become safe and supportive environments for all people. Issues examined include the needs of lesbian and gay youth and related school-based intervention, counseling, and education; effects of empowerment training on the attitudes of lesbian and gay educators; lesbian and gay students' perceptions of the attitudes and abilities of their counselors and teachers; a critique of the current failings in graduate training programs for mental health professionals; images of lesbian and gay people in health and sexuality textbooks; empowerment theory and curricula modification suggestions; HIV/AIDS education; and a history of the treatment of lesbian and gay educators and their current legal rights. One of the twenty-five court cases examined, *Woo v. University of California at Berkeley,* has received widespread coverage in the community press. Karen M. Harbeck writes, "Given the high cost of employment discrimination litigation in time, money, and emotional and physical health, I would urge any person in a similar situation to follow the example set forth in the Woo controversy and elicit the collective support of gay men and lesbians both locally and nationally" (p. 134). Harbeck, who specializes in school law, educational history, and minority issues in education, summarizes the goals of this empowering book, "It is our hope that this volume of research on homosexuality and education will serve three major functions: address the lack of available research on the topic; encourage lesbians, gay, and bisexuals in education as they struggle within the system; and provide concerned individuals with some of the knowledge needed to empower themselves and to educate others. *Coming Out of the Classroom Closet* includes attitudinal survey results, interview excerpts, course outlines, charts, tables, extensive chapter notes and bibliographies, a table of court cases, and an index. *Topics*: Coming Out, Court Cases, Education, Research Results.

Harbeck, Karen M. *Gay and Lesbian Educators: Personal Freedoms, Public Constraints.* Amethyst Press and Productions, 1997. Hardcover $24.00 (ISBN 1889393487); Paper $17.95 (ISBN 1889393517).

In this meticulously researched history of lesbian and gay educators in the United States, Karen M. Harbeck combines legal and political analysis with her field research. She provides a thorough examination of statewide movements against lesbian and gay educators that were led by Anita Bryant in Florida, John Briggs in California, and other conservatives in Oklahoma. More than 150 court cases are referenced throughout the book, documenting the discrimination and intimidation that lesbian and gay educators have experienced. Drawing upon historical research, legal case studies, newspaper accounts, personal interviews, and articles in magazines and journals, Harbeck provides a comprehensive examination of the controversies involved. Excerpts from speeches, articles, and books, along with Harbeck's insights and clarity, add to the readability of this important book. A table of cases, extensive endnotes, a timeline of GLBT Educators' Rights, constitutional provisions and statutes, information on the status of sodomy laws in the United States, and an index are included. Harbeck, an educator and attorney, is Executive Director of the National Institute for GLBT Concerns in Education, Inc., a nonprofit organization committed to helping create safe school/college environments for gay, lesbian, bisexual, and transgender youth and adults. She writes, "Prejudice, hatred, ignorance, and violence hurt us all, especially if they occur in our major social institutions of family, school, and church" (p. 10). Her courage, commitment, intelligence, and hard work are evident in her books. *Topics*: Court Cases, Educational Law, Lesbian and Gay Educators.

Harris, Mary D. *School Experiences of Gay and Lesbian Youth: The Invisible Minority*. Haworth Press, 1997. Hardcover $29.95 (ISBN 0789003767); Paper $14.95 (ISBN 1560231092).

Series: Journal of Gay and Lesbian Social Services. Written for educators, board members, preservice teachers, policymakers, and other school personnel, this title offers seven scholarly papers that document hostile school climates, active silencing, and institutionalized homophobia and heterosexism. Combining qualitative and quantitative research, the papers explore the needs of lesbian and gay youth, explain how to meet those needs, and examine the consequences of failure to do so. Susan L. Morrow considers the effects of lesbian/gay identity development, the coming-out process, and homophobia on the career development process. Karen M. Jordan, Jill S. Vaughan, and Katharine J. Woodworth explore harassment, hostility, and hate crimes and elucidate the positive coping skills, traits, and experiences of lesbian, gay, and bisexual students. Kathleen P. Malinsky's study on invisibility is based on e-mail interviews with twenty-seven self-identified lesbian and bisexual female high school students. Kathryn Herr's case study demonstrates how interrupting harassment and correcting stereotypes and misinformation could have made a difference in the life of one young lesbian dropout. Amy M. Rey and Pamela Reed Gibson examine self-reported anti-gay/lesbian behaviors of heterosexual college students. Mary B. Harris and Gail K. Bliss studied lesbian and gay students' experiences and opinions about coming out in a school setting. Janet H. Fontaine's study shows that attitudes of students and educators toward homosexuals have changed little over the past ten years. She provides suggestions for developing gay/lesbian supportive school environments. Excellent bibliographies are included with each chapter. *Topics*: Career Development, Coping Skills, Dropouts, Education, Schools.

Jennings, Kevin, editor. *One Teacher in Ten: Gay and Lesbian Educators Tell Their Stories*. Alyson Publications, 1994. Paper $9.95 (ISBN 1555832636).

This powerful collection of personal stories written by lesbian and gay educators provides an overview of the unique obstacles they encounter in a profession that is rife with homophobia and heterosexism. Thirty-four courageous contributors from all regions of the United States and one from Australia share their memories and journeys, their struggles and victories, and their disillusionments and inspirations. Jennings writes about his disappointment that he was unable to bring greater cultural diversity to the collection. "Over and over, gay and lesbian teachers of color expressed their tremendous anxiety over contributing to the book. In the process, they educated me on how homophobia, racism, and sexism can intersect in an individual's life in truly powerful and destructive ways" (p. 13). Several contributors draw parallels between their experiences as students and as educators. In "Wanda and the Wastebasket" Arthur Lipkin writes, "My decision to become a teacher had its origin in that singular place where I could be a Jew and a sissy and not only survive but thrive" (p. 39). Many contributors reminisce about lesbian and gay students whose lives they have touched. Their sentiments are expressed in the words of Ron Ritchard in "Teaching with the Heart," in which he writes, "a simple act of caring can rescue a person and make all the difference. A difference of which we might never be aware" (p. 53). Some contributors write about being harassed by students and even by co-workers and how they persevered and triumphed. Most often the pressure to conform and be silent comes in the form of vague, euphemistic threats and policies that are so insidious that it is difficult to confront them. Several pieces stir memories of colleagues who whispered private encouragement while maintaining public distance. Fear of losing their jobs leads many teachers to collaborate in their own misnaming; self-censorship is a common survival technique. However, more and more teachers are finding the courage to come out. Jennings notes that publication of this collection marks the beginning of the destruction of one of the most well-fortified closets in our community. In "Out and Outcome," Jan Smith, an elementary teacher in Sands Montessori School in Cincinnati, Ohio, writes about her experiences after she came out in an article in the local newspaper and to her class of six- to nine-year-olds the next day. The response from colleagues and most parents was positive. She includes copies of several of the notes and letters she received and summarizes others. She concludes, "If I had the whole ordeal to do over again, I think I would write a note to the parents on the Friday before the article came out, suggesting that they read and discuss the article with their children" (p. 217). Gretchen Hildenbrand Coburn, an elementary teacher in a small town in New Hampshire, like many others survived the initial shock and ostracism after she came out. She writes, "I must live honestly, albeit dangerously, rather than in a cocoon or a web of deceptions" (p. 227). This important book ends with "A Legal Overview of the Rights of Gay, Lesbian, and Bisexual Teachers" and a list of gay and lesbian teacher organizations. *Topic*: Lesbian and Gay Teachers.

Kissen, Rita M. *The Last Closet: The Real Lives of Lesbian and Gay Teachers.* Heinemann, 1996. Hardcover $23.95 (ISBN 0435070053); Paper $15.95 (ISBN 0435081470). *Award: Choice* Magazine Outstanding Academic Book.

Lesbian and gay teachers, librarians, counselors, and administrators are widely harassed, silenced, erased, pressured to resign, or fired outright solely because of their sexual identity. Rita M. Kissen interviewed more than 100 gay and lesbian educators in public and private schools in nineteen states from Massachusetts to Oregon, encompassing preschool through senior high. Caught between their commitment to authenticity and their need for safety, her respondents describe their daily struggles for dignity. Kissen, who is heterosexual, a founding member and past president of the Portland, Maine chapter of PFLAG, and an associate professor in the College of Education at the University of Southern Maine, was inspired to write this book after her lesbian daughter became a high school English teacher. Kissen found that "vast numbers of dedicated teachers do not feel safe in school, for reasons that have nothing to do with their merit as educators" (p. 4). Often forced to hide their significant relationships, monitor their appearance, and censor their behavior and language, lesbian and gay educators' lives are complicated by stresses of which most of their heterosexual colleagues are completely unaware. Kissen found the interviewees to be conscientious professionals who often overcompensated because of their fear that being average is not good enough. One teacher noted, "you have to be the absolute best, perfect model of a teacher all the time. You just end up driven" (p. 41). Always planning for the worst, another added, "I had to be twice as good" (p. 73). Anti-gay referendum questions on ballots in Colorado, Oregon, Idaho, and Maine subjected lesbian and gay educators to enormous pain, anxiety, and fear. A teacher from Colorado Springs said, "I felt like I was in an aquarium, out in the middle of the street, and everybody was pointing, 'there's one, there's one'" (p. 112). Kissen suggests survival strategies for lesbian and gay educators and offers ideas for ways their allies can support them. In the foreword, Kevin Jenning, Executive Director of the Gay, Lesbian, and Straight Education Network, writes, "In Rita's moving and superbly documented book, we learn what really goes on with lesbian, gay, and bisexual teachers. In the place of the predatory monsters created by [Lou] Sheldon (head of Traditional Values Coalition), Kissen paints a picture of dedicated professionals, often torn between their desire to serve their students and their need to be themselves. [They] often pay an immense personal price because they so desperately want to make life better for the next generation" (p. x). *Topics*: Gay Educators, Lesbian Educators.

Mitchell, Leif, editor. *Tackling Gay Issues in School: A Resource Module*. GLSEN of Connecticut and Planned Parenthood of CT, 1998. Hardcover $20.00. No ISBN: Available through GLSEN at (212) 627–7707.

This comprehensive resource is a compilation of practical information, staff development activities, useful strategies, and thoughtful lesson plans. Gathered together in a sturdy binder are hard-to-find materials such as mission statements, needs assessments, ground rules, a lesbian and gay history timeline, bibliographies, action points, guided journeys, checklists, questionnaires, lists, handouts, policy statements, suggestions on how to start a gay/straight alliance, a glossary, and much more. Teacher-friendly curricula include fascinating suggestions for icebreakers, debunking myths, understanding oppression, and making connections between homophobia and other forms of oppression. Thirteen excellent recommendations and strategies from Safe Schools Coalition of Washington provide rationales and ideas for retaining a diverse staff, building an inclusive library collection, creating a bias-free curriculum, and intervening in harassment. A legal perspective on stopping the abuse of lesbian and gay students is provided by the Lambda Legal Defense and Education Fund. Other interesting sections of the book offer practical ideas for building support networks and for responding to resistance from teachers, administrators, students, and community members. *Tackling Gay Issues in School* has received endorsements from numerous educational organizations including the Connecticut State Department of Education. *Topics*: Curriculum, Gay/Straight Alliances, Staff Development.

Nilsen, Alleen Pace. *Presenting M. E. Kerr*, updated edition. Twayne, 1997. Hardcover $24.95 (ISBN 0805792481).

Series: Twayne's United States Authors Series: Young Adult Authors. "M. E. Kerr breezes into teenagers' lives like an Auntie Mame—more experienced and worldly than their friends and less uptight and protective than their parents. Her literary style flatters young readers because she makes them feel as though they are respected party guests worthy of her wittiest and most charming efforts" (p. 108). This updated version of the 1986 edition inspects the substantial body of work produced by Kerr, covers her personal and professional life, touches on her recent foray into books for intermediate readers, and celebrates her literary style, her humor, her defense of the underdog, and her intriguing names. The four highly acclaimed books cited by the Margaret A. Edwards Award selection committee are examined in one chapter along with *Deliver Us from Evie*, which Nilsen feels would have been included if the award had been given a few years later. The last chapter is devoted to tracing the ways in which Kerr encourages young readers to think about anti-Semitism, socioeconomic issues, and lesbian and gay themes. "One of the chief values of both *Night Kites* and *Deliver Us from Evie* is the way they discuss stereotypes and illustrate that homosexuals are individuals; some fit cultural expectations and some do not" (p. 148). Nilsen acknowledges the contribution Kerr has made in providing information "about what it means to be different from the majority, whether through sexual orientation, ethnic identification, socioeconomic status, physical condition, or intellectual ability" (p. 158). Written with enthusiasm, this well-researched book includes a preface, chronology, notes and references, selected bibliography, appendix of honors and prizes won by M. E. Kerr, and an index. For more information about M. E. Kerr, see Chapter 7 of this book. *Topics*: Authorship, Biography, Writers.

Owens, Robert E., Jr. *Queer Kids: The Challenges and Promise for Lesbian, Gay, and Bisexual Youth.* Haworth Press, 1998. Hardcover $49.95 (ISBN 0789004399); Paper $24.95 (ISBN 1560239298).

This useful book examines the multiple challenges confronting queer kids and offers suggestions that adults might use to help them cope with self-definition, coming out, relationships, sexuality, and homophobia. Written primarily for parents, counselors, educators, youth workers, and queer adults, the book blends an amazing amount of research with the candid voices of young lesbian, gay, and bisexual people. Practical suggestions for combatting stereotypes and addressing societal misconceptions are provided, along with definitions, statistics, tables, and chapter summaries. Over forty-five pages are devoted to print, video, and on-line resources as well as extensive lists of organizations, hotlines, and youth groups. The voices of young people cry out from the pages. "I was spit on, pushed, and ridiculed. My school life was hell" (p. 73). "I've spent more than one lonely night sobbing . . . and I've planned out my suicide more than once" (p. 131). Owen, who is gay, writes, "I find it almost impossible to remain objective about human rights. . . . I am unable to fully comprehend the thinking of those who are hostile toward diversity" (p. xiii). His concern for the well-being of young lesbian, gay, and bisexual people is apparent throughout his well-researched book. In the last chapter, "Letter to a Queer Kid," Owens encourages them to be truthful to themselves, to trust their feelings, to surround themselves with supportive people, and to celebrate themselves. He writes, "Just remember, *there's nothing wrong with you.* There *is* something wrong with a society that makes people feel guilty for loving each other" (p. 219). This comprehensive book ends with extensive chapter notes and a helpful index. *Topics*: Coming Out, Counseling, Educating, Parenting.

Peabody, Barbara. *The Screaming Room: A Mother's Journal of Her Son's Struggle with AIDS—A True Story of Love, Dedication and Courage.* Oak Tree Publications, 1986. Hardcover $ 15.95 (ISBN 0866790306); Avon, 1987. Paper $4.99 (ISBN 0380703459).

This excruciatingly painful account of a gay man's courageous struggle against AIDS is told by his mother, who took care of him during the last year of his life. Peter Vom Lehn (1955–1984) moved to San Diego from New York to live with his mother after becoming seriously ill. Barbara Peabody writes poignantly about Peter's independence and dignity, his hope and denial, and his determination to concentrate on living, on surviving. She includes many details about countless appointments with doctors, numerous hospitalizations, endless procedures, tests, and medications, and heartbreakingly, the deterioration of her son's condition. "His indomitable will to survive continues to amaze me. . . . here he is, barely surviving—but indeed surviving. It's as if he's made survival the purpose of his life, to prove to himself and others that this strange and vicious disease can indeed be battled, and that Peter Vom Lehm is going to win. It is his greatest challenge and he has met it head-on and un-flinchingly" (p. 193). Peabody also chronicles her own anguished ordeal, from innocence and hope to knowledge, fear, and despair. "Our life is fast becoming a nightmare. Thoughts and fears jostle, fall over each other, and I want to scream. . . . If only I could go somewhere and scream myself inside-out" (p. 66). Exhausted physically and emotionally, she still found the time and energy to give art classes for AIDS patients. After her son's death she continued offering this intensive artwork, which was exhibited in a gallery her students named after Peter. She also helped found Mothers for AIDS Patients (MAP), an organization which offers support and "substitute mothers" for patients rejected by their families. Although *The Screaming Room* was written in the 1980s, it is still impor-tant reading. It is the inspiring story of a strong woman who accepted her gay son wholeheartedly and supported him in life and while he was dying with love, dedication, and courage. *Topics*: AIDS, Dying and Death, Mother-Son Relationship.

Rafkin, Louise, editor. *Different Daughters: A Book by Mothers of Lesbi-ans.* Cleis Press, 1996. Hardcover $24.95 (ISBN 1573440515); Paper $12.95 (ISBN 1573440507).

Twenty-nine mothers of lesbians trace their journeys toward accep-tance of their daughters in the second edition of this valuable book. Con-fronting their prejudice and misunderstandings, fear, and confusion, these women write honestly and bravely about the difficulties and joys of their relationships with their "different daughters." Writing about expectations, hopes, fears, dreams, and concerns, they raise questions shared by many mothers: What will the neighbors and relatives think? How can my daughter find happiness in a homophobic world? Many of these women write about the important role books played in helping them understand their daughters. "I read furiously everything I could find" (p. 35); "I realized I had to get myself informed about homosexuality" (p. 134). One mother reports that the books at her library were all locked inside a cabinet. Another found that writing helped her sort out her feelings and thoughts. Some mothers were not at all surprised when their daughters came out. One even initiated a family gathering to celebrate her daughter's coming out. Editor Louise Rafkin's mother writes about the period of soul-searching and growth in accepting her daughter's sexual identity. In an update written ten years later she writes, "Our contact with gay men and lesbians has been very positive, and our lives have been enriched by the people we have met" (p. 54). Another mother writes that she feels that she is a better person for having been exposed to a whole different world. "I have been forced to grow as a person" (p. 110). One mother testified in favor of a civil rights bill being considered before the Illinois legislature. Several women write about having more than one lesbian daughter, and one even watched her own widowed mother fall head over heels in love with a woman. Another declared herself to be a lesbian years after her daughter came out. Not all of the stories are as positive as these, however. Some mothers are still struggling with the grandchildren issue, and a few continue to be uncomfortable with lesbians who are openly affectionate with each other. But they all reiterate their love for their daughters, their determination to examine their own prejudices, and their commitment to preserving the mother-daughter bond. These journeys from misconception to acceptance are heartwarming and hopeful. Some use misleading terms such as "lifestyle" and "choice," but they otherwise write with awareness and sensitivity. *Topic*: Mother-Daughter Relationships.

Remafedi, Gary, editor. *Death by Denial: Studies of Suicide in Gay and Lesbian Teenagers.* Alyson Publications, 1994. Paper $9.95 (ISBN 1555832601).

A federal study in 1989 found that teenagers struggling with issues of sexual identity were three times more likely than their peers to commit suicide. This alarming and hotly contested report was swept aside by the Bush administration. *Death by Denial* includes the full findings of the *Report of the Secretary's Task Force on Youth Suicide* and of several other studies, documenting the difficulties confronting teenagers who are coming out, and proposing ways to ease that process. Editor Remafedi writes, "In preparing this book . . . it has been my intention to stimulate critical thinking about youth suicide and sexual orientation by gathering the existing sources of information for your deliberation" (p. 13). The book is a complete collection of all the peer-reviewed and previously published journal articles that specifically treat the subject up until 1993. Contributors ask urgent questions and encourage further research. They make it clear that the lack of information and the suppression of the data available are reflections of the homophobia of our society. Researchers analyze the risk factors in lesbian and gay youth suicide and offer suggestions for counseling. Recommendations from the Massachusetts Governor's Commission on Gay and Lesbian Youth include: school policies protecting gay and lesbian students from harassment, violence, and discrimination; training teachers/counselors/school staff in crisis intervention and violence prevention; school-based support groups for gay and straight students; information in school libraries for gay and lesbian adolescents; and curriculum which includes lesbian and gay issues. Remafedi concludes, "In my own mind, there is no doubt that the existing evidence points to an inordinate risk of suicide facing homosexual and bisexual youth. . . . To ignore the problem now is a missed opportunity to save thousands of young lives, tantamount to sanctioning death by denial" (p. 13). *Topic*: Suicide Prevention.

Rottnek, Matthew, editor. *Sissies and Tomboys: Gender Nonconformity and Homosexual Childhood.* Hardcover $55.00 (ISBN 0814774830); Paper $18.95 (ISBN 0814774849).

After homosexuality was officially depathologized with a revision in the *Diagnostic and Statistical Manual* of psychiatry in 1973, a new diagnosis appeared: Gender Identity Disorder of Childhood (GID). *Sissies and Tomboys*, which is comprised of eight scholarly essays and seven personal narratives, grew out of a February 1995 conference sponsored by the Center for Lesbian and Gay Studies of the City University of New York. Rottnek writes, "We need to open a conceptual space in which to look at the experience of homosexual childhood in a way that respects and values gender diversity and homosexual development and in a way that values homosexuals as human beings" (p. 2). The first part of the book considers ethical issues in the diagnosis and treatment of GID. Part II, "Theorizing Gender Nonconformity," includes scholarly examinations of homosexual boyhoods and tomboy girlhoods. Part III, "Sissies and Tomboys Speak," is the most accessible section of the book. These personal narratives are the strongest testimonies to the need for an end to the tyranny of gender conformity. In "Butch in a Tutu," Sara Cytron writes about her harrowing journey from tomboy childhood to butch lesbian adulthood. "I . . . feel that the hysteria my parents brought to my developing femaleness made me respond with a kind of defensive hysteria about my butchness. There was a panic and rigidity on both sides. Certainly we all lacked a sense of play and freedom; gender and sexuality were deadly serious matters" (p. 224). In "Such a Polite Little Boy," Arnie Kantrowitz recalls hormone shots, boxing lessons, summer camps, and suicide attempts. His mother encouraged his friends to attack him so that he would learn to fight back. After years of feeling ashamed of what made him different, he now writes, "It no longer matters to me what society thinks. . . . I don't feel like a manly man or a womanly man or a woman trapped in a man's body. I feel like a person in a human being's body" (p. 235). These and other essays challenge the stigma of illness and expose the ways in which it influences a child's development. The contributors make it clear that the real disorder is in a society that tortures young people by trying to force them all to fit a heterosexual mold. Indeed, the courageous resistance and robust defiance of young tomboys and sissies are cause for celebration! This important book includes a bibliography and an index. *Topics*: Appearance, Identity, Psychology.

Sears, James T. and Walter L. Williams. *Overcoming Heterosexism and Homophobia: Strategies That Work*. Columbia University Press, 1997. Paper $18.50 (ISBN 0231104235). *Award*: GLSEN Contribution Toward Excellence in Education Award.

Series: Between Men—Between Women: Lesbian and Gay Studies. How can heterosexism and homophobia be unlearned? What can be done to foster a climate that promotes the acceptance of differences? More than thirty original essays written by scholars, activists, and practitioners provide strategies for overcoming heterosexism and homophobia in a wide variety of cultural and occupational settings, including schools, churches, the police force, the mass media, and the corporate world. Grounded in research and theory, contributors offer ideas for educators, counselors, social workers, clergy, community activists, and those working in the lesbian and gay community. Role-playing exercises, suggestions for beginning a dialogue, methods of coming out effectively to family members and coworkers, and outlines for workshops are provided. The editors decided not to include political and legal strategies in this volume because they felt "that so much attention has been focused on political issues that other significant areas of social change are being relatively ignored" (p. 3). Among the many approaches is one suggested by Glenda M. Russell in "Using Music to Reduce Homophobia and Heterosexism" in which she writes, "Not only does [music] convey information, it also allows participants to access and explore their emotional reactions to issues around sexual orientation and homophobia. Music often operates as a tool to facilitate understanding at a level beyond the purely cognitive" (p. 164). Another section of the book includes essays that address issues concerning Asian-American, Latino/a Immigrant, African-American, and Jewish communities. Strategies suggested in "Reducing Homophobia in African American Communities" by Sylvia Rhue and Thom Rhue include: Come Out, Be Confrontive, Learn How to Deal with the Media, Build and Maintain Institutions That Nourish Us, Build Alliances, Speak the Truth, and Celebrate Heroes. This collection augments the increasing body of literature on proactive strategies to confront discrimination and prejudice. Extensive notes, bibliographies, and an index are included. *Topics*: Behavior Modification, Education.

Tasker, Fiona L. and Susan Golombok. *Growing Up in a Lesbian Family: Effects on Child Development*. Guilford, 1998. Paper $17.95 (ISBN 157230412X). Ages 17 up. *Award*: Benjamin Franklin Award for Editorial and Design Excellence.

Legal battles over custody of children and same-sex marriage have drawn increasing public attention to the question of whether lesbians can raise happy, healthy children. This pioneering book provides an objective and long-overdue analysis of the experiences of the children themselves. Presenting a controlled longitudinal study of the social and psychological effects on twenty-five children raised in lesbian mother families, this book challenges assumptions and confronts a range of myths and stereotypes. The researchers report that young people from lesbian mother families were no more likely to be anxious or depressed or to have sought professional help for mental heath problems. The commonly held assumption that children raised by lesbians will grow up to have a lesbian or gay sexual identity is not supported by the findings of this study. These and other results are reported in language accessible enough for beginning college students and comprehensive enough for adults. Fiona L. Tasker is a Lecturer in Psychology at the University of London and Susan Golombok is a Professor of Psychology at City University in London. *Topics*: Lesbian Mothers, Research.

Unks, Gerald, editor. *The Gay Teen: Educational Practice and Theory for Lesbian, Gay, and Bisexual Adolescents*. Routledge, 1995. Paper $18.99 (ISBN 0415910951).

Written by and for lesbian, gay, and heterosexual educators, *The Gay Teen* explores lesbian/gay adolescence from both practical and theoretical perspectives. Opening essays focus on the problems confronting lesbian/gay teens in today's high schools—alienation from peer groups, low academic achievement, substance abuse, violence, and the absence of lesbian/gay role models. Other essays focus on the subject matter and teaching methodology central to the successful education of lesbian, gay, and bisexual high school students—how to develop lesbian/gay-friendly curricula in literature, social studies, sports, and sex education, teaching strategies, intervention techniques for reducing homophobia, and recommendations for sensitizing staff to lesbian/gay students' needs. The closing essays showcase safe spaces that educators have created for lesbian/gay students and their heterosexual allies: Project 10, Gay/Straight Alliances, and OutRight, an out-of-school gay/lesbian youth group. In "Gay Teens in Literature," Jim Brogan discusses nonexplicit and submerged themes in early fiction and touches briefly on contemporary lesbian/gay themed young adult fiction. James T. Sears, in "Black-Gay or Gay-Black? Choosing Identities and Identifying Choices," writes, "If we wish to convey to young people the presence and value of diversity, then our discussion of homosexuality must be multicultural and critical" (p. 150). He also touches briefly on contemporary novels that include lesbians and gays of color as central characters, including *Ruby* by Rosa Guy and *Coffee Will Make You Black* by April Sinclair. Most essays are followed by a list of helpful references. The book ends with a list of selected resources including organizations, curricular units, a bibliography, contributor profiles, and an index. *Topics*: Curriculum, Gay/Straight Alliances, Project 10, Resources for Educators.

Walling, Donovan R., editor. *Open Lives, Safe Schools: Addressing Gay and Lesbian Issues in Education.* Phi Delta Kappa Educational Foundation, 1996. Paper $30.00 (ISBN 0873674855).

Written for educators and others concerned with schooling from kindergarten through graduate school, this diverse collection of essays addresses a number of important lesbian and gay issues in education, from the coming-out processes of students and staff to gay/lesbian-positive curricula to parenting and family concerns. The central premise of the book is that everyone benefits when students, educators, parents, and others in the educational community are allowed to live openly in terms of sexual identity. By probing these issues, honest dialogue can be generated and constructive solutions can be found to problems and concerns that arise. The book opens with an excellent essay by Jan Goodman in which she challenges false assumptions about homosexuality that serve as excuses for denying human rights to one-tenth of our school population. She writes, "The price of our ignorance can be fatal" (p. 11). Curricular issues are addressed in several essays including "The Case for a Gay and Lesbian Curriculum" by Arthur Lipkin. Two essays are of particular interest to educators searching for information about the use of lesbian/gay positive literature: "Self-Censorship of Picture Books About Gay and Lesbian Families" by John Warren Stewig and "Bringing Gay and Lesbian Literature Out of the Closet" by Vicky Greenbaum. The section that focuses on youth, parents, and families opens with the landmark coming-out story from Lynn Johnston's popular newspaper comic strip, "For Better or for Worse," printed in its entirety. Three pieces examine lesbian and gay studies programs in higher education in the United Kingdom, Australia, and Montana. Other essays describe effective resource programs: Project 10, IYG Youth Hotline, and GLSTN (now GLSEN). This accessible book ends with an essay by Frances Snowder in which she examines lesbian/gay teen suicide and ways to prevent it. A list of resources available for educators, students, and parents is appended. *Topics*: Curriculum, Lesbian and Gay Studies, Suicide Prevention, Youth Groups.

Woog, Dan. *School's Out: The Impact of Gay and Lesbian Issues on America's Schools*. Alyson Publications, 1995. Paper $12.95 (ISBN 1555832490).

In chronicling the stories for *School's Out*, journalist Dan Woog conducted nearly 300 interviews of lesbian, gay, and heterosexual teachers, administrators, guidance counselors, coaches, nurses, school board members, curriculum specialists, students, and parents across the United States. He discovered a wide variety of experiences: openly gay and lesbian teachers and coaches who are valued mentors to young people; a teenager who was harassed in one school but accepted in another; another teen who became more popular after coming out because his schoolmates admired his courage; a small-town Nebraska man who, dying of AIDS, found the courage to talk to students about his life; a lesbian parent who helped organize a citywide lesbian and gay parent organization; a director of support services who develops lesson plans and resources; and a student who announced that she was a lesbian at a schoolwide assembly. Woog interviewed the people involved in a number of organizations and groups such as Project 10, Lesbian Teachers Network, Gay/Straight Alliance, Project 21, Harvey Milk School, and Outreach to Rural Youth Project. He provides a detailed account of the attempts to censor books such as *Annie on My Mind* by Nancy Garden. Woog states, "Courageous men and women, heroic boys and girls have helped place lesbian and gay issues in the forefront of school consciousness. Some have done so at great personal risk. . . . Some of their stories are inspiring, some are heartbreaking. Each is unique" (p. 135). "In the end," Woog adds, "I came away exhilarated by the joy that so much is changing for the better" (p. 16). This upbeat, readable book includes black-and-white photographs of some of the interviewees and a guide to books, curriculum materials, films, organizations, and training programs. *Topics*: Challenged Books, Gay Educators, Lesbian Educators.

7

Author Profiles

Marion Dane Bauer (1938)

Stories help us make sense of our world. They teach us what is possible. They let us know that others before us have struggled as we do.
What's Your Story? p. ix

I was a "different" child, even an odd one. I am not exactly a typical adult, either, but differentness is usually dealt with somewhat more gently among adults than among schoolmates. . . . In the adult world, that inclination to stand apart, to make my own choices, even to be different, works well for me most of the time.
A Writer's Story, pp. 129–130

I write for children because there is a child in me who refuses to be subjugated into all the proper forms of adulthood. I write for children because such writing allows me to deal with all my old feeling issues in a context that approximates the original experience.
Contemporary Authors: New Revision Series, Volume 11, p. 47

LESBIAN/GAY-THEMED WORKS BY MARION DANE BAUER

Am I Blue? Coming Out from the Silence (editor). HarperCollins, 1994. (See Chapter 3)

"Dancing Backwards." In *Am I Blue? Coming Out from the Silence* (editor). HarperCollins, 1994. (See Chapter 3)

Marion Dane Bauer, the author of more than twenty books for young people, was born on November 20, 1938 in Oglesby, Illinois, a small town in the Illinois River Valley. Her mother, Elsie Hempstead Dane, was a teacher and her father, Chester Bauer, was a chemical engineer. During her early years, a lively imagination helped Bauer deal with her parents' emotional restraint and her loneliness at school. "I was the youngest in my class, having started kindergarten at four, and my isolated childhood had left me entirely without social skills . . ." (*Something About the Author Autobiography Series [SATAAS]*, Volume 9, p. 3). Bauer describes the years she attended seventh and eighth grades as the worst two years of her life. "I belonged nowhere" (*A Writer's Story*, p. 90).

Bauer's head was constantly spinning with stories, and she knew from an early age that she would be a writer. "I constantly made [stories] up in my head, for my dolls, for my friends. I acted them out using my cigar box filled with marbles as characters" (*What's Your Story?* p. 14). Although the emphasis at school was on penmanship, not creativity, Bauer was inspired by her Aunt Dyllone, who not only encouraged her to write but took her own writing very seriously. "That example, the example of someone who loved writing and found doing it both good and important, probably influenced me more deeply than any other" (*Authors and Artists*, p. 16).

In high school, she found her way to the yearbook staff, where she blossomed and made friends. She also wrote the script for and directed the school talent show each year. After graduating from the local junior college she attended the University of Missouri, where she studied journalism. A year later she switched to English and moved to Oklahoma, where she completed her B.A. at the University of Norman. Through college, marriage, and raising children, Bauer always wrote, keeping her dream of being a full-time writer alive.

When Bauer was in her early thirties, she realized that it was time to make writing a priority. Many aspiring writers dream about the lucky break that will gain them recognition. For Bauer, that moment came when she attended a writers' conference in St. Paul, Minnesota, where Maia Wojciechowska praised her manuscript *Foster Child*. "I sat in the audience, fragile, tentative hope blooming into confidence for the first time, and knew there would never be another moment in my life to match that one . . . at least not one connected to my writing" (*SATAAS*, p. 9). That experience gave her wings. Since then Bauer has written numerous award-winning books, including *On My Honor*, a 1987 Newbery Honor Book, which came out at a time when she was going through a transition in her personal life, including a divorce after twenty-eight years of marriage.

While Bauer is best known for her young adult novels, she has recently branched out into other genres, including several picture books and two nonfiction books about the literary life. In 1994 Bauer edited *Am I Blue?*, a collection of short stories for young people about growing up lesbian or gay, or with lesbian or gay friends or parents. Dedicated "to all young people in their search for themselves," with a portion of the proceeds from its sales earmarked for PFLAG, the collection has been widely praised. Bauer conceived of the idea and gathered the authors for the anthology out of a conviction that those who write for young people have a responsibility to speak out on subjects, such as homosexuality, that society attempts to shroud in silence.

Bauer ends *Am I Blue?* with her own story, "Dancing Backwards," about two young women in a private school who "do not discover what they unconsciously already know about their closeness until they experience the accusatory and harsh reactions of the nuns in charge" (*Authors and Artists*, p. 20). Bauer writes, "I was a counselor for an Episcopal Church girls' camp . . . and the young woman I loved—two of the best counselors the sisters had—were not invited back after that summer. We were as innocent in our love as two young women could be, and we were never even able to bring ourselves to speak of the reason our services would no longer be required, though we both understood. We never discovered the full sweetness possible between us, either" (*Am I Blue?* p. 273).

The book jacket of *Am I Blue?* tells us that Bauer lives in Minneapolis with her partner. In addition to writing, Bauer's interests include camping, hiking, cats, and theater. Her passion for live theater led her to write a one-woman show called *God's Tears: A Woman's Journey*, a feminist piece which has been performed by Melliss Kenworthy, a professional actor. Bauer is active in the children's literature community and teaches fiction writing to adults at Vermont College in Montpelier, Vermont.

"I am each day enormously grateful that I can take the substance of my life, even the essence of my pain, and out of it offer a gift by which other people can find themselves, understand their own pain, discover their own possibilities for joy" (*SATAAS*, p. 15).

MORE INFORMATION ABOUT MARION DANE BAUER

Authors and Artists for Young Adults, Volume 19, pp. 13–21.
Contemporary Authors, Volumes 69–72, p. 54.
Contemporary Authors: New Revision Series, Volume 11, p. 47.
Contemporary Authors: New Revision Series, Volume 26, p. 40.
Something About the Author Autobiography Series, Volume 9, pp. 1–16.
What's Your Story? A Young Person's Guide to Writing Fiction. Clarion Books, 1992.
A Writer's Story: From Life to Fiction. Clarion Books, 1995.

Beth Brant (1941)

Photo by Tee A. Corinne

I write because to not write is a breach of faith.

Mohawk Trail, p. 93

I want to bring lasting beauty to this world we inhabit. . . . I want to tell that I don't write as an "individual," but as a member of many communities—Indian, working class, gay and lesbian, feminist, recovering, human, mammal, living entity among other living entities. I write for my People and because of my People.

Reinventing the Enemy's Language, p. 353

Being a Native lesbian is like living in the eye of the hurricane— terrible, beautiful, filled with sounds and silences, the music of life-affirmation and the disharmony of life-despising. To balance, to create in this midst is a gift of honor and respect.

Completely Queer, p. 99

WORKS BY BETH BRANT

Food and Spirits. Firebrand Books, 1991. (See Chapter 3)
A Gathering of Spirit: North American Indian Women's Issue (editor). Sinister Wisdom 22/23, 1983; reissued as *A Gathering of Spirit: A Collection by North American Indian Women.* Firebrand Books, 1988.
Mohawk Trail. Firebrand Books, 1985. (See Chapter 3)

Beth Brant, a writer, editor, archivist, and activist, is a Bay of Quinte Mohawk from Theyindenaga reserve in Deseronto, Ontario. She was born on May 6, 1941 in Grandma and Grandpa Brant's house in Detroit, Michigan. According to her mother, it was a very hot day but Grandpa shoveled coal into the furnace and then lit the fire, "just in case." Her grandparents had moved to Detroit from Canada, hoping for better opportunities for their children. In Detroit all of the children married white people, and Brant writes about being teased for being a "half-breed."

After dropping out of high school, Brant married at seventeen, and had three daughters—Kim, Jenny, and Jill. She worked at various jobs after her divorce: salesclerk, waitress, sweeper, cleaning woman, and Title IV coordinator.

Brant did not begin her career as a writer until she was forty years old. She tells about an encounter with Eagle as she and her lover were driving through the Mohawk Valley. "He swooped in front of our car. . . . I got out and faced him as he sat in a tree, his wings folded so gracefully, his magnificent head gleaming in the October afternoon sun. We looked into each other's eyes. Perhaps we were ten feet away from one another and I was marked by him. I remember that I felt in another place, maybe another time. He stared at me for minutes, maybe hours, maybe a thousand years. I knew I had received a message to write" ("To Be or Not to Be Was Never the Question," p. 17). Brant has been writing since that day.

With the gift of writing brought by Eagle, Brant sent her first stories, "Mohawk Trail" and "Native Origin," to *Sinister Wisdom*, a lesbian feminist journal. Encouraged by Adrienne Rich and Michelle Cliff, who were editors of the journal at that time, Brant edited *A Gathering of Spirit: A North American Indian Women's Issue*, which was published as a special issue of *Sinister Wisdom*. In the introduction Brant writes about the feelings she experienced when Rich and Cliff first invited her to edit the issue.

There is panic in my gut. I am not an "established" writer. (To this day, I am not sure what those words mean.) I have never edited any work but my own. And I do not have the education. . . . As I lay in bed that night, I wrestle with this very complicated question. And I struggle with the complicated realities of my life. I am uneducated, a half-breed, a *light-skinned* half-breed, a lesbian, a feminist, an economically poor woman. (*A Gathering of Spirit*, p. 5)

With these awarenesses, Brant took on the project. It was the first anthology of Native writing edited by a Native woman. This highly acclaimed collection includes works by a number of women who have written on lesbian themes, including Paula Gunn Allen, Chrystos, Janice Gould, Mary Moran, Vickie Sears, and Midnight Sun.

In her powerful short story collections, *Mohawk Trail* and *Food and Spirits*, Brant writes about survival and endurance. The cover of *Mohawk Trail* is based on a quilt design, "Mohawk Trail," created by Beth Brant's grandmother, Margaret Brant, almost fifty years before the book was published. One of the stories, "A Simple Act," is about two girls who were best friends from third to seventh grades. "Spending nights at each other's houses, our girl bodies hugging tight" (p. 88). Then one day a neighbor looked through the bedroom window and saw them together. Their parents forbade them to see each other again. Their rebellions failed and gradually "something hard, yet invisible, had formed over our memories. We went the way of boys, back seats of cars, self-destruction" (p. 89). Twenty-five years later, the narrator writes about her memories. "Sandra, I am remembering our loss" (p. 90). She tells Sandra that she now has a woman lover and that she is a writer. This is a poignant story about two young women torn apart and shamed into denying their love for each other. Brant's stories are intensely personal and reflect her strong sense of tribal identity. Her acknowledgments include Denise, her "lover and mate," and "My mom and dad I want to thank for giving me just the right blend of Indian spirit and Irish/Scots practicality."

The Michigan Council for the Arts recognized Brant's work with grants in 1984 and 1986. The Ontario Arts Council awarded her a grant in 1989, and she received a literary fellowship from the National Endowment for the Arts in 1991. Brant was a judge for the Astraea Foundation National Lesbian Writer Award series in 1992. Known for her inspirational voice, Brant is a popular lecturer at lesbian, feminist, university, and Indian events. She lives in Michigan with her life partner, Denise. They have co-founded Turtle Grandmother, an archive and library of information about North American Indian women. Turtle Grandmother is also a clearinghouse for manuscripts, published and unpublished, by Indian women.

Brant belongs to the Turtle clan, as have all the women before her. She loves fry bread, corn soup, Heaven Hill bourbon, and being alive. She says,

In [my] writing, I have tried to convey and speak the truth about my people. When Eagle came to me, He did so when I was ready to accept the challenge and responsibility that such a gift brings. It has not been easy, but writing is like life—you either do it fully, with compassion and strength, or you cheat yourself and others of that joy. (*Reinventing the Enemy's Language*, p. 352)

MORE INFORMATION ABOUT BETH BRANT

Completely Queer: The Gay and Lesbian Encyclopedia, edited by Steve Hogan and Lee Hudson. Holt, 1998, p. 99.

Contemporary Lesbian Writers of the United States: A Bio-Bibliographical Critical Sourcebook, edited by Sandra Pollack and Denise D. Knight. Greenwood Press, 1993.

Reinventing the Enemy's Language: Contemporary Native Women's Writings of North America, edited by Joy Harjo and Gloria Bird. W. W. Norton, 1997.

"To Be or Not to Be Was Never the Question." In *Inversions*, edited by Betsy Warland. Press Gang, 1991, pp. 17–23.

Larry Dane Brimner (1949)

In every school, in every city, in every state, in every country, there are sexual-minority youths who are wishing desperately to find themselves portrayed in books.

Being Different, p. 23

I ... have a firm belief in fairness. ... I believe that a democratic government has a responsibility to guarantee equal treatment of all people. I believe that the freedom of speech does not include the right to silence others.

Being Different, pp. 17–18

LESBIAN/GAY-THEMED WORKS BY LARRY DANE BRIMNER

Being Different: Lambda Youths Speak Out. Franklin Watts, 1995. (See Chapter 4)
Letters to Our Children: Lesbian and Gay Adults Speak to the New Generation. Franklin Watts, 1997. (See Chapter 4)
The NAMES Project. Children's Press, 1999. (See Chapter 4)

Larry Dane Brimner, a writer, editor, and educational consultant, was born on November 5, 1949 in St. Petersburg, Florida to Evelyn A. Brimner, a homemaker, and George Frederick Brimner, a military officer. He is the author of more than twenty books on diverse subjects for young readers.

His childhood on Kodiak Island, Alaska nurtured his love for nature, sports, and fiction. With no television and only sporadic radio reception, he learned early to enjoy listening to and reading stories. "[T]hat's why I'm a writer" (*Something About the Author*, p. 29). Those early experiences in Alaska explain why he enjoys a snowy environment surrounded by nature, and why winter is his favorite season of the year. Alaskan influences on his writing are apparent in his books about hibernation and ice skating. Brimner started ice skating soon after he learned to walk.

After graduating from San Diego State University in 1971, Brimner taught at several schools before taking a position as a writing teacher at Central Union High School in El Centro, California, where he worked for ten years. In 1984 he earned his M.A. at San Diego State University and several years later began teaching there. Subsequently, Brimner became a full-time writer, lecturer, and writing consultant to school systems nationwide.

"In college, I became acutely aware—as opposed to the *vague* awareness I had when I was four or five—of my attraction to other men. Although I always had girlfriends, my eyes and mind wandered when I was with them, and it wasn't long before I was visiting the library to look up *homosexuality*" (*Being Different*, p. 20). Brimner's high school library did not have books on the subject, but the university library did. However, because these books were on reserve and had to be requested at the desk, making them essentially unavailable, Brimner's reading was limited to case studies in psychology textbooks. Because he didn't fit the descriptions in these books, he went into a long period of denial.

After his parents became suspicious and confronted him, they told him that they would withdraw support if he was gay. "To hammer home the point, my mother said I could forget about a teaching career as well; she would see to it that I never set foot in a classroom" (*Being Different*, pp. 20–21). They ridiculed and pressured him until he agreed to see a psychiatrist. "The ensuing months were a blur of psychiatric appointments, electroshock treatments, arguments, and tears that ultimately led to two suicide attempts" (*Being Different*, p. 21).

Even though Brimner graduated with honors and was named "Outstanding Student Teacher of the Year," he was rejected for a position with the Escondido, California school system, which told him that it didn't hire homosexuals. Eventually, Brimner found a teaching job and devoted many years to his profession. In time, he embraced his sexual identity, established a nurturing relationship, and reunited bonds with his family.

Year later, when his editor invited him to write a book about lesbian and gay teenagers, he asked for a few days to think about it. While considering the project he traveled to the South to fulfill a speaking engagement at a reading conference. That evening at dinner, one of the librarians asked about the topic of his next book. When he told her that he was considering a book about lesbian and gay teens, she told him that he would never sell another book in her school system if he wrote a book on *that* topic. Brimner came home determined to do what he could to spare young lesbian and gay people the pain, confusion, and isolation he experienced. Subsequently, he has written or edited three excellent books that will nurture pride and dignity in gay and lesbian youth.

In addition to writing, Brimner's interests include reading, snow skiing, animals, pine furniture, travel, and American folk art.

MORE INFORMATION ABOUT LARRY DANE BRIMNER

Being Different: Lambda Youths Speak Out. Franklin Watts, 1995, pp. 17–23.
Something About the Author. Volume 79, pp. 28–30.
Who's Who in America, 1996.

Michael Cart (1941)

[B]ooks are important . . . because they offer engagement and enlightenment—first for the mind by stimulating thought but then for the spirit, too, since by giving readers the opportunity to eavesdrop on the hearts of others, books stimulate empathy and sympathy. In short, books are important because they have the power to enlarge and change both minds and lives. This is why it is so important to have books for and about gay and lesbian young adults. Not only so that homosexual youth can see themselves positively represented in literature . . . but also so that heterosexual teenagers can read about the homosexual experience and, accordingly educate and expand their own hearts and minds.

Gay and Lesbian Literature: Volume 2, p. 77

Too often [lesbian and gay] teens, despairing of a better life, resort to self-inflicted violence. . . . What better way to give them assurance than to share good books that deal compassionately and honestly with homosexual themes and issues?

"YA Talk," *Booklist*, June 1 and 15, 1999, p. 1810

Everyone who cares about literature and about young people has a dead-serious responsibility to focus attention on, support, and defend the very best, most courageously outspoken, and bluntly honest of young adult books. By doing so, we strengthen its voice; we amplify it so that it can be heard by those who most need to hear it: the most-at-risk-ever young adults themselves.

From Romance to Realism, p. 278.

WORKS BY MICHAEL CART

Lesbian/Gay Themed Works for Young Adults

My Father's Scar. Simon & Schuster, 1996. (See Chapter 2)

Literary Criticism

From Romance to Realism: 50 Years of Growth and Change in Young Adult Literature. HarperCollins, 1996.
The Heart Has Its Reasons: Homosexuality in Young Adult Literature. Scarecrow Press, forthcoming.

Michael Cart, a nationally recognized expert in children's and young adult literature, was born on March 6, 1941 in Logansport, Indiana. He earned degrees in journalism from Northwestern University, where he was a McCormick Scholar, and in library science from Columbia University, where he graduated with honors in 1964. Cart served in the United States Army from 1964 to 1967 and received an Army Commendation Medal.

Currently a columnist for *Booklist* magazine and a book reviewer for The *Los Angeles Times*, Cart has taught at UCLA and Texas Woman's University. From 1979 to 1991 he served as Director of the Beverly Hills Public Library in California, and for ten years he also hosted and co-produced the nationally syndicated cable TV author-interview program *In Print*. He is the author of more than 250 articles and reviews, which have appeared in *The New York Times Book Review, School Library Journal, Children's Literature in Education, The Lion and the Unicorn,* and many other professional magazines and journals.

Active in the American Library Association and a frequent speaker at conferences, Cart is known for his wide-ranging erudition and acerbic wit. He has been a member of numerous committees including the Caldecott Medal Committee and the USBBY Hans Christian Andersen Medal Committee. Cart was on the board of directors for the Young Adult Library Service Association from 1994 to 1996 and then served as vice-president/president-elect from 1996 to 1997.

Cart has been recognized with many awards, including the Dorothy C. McKenzie Award for Service to Children and Literature in 1983, the Educational Press Association of America Distinguished Achievement Award in 1994, and the National Association of Television Officials and Administrators Award in 1990 and 1996.

Since his retirement in 1991, Cart has been a full-time writer. His books include literary biographies of Francesca Lia Block and Robert Lipsyte, a book on humor in children's literature, an overview of the young adult novel in the United States, a young adult novel, and several books of short stories for young adults. His forthcoming book, *The Heart Has Its Reasons*, is a critical study of homosexuality—in theme and character—in young adult literature.

In *From Romance to Realism* Cart issues a passionate call for literature that has the power to change and improve troubled lives. He envisions young adult literature that tackles significant subjects with authenticity, honesty, and integrity. "He issues a manifesto for the inclusion of topics that are relevant, immediate, and important in the lives of young people. . . . Cart writes at length about the inadequacy of the treatment of homosexuality in young adult literature" (*Gay and Lesbian Literature: Volume 2*, p. 77). He believes that there must be more good books that present homosexuality in the context of respect, acceptance, and love. "Silence equals death—not only of the body but of the spirit" (*Gay and Lesbian Literature: Volume 2*, p. 77).

Drawing on his own experiences, Cart wrote *My Father's Scar*, a powerful story of how one gay person survived his anguished childhood to find love and acceptance. One of the many strengths of the book is the portrayal of a gay uncle who extends a lifeline to the protagonist, validating his love for books and encouraging him to believe in himself. This memorable book will touch the hearts and minds of both gay and heterosexual teenagers, as well as adults. Cart writes,

[I]f we are to ensure that love—not ignorance and its evil twin, hatred—wins, then it is imperative that good books on the homosexual experience be read not only by gay and lesbian teens but also by their heterosexual peers. Ignorance demonizes those who are different. Good books show us the commonalities shared by our hearts. ("YA Talk," *Booklist*, June 1 and 15, 1999, p. 1811)

From 1980 to 1992 Cart's life partner was John V. Ledwith, Jr., a motion picture executive. The partnership ended amicably and, indeed, Cart's book *From Romance to Realism* is dedicated to Ledwith, who remains the author's closest friend.

MORE INFORMATION ABOUT MICHAEL CART

Gay and Lesbian Literature: Volume 2, edited by Tom Pendergast and Sara Pendergast. St. James Press, 1997, pp. 76–78.

Michael Thomas Ford (1968)

Photo by Becket Logan

If you are in a situation right now where you feel all alone or depressed, I hope that you will see that you are not really alone. . . . The gay community is filled with wonderful people doing exciting things with their lives, and you can be a part of that. . . . And no matter what anyone tells you, you are special and you are worth caring about.

The World Out There, p. 189

We all deserve to be told that we are worthwhile. . . . [E]very one of us deserves the chance to be happy. No matter what people tell you—your parents, your friends, your priests or rabbis or ministers, your teachers, people at school or work, your coaches—you are someone who deserves to be treated well. It doesn't matter what your grades are, what sports you play, what activities you are involved in, what you're good at, or what job you have. The person you are right now is a person who deserves respect.

The World Out There, pp. 88–89

WORKS BY MICHAEL THOMAS FORD

For Young Adults

100 Questions and Answers About AIDS: A Guide for Young People. Macmillan, 1992.
   (See Chapter 4)

Outspoken: Role Models from the Lesbian and Gay Community. Morrow, 1998. (See
    Chapter 4)
The Voices of AIDS. Morrow, 1995. (See Chapter 4)
The World Out There: Becoming Part of the Lesbian and Gay Community. The New
    Press, 1996. (See Chapter 4)

For Adults

Alec Baldwin Doesn't Love Me & Other Trials from My Queer Life. Alyson
    Publications, 1998. (Lambda Literary Award Winner for Best Humor
    Book)
That's Mr. Faggot to You: Further Trials from My Queer Life. Alyson Publications,
    1999.
Voices of the Spirit: Conversations About Faith and Spirituality. Simon & Schuster,
    forthcoming.

Michael Thomas Ford is the author of more than twenty books, including several for young adults. His syndicated humor column, "My
Queer Life" appears monthly in newspapers across the country. His essays, fiction, and articles have appeared in numerous magazines and
anthologies.

In his irreverent, humorous biographical essays, Ford reminisces about
growing up in the 1970s with a strict Baptist mother. When he was seven,
he "was convinced that Jesus was going to come and snatch [him] up
into the clouds (*Alec Baldwin Doesn't Love Me*, p. vii). An introverted
child, he was an avid reader. He knew Judy Blume's books inside and
out. Two of his favorites were *Forever* and *Then Again, Maybe I Won't.*

When Ford was about to enter fifth grade his father retired from his
government job and moved the family to a small town in upstate New
York. Dropped into the middle of a farming town where everyone had
grown up together, he did not fit in. "Within ten minutes of my first day
there, I became the school queer" (*That's Mr. Faggot to You*, p. 75). Years
later, Ford remembered what it felt like the day he saw the class roster
taped to his teacher's desk with the word "faggot" written next to his
name in red. The teacher had not bothered to remove the word. Although he was never physically abused, the emotional abuse was so
severe that he refused to go back to school after the eleventh grade.
Instead, he went to college a year early.

The first books Ford read about gay people were written by Gordon
Merrick. When he was twelve, he bought these books at Waldenbooks
while his father waited, oblivious. At his "small religious college outside
of New York where being gay was the worst offense imaginable" (*The
World Out There*, p. 11), Ford secretly read books about gay history. After
graduation he moved to Greenwich Village. "Finally I was surrounded

by the culture I'd been waiting my whole life for" (*That's Mr. Faggot to You*, p. 230).

Ford has also written several excellent books for young adults. *100 Questions and Answers About AIDS* is a frank, nonjudgmental book that combines comprehensive information with poignant personal stories. Direct answers to questions cover modes of transmission, stages of infection, myths, prevention, diagnosis, and treatment. Using a reassuring tone, Ford successfully conveys the message that young people *can* take control over their own destinies and avoid infection. *Outspoken*, a highly acclaimed book, is an inspiring collection of interviews with eleven "out" lesbians and gay men. Designed to provide young people with positive images of individuals who are leading happy, healthy, and productive lives, the interviewees include Nancy Garden and Kevin Jennings. Ford's questions are individualized for each interviewee and the engaging responses demonstrate the diversity within the lesbian/gay community.

In his compassionate book, *The Voices of AIDS*, Ford interviews twelve people whose lives have been touched by AIDS. This book has been praised for its unflinching, succinct information; honest, moving interviews; and examination of themes of self-esteem, self-respect, and respect for others. Ford's fourth book for young adults, *The World Out There*, provides basic information about what it means to be part of a lesbian and gay community. In a reassuring tone, Ford answers questions such as "What is a Gay Community?" "Why Should I Become Involved in the Gay Community?" and "How Can I Find the Gay Community?"

Currently Ford lives in Massachusetts, where he is a full-time writer. After the publication of his award-winning collection of essays, *Alec Baldwin Doesn't Love Me*, he traveled around the country doing readings and meeting the people who enjoyed the book. He was interviewed by a number of gay newspapers, radio shows, and television programs. Because the book was so successful, a second collection of essays was published.

Nancy Garden (1938)

Photo by Midge Eliassen

One of the things I try to say in my books is "you have a right to be whoever you are. Be true to yourself, whoever that self is, and follow your dreams, whatever they are."

Personal Communication

Understand that you're not the only [lesbian or gay person]. . . . You have to hang on to the fact that you have every right to be here and to be exactly who you are. . . . You're a unique, special person, and you have a right to live your own life.

Outspoken, p. 66

Children's books can be mind-stretchers and imagination-ticklers and builders of good taste in a way that adult books cannot, because young people usually come to books with more open minds. It's exciting to be able to contribute to that in a small way.

Contemporary Authors, New Revision Series, Volume 30, p. 147

LESBIAN/GAY-THEMED WORKS BY NANCY GARDEN

Annie on My Mind. Farrar, Straus & Giroux. 1982; 1992. (See Chapter 2)
Good Moon Rising. Farrar, Straus & Giroux, 1996. (See Chapter 2)
Holly's Secret, Farrar, Straus & Giroux, forthcoming. (See Chapter 2)

Lark in the Morning. Farrar, Straus & Giroux, 1991. (See Chapter 2)
Molly's Family. Farrar, Straus & Giroux, forthcoming.
"Parents' Night." In *Am I Blue? Coming Out from the Silence,* edited by Marion
    Dane Bauer. HarperCollins, 1994. (See Chapter 3)
The Year They Burned the Books. Farrar, Straus & Giroux, 1999. (See Chapter 2)

Nancy Garden is the highly acclaimed author of more than twenty-five books for children and young adults. She is best known for her landmark book *Annie on My Mind,* which features two young women who fall in love. Garden notes, "I wrote it to give solace to young gay people, to let them know they were not alone, that they could be happy and well adjusted and also to let heterosexual kids know that we gay people aren't monsters" (*Booklist,* April 15, 1996).

Born in Boston, Massachusetts on May 15, 1938, Garden has lived most of her life in New England and New York. She is an only child and her family moved frequently. "I was shy, and I think I took refuge in books, in writing, and in telling long stories to myself and sometimes acting them out" (*Something About the Author* [*SATA*], Volume 12, p. 86). She recalls her first and second grade teacher, who encouraged her "love of storytelling and acting by asking [her] to supervise the performance, in assembly, of an ongoing recess-time saga [she'd] invented involving a cat family" (*SATA,* p. 80). Garden started writing poetry and stories when she was eight; one of her early projects, "Dogs I Have Known," was a collection of biographies of every dog she had ever met.

In high school Garden became interested in theater, first in acting and then in lighting design and directing. It was while she was in a group of one-act plays that she fell in love with Sandra Scott, who was also active in theater. "We got to talking at rehearsals, and we found out we had a lot in common. We became close very quickly, and it was very romantic" (*Outspoken,* p. 52). The bond they formed "soon became and has remained, the most important one in my life" (*Something About the Author Autobiography Series* [*SATAAS*], Volume 8, p. 88). They, like many others, searched in vain for positive information about lesbianism, but almost all of the books that they found ended in mental illness, suicide, or with the lesbian(s) becoming heterosexual. After reading Radclyffe Hall's *The Well of Loneliness,* which ends sadly but with an impassioned plea for justice, Garden vowed that she would someday write a book about young lesbians that ended happily.

Both during and after completing her B.F.A. at Columbia School of Dramatic Arts and her M.A. at Columbia Teachers College, Garden worked in theater, did office work, and worked as a teacher and editor. During that time she continued to write in the evenings, on weekends, and during vacations. Now she writes as close to full-time as possible, along with teaching a correspondence course, visiting schools, and speaking at conferences. In 1982 Garden fulfilled her vow to write a book with positive images of young lesbians. She says, "I've written many books for young people, but closest to my heart is *Annie on My Mind*, a lesbian love and coming-out story" (*Am I Blue?* p. 145). Michael Thomas Ford adds, "It was the first time I'd ever read that gay and lesbian people could have happy lives filled with love and laughter. Many people I know—especially lesbians—said the same thing about the book" (*Outspoken*, p. 48).

In 1993 the award-winning *Annie on My Mind* came under attack in Kansas. Unknown to Garden, *Annie* was donated, along with Frank Mosca's *All American Boys*, to forty-two schools in and around Kansas City, Kansas and Missouri. A fundamentalist minister burned *Annie* in front of the building housing the the Kansas City school board, and school officials in several districts ordered it to be removed from library shelves. A group of students and parents in Olathe, Kansas successfully sued to have it returned to circulation.

Meanwhile, Garden's second lesbian-themed book for young adults was published in 1991. *Lark in the Morning* is one of the few books about young lesbian and gay people that is not a coming-out story. Garden notes, "I wrote *Lark* partly because I feel there should be books about gay kids in which being gay is important but not necessarily pivotal in itself—as being straight is in most other young adult books" (*Am I Blue?* p. 145). Next came *Good Moon Rising*, a beautifully written love story that Garden had written in the 1970s. She recalls, "Writing *Good Moon Rising*—which on the one hand was gay and on the other was about theater—was a real catharsis for me. I thought it wasn't any good though, and put it away" (*Outspoken*, p. 60). Years later, she got it out, revised it, and, happily for her readers, published it in 1996.

Her feelings about censorship in general and the attempts to censor *Annie on My Mind* led Garden to write her fourth lesbian-themed book for young adults, *The Year They Burned the Books*. Forthcoming books include *Holly's Secret* and *Molly's Family*. Garden says, "I keep feeling there's a book just out of reach, no matter how many I write" (*SATAAS*, p. 97).

Garden enjoys reading, hiking, gardening, the outdoors, and anything to do with dogs. She and Sandy live in Carlisle, Massachusetts, with their various dogs and cats. They spend as much time as they can at their log cabin in Maine.

MORE INFORMATION ABOUT NANCY GARDEN

Journals

Nancy Garden, "Annie on Trial: How It Feels to Be the Author of a Challenged Book," *Voice of Youth Advocates*, February 1996.

Books

Authors and Artists for Young Adults, Volume 18, pp. 105–111.
Contemporary Authors: New Revision Series, Volume 30, p. 147.
Outspoken: Role Models from the Lesbian and Gay Community, edited by Michael Thomas Ford. Morrow, 1998, pp. 48–66.
Something About the Author, Volume 12, pp. 85–86.
Something About the Author Autobiography Series, Volume 8, pp. 79–98.

Kevin Jennings (1963)

Our stories are our best weapons in the fight against homophobia.
Telling Tales Out of School, p. xiv

[T]he only people who have created real change in history are those who were convinced that the impossible could be achieved. . . . The first and foremost essential step toward achieving justice is to believe that justice can be achieved. We must believe this deep in our hearts, and hold onto that belief even when other people and the circumstances in which we find ourselves would suggest that we are naive, foolish and perhaps crazy to do so.
Blackboard: The Newsletter of the Gay, Lesbian, and Straight Education Network, Summer 1998, p. 5

We, as gay students and gay teachers, are going to make it, no matter how many obstacles and barriers stand in the way of our liberation.
One Teacher in Ten, p. 28

WORKS BY KEVIN JENNINGS

Becoming Visible: A Reader in Gay and Lesbian History for High School and College Students. Alyson Publications, 1994. (See Chapter 4)
One Teacher in Ten: Gay and Lesbian Educators Tell Their Stories (editor). Alyson Publications, 1994. (See Chapter 6)
Telling Tales Out of School: Gays, Lesbians, and Bisexuals Revisit Their School Days (editor). Alyson Publications, 1998. (See Chapter 5)

Kevin Jennings is the energetic co-founder and Executive Director of the Gay, Lesbian, Straight Education Network, an organization that brings together educators, parents, and community members who are working together to end anti-gay bias in schools. Jennings was named one of *Out Magazine*'s "Top 100 Newsmakers and Earthshakers" for his work in both 1995 and 1996. In 1997 he was named to *Newsweek*'s "Century Club" as one of 100 people to watch in the next century.

Born in 1963, Jennings grew up in a Southern Baptist fundamentalist home in the rural community of Lewisville, North Carolina, just outside of Winston-Salem. Poor white people descended from Confederate veterans, his relatives sought out scapegoats for their failure to succeed. His uncles and cousins joined the Ku Klux Klan, while his father, a fundamentalist minister, used religion to justify his prejudices against every minority group, including gay and lesbian people.

Even though he loved sports, Jennings stopped playing on organized school teams after being humiliated by his seventh grade gym teacher. Haunted by this "outing," he was taunted daily in the locker room, in the hallways, and in the classroom. "Whenever I volunteered to answer a question or write on the board, a slightly audible murmur from my classmates would arise. 'Faggot,' I would hear. I learned not to volunteer or raise my hand" ("I Remember," p. 20).

Jennings knew that he was gay from the age of six but, with his religious upbringing and his determination to achieve the American Dream, he spent many years in denial. By his senior year in high school he was drunk or stoned almost every day. After he fell in love with a classmate and they made love, he tried to kill himself but was saved by a friend. "Those moments of desperation helped me understand why one out of every three gay teens tries to commit suicide" ("American Dreams," p. 5).

Jennings' father died when he was eight, and his mother went to work at McDonald's. She was determined that her youngest son was going to achieve the dream that had been denied to her and her other children. (Years later, she founded the first chapter of Parents, Families, and Friends of Lesbians and Gays (PFLAG) in the state of North Carolina.) Jennings earned a scholarship to Harvard, where he was an openly gay activist. He graduated magna cum laude and delivered the Harvard Oration at the 1985 commencement. He taught history at Moses Brown School in Providence, Rhode Island from 1985 to 1987, and Concord Academy in Concord, Massachusetts from 1987 to 1994. In 1992 he was named one of fifty "Terrific Teachers Making a Difference" by the Edward Calesa Foundation.

In 1993 Jennings was named a Joseph Klingenstein Fellow at Columbia University, from which he received his M.A. in 1994. In 1999 he received his M.B.A. from the Leonard N. Stern School of Business at New York University. He currently lives in New York with his partner, Jeff Davis.

Best known for his work in the fight for equality for lesbian and gay youth, Jennings is the author of several related books. His goals are to embolden educators to come out, serve as role models for lesbian and gay youth, and get involved in creating support systems in school environments. Jennings is a dynamic speaker and an inspirational leader. He states, "Teaching a kid to hate himself [or herself] so much that he or she wants to die is abuse" (source unknown).

MORE INFORMATION ABOUT KEVIN JENNINGS

"American Dreams." In *Growing Up Gay, Growing Up Lesbian: A Literary Anthology*, edited by Bennett L. Singer. New Press, 1994.

"GLSTN Shines Its Light." In *School's Out: The Impact of Gay and Lesbian Issues on America's Schools* by Dan Woog. Alyson Publications, 1995.

"Half-Breed." In *Telling Tales Out of School: Gays, Lesbians, and Bisexuals Revisit Their School Days.* Alyson Publications, 1998.

"I Remember." In *One Teacher in Ten: Gay and Lesbian Educators Tell Their Stories.* Alyson Publications, 1994.

Outspoken: Role Models from the Lesbian and Gay Community by Michael Thomas Ford. Morrow, 1998.

"The Truth, the Whole Truth, and Nothing But the Truth," Foreword to *The Last Closet: The Real Lives of Lesbian and Gay Teachers* by Rita M. Kissen. Heinemann, 1996.

Who's Who in the East, 1999.

M. E. Kerr (1927)

[T]here was an inner restless feeling that I was somehow different
... that I was out-of-step with my peers, faking my way through
many of the tribal rites of the times. I felt like a Kafkaish character
with a secret, who didn't know what the secret was.

> "Books Remembered," *Children's Book Council Features*,
> Fall-Winter 1995, unpaginated

... I thought of what this book [*Hearing Us Out*] might have meant
not just to someone like me, growing up gay, but also to a parent
like my mother, who was not that different from many of her time.
If only there had been literature for her to read, besides the heavy
and pathetic *Well of Loneliness*. If only she had some confirmation
that this blight on our family was not as rare and terrible as she
believed it was. My father could not even speak about it.

> *Hearing Us Out*, p. ix

This anthology is dedicated to a better understanding of all the [les-
bians], in all the cities, in all the countries of the world. It is not
intended to glorify her, nor to defame her, but to further explain her,
in the hope that one day society may receive her less with shock or
morbid curiosity, more with an intelligent, tolerant disposition.

> *Carol in a Thousand Cities*

LESBIAN/GAY THEMED WORKS BY M. E. KERR

For Young Adults

Deliver Us from Evie. HarperCollins, 1994. (See Chapter 2)
"Hello," I Lied. HarperCollins, 1997. (See Chapter 2)
Night Kites. HarperCollins, 1986. (See Chapter 2)
"We Might As Well All Be Strangers." In *Am I Blue? Coming Out from the Silence*,
    edited by Marion Dane Bauer. HarperCollins, 1994. (See Chapter 3)

For Adults (Under Pseudonym Vin Packer)

Spring Fire. Gold Medal Books, 1952.

For Adults (Under Pseudonym Ann Aldrich)

Carol in a Thousand Cities. Gold Medal Books, 1960.
Take a Lesbian to Lunch. MacFadden-Bartell, 1972.
We Too Must Love. Gold Medal Books, 1958.
We Two Won't Last. Gold Medal Books, 1963.
We Walk Alone. Gold Medal Books, 1955.

   M. E. Kerr is the highly acclaimed author of more than twenty books
for young readers. Born Marijane Meaker on May 27, 1927 in Auburn,
New York, she is the middle child and only daughter of Ellis R. Meaker,
a mayonnaise manufacturer, and Ida T. Meaker. Although she grew up
in an affluent home and had what most people would consider a privileged childhood, she always felt like an outsider. "My arms and knees
were full of scabs from falls out of trees and off my bicycle. I was hap-
piest wearing the pants my brother'd grown out of, the vest to one of
my father's business suits over one of my brother's old shirts. . . . Everything I said came out of the side of my mouth, and I strolled around
with my fists inside my trouser pockets" (*ME ME ME ME ME*, p. 36).
The year she turned twelve, her younger brother was born and her older
brother went off to military school. "I was suddenly the nothing, sand-
wiched between two stars" (*ME*, p. 60.) She couldn't endure the misery
of wearing a dress and acting like most girls, even though she knew that
would have earned her the attention she so desperately needed.
   Kerr had always loved reading and knew from an early age that she
wanted to become a writer, so at thirteen she locked herself in her room
and wrote stories about murder and suicide. Her mother enrolled her in
dance classes, and both parents encouraged her to date boys. While waiting in the living room with her parents before one date, she remembers
wishing she was "back upstairs where I belonged, writing about life
instead of enduring it" (*ME*, p. 122). In 1943 she left Auburn to attend a
boarding school for young women in Staunton, Virginia, where she en-
gaged in kissing games with some of her classmates. Her penchant for

being the class cutup resulted in her suspension, but she returned in time to graduate with her class in 1945. After attending Vermont Junior College, where she edited the school newspaper, Kerr enrolled at the University of Missouri. There she joined the Communist Party, volunteered at the local mental hospital, and wrote story after story, which she sent off to New York–based magazines.

After graduating from the University of Missouri with a major in English literature, Kerr moved to New York City, where she found a job as a file clerk at Dutton Publishing. She continued to write, turning out volumes of confession stories, articles, and poetry. Finally, at age twenty-three, Kerr sold her first story to *Ladies Home Journal* (under the pen name Laura Winston). After this success, she never worked at a full-time job again. Her first novel, *Spring Fire*, written under the pen name Vin Packer, sold 1,463,917 copies in 1952. *Spring Fire* was followed by four books under the pen name Ann Aldrich, all of which were about lesbian relationships. She wrote seventeen mysteries under the pen name Vin Packer over the next seventeen years.

It wasn't until 1972 that Kerr's first book for young adults was published. Her close friend, Louise Fitzhugh, the author of *Harriet the Spy*, had been encouraging her to try writing for young people for several years. "I came to children's literature late in life, after some twenty-two novels, hard- and softcover, most of them crime or suspense stories" (*Youth Services in Libraries* [*YSL*], Fall 1993, p. 28). To date she has written over twenty books for young readers and is one of the most respected and popular writers in the field. "M. E. Kerr breezes into teenagers' lives like an Auntie Mame—more experienced and worldly than their friends and less uptight and protective than their parents. Her literary style flatters young readers because she makes them feel as though they are respected guests worthy of her wittiest and most charming efforts" (*Presenting M. E. Kerr*, Updated Edition, p. 108). Her award-winning books have been praised for their lively humor, irreverent tone, punny names, clever dialogue, wordplay, significant themes, and defense of the underdog.

In reflecting on early influences, Kerr writes, "I was a real library addict; I hung out at the library and the librarians would watch and direct my growth as a reader. They all knew I wanted to be a writer, so they would give me biographies and autobiographies of writers" (*Contemporary Authors*, Volume 107, p. 334). She remembers reading *The Well of Loneliness* when she was twelve years old, with "my hands shaking and my heart beating, knowing that I had stumbled upon myself" (*Children's Book Council Features*, Fall-Winter 1995, unpaginated). Because she did not dare check it out, she "read it quickly in one afternoon, and then went back and read it more carefully, piecemeal, day by day." Although she, like many others, found the book to be depressing, it reassured her that she was not alone. Reading the book was her first step toward self-acceptance.

Years later she included minor lesbian or gay characters in many of her books for young readers. Then in 1986 she wrote *Night Kites*, the first novel for young adults about AIDS. "It was the most difficult book I ever wrote. I stopped and started it again and again" (*YSL*, p. 30). After the book was released, principals of high schools where she was scheduled to speak would meet her in the parking lots and ask her not to mention the book. However, *Night Kites* was one of the four books cited by the selection committee when Kerr won the 1993 Margaret A. Edwards Award, sponsored by *School Library Journal* and administered by ALA's Young Adult Library Services Association. The award was created to honor an author whose work has been taken to heart by young adults over a period of years, and provides an authentic voice that continues to illuminate their experiences and emotions, giving insight into their lives. The next year, *Deliver Us from Evie* featured one of the strongest lesbians in young adult fiction history. Evie, who has remained true to herself through eighteen years of heterosexist pressure from family, church, and community, apologizes to no one for her sexual identity.

Once a psychologist asked Kerr, "How do you know so much about the denial and intragroup prejudice and the rest?" Kerr responded, "growing up homosexual in the late '30s and early '40s had given me all my insights." She continues, "So formed by what others thought, so in thrall to convention and conformity, both my parents missed the chance to know my warm and loving friends—as well as to know me better. I feel sorry for people who miss the chance to know us" (*Hearing Us Out*, pp. ix–x).

M. E. Kerr is currently working on her Ph.D. Her manuscripts are housed in the Kerlan Collection at the University of Minnesota.

MORE INFORMATION ABOUT M. E. KERR

Journals

"An Interview with M. E. Kerr," by Joyce L. Graham. *Youth Services in Libraries* (Fall 1993), pp. 31–36.
"An Interview with M. E. Kerr," by Paul Janeczko. *English Journal* (December 1975), pp. 75–77.
"Books Remembered," by M. E. Kerr. *Children's Book Council Features* (Fall–Winter 1995), unpaginated.
"1993 Margaret A. Edwards Award Acceptance Speech," by M. E. Kerr. *Youth Services in Libraries* (Fall 1993), pp. 25–29.

Books

"As I See It." In *Whole Language, Whole Learning: Creating a Literature Centered Classroom*, edited by Laura Robb. Morrow, 1994.

Authors and Artists for Young Adults, Volume 2, pp. 123–138.

Contemporary Authors, Volume 107, pp. 332–336,

Contemporary Literary Criticism, Volume 35, pp. 247–252.

ME ME ME ME ME: Not a Novel (Autobiography). HarperCollins, 1983.

The 100 Most Popular Young Adult Authors by Bernard A. Drew. Libraries Unlimited, 1997.

Presenting M. E. Kerr, Updated Edition by Alleen Pace Nilsen. Twayne Publishers, 1997. (See Chapter 6)

Something About the Author Autobiography Series, Volume 1, pp. 141–154.

Michael Nava (1954)

Photo by C. F. Berkstresser

Childhood had been a form of imprisonment for me. . . . [M]y mother and grandmother . . . had no idea what to do with me, a moody boy, precocious at one moment and withdrawn the next, who sometimes accepted their solicitude and other times angrily rejected it. And it was beyond their power—because it was beyond my understanding—to tell them I hurt . . . I could have only told them, though not in these words, that I was waiting for my life to begin.

"Abuelo: My Grandfather, Raymond Acuña," p. 18

The aberration in my life is not that I'm a lawyer who writes, but that I'm a writer who practices law.

Bloomsbury Review, p. 1

I'm an outsider. . . . I'm no one's stereotype . . . I think that the great mass of the American public still thinks that all homosexuals are white hairdressers, are promiscuous, are . . . well, fill in the blank. I'm here to say, Look at me: I'm Latino, I'm a lawyer . . . you can't make generalizations about my people, Latino or gay.

Bloomsbury Review, p. 1

WORKS BY MICHAEL NAVA

For Young Adults

"Abuelo: My Grandfather, Raymond Acuña." In *A Member of the Family: Gay Men Write About Their Families*, edited by John Preston, Dutton, 1992. (See Chapter 5)

Created Equal: Why Gay Rights Matter to America, written with Robert Dawidoff. St. Martin's Press, 1994. (See Chapter 4)

"The Marriage of Michael and Bill." In *Friends and Lovers: Gay Men Write About the Families They Create*, edited by John Preston. Dutton, 1995. (See Chapter 5)

For Adults

"Boys Like Us." In *Boys Like Us: Gay Writers Tell Their Coming Out Stories*, edited by Patrick Merla. Avon, 1996, 1997.

The Burning Plain. Putnam, 1997.

The Death of Friends. Putnam, 1996.

Finale: Short Stories of Mystery and Suspense (editor). Alyson Publications, 1989.

Goldenboy. Alyson Publications, 1988.

The Hidden Law. HarperCollins, 1992.

How Town. Harper and Row, 1990.

The Little Death. Alyson Publications, 1986.

Michael Nava, writer and lawyer, is best known for his award-winning mystery series featuring a gay Latino lawyer. Recognized as an accomplished novelist, Nava's work is distinguished by its insight, compassion, and sense of social justice. He has also written several short pieces about his childhood that poignantly express the confusion, isolation, and anguish a young person experiences growing up gay in a homophobic society.

The second oldest of six children, Nava was born on September 16, 1954 in Stockton, California and grew up in Gardenland, a semi-rural barrio, on the outskirts of Sacramento, California. His great-grandparents came to the United States from Mexico during the Mexican Revolution, starting as migrant workers and working their way to the Sacramento Valley, where they stayed. "[T]he son of a man with whom my mother, then married, had had an affair, to the lasting shame of her Mexican-Catholic family" ("Abuelo," p. 15), Nava was a moody, unhappy child who turned to books for solace. "At that early age, in my innermost self, I was no one's child, and as I grew older my sense of estrangement from my family deepened" ("Abuelo," p. 16). He felt cast off completely when, at the age of eleven, he was sexually molested by an adult family member. "Fat, myopic, and brainy, I escaped sissyhood only because of the aggressive gloominess I shared with my grandfather" ("Abuelo," p. 17). At twelve, the final, crushing blow came when he realized that he was gay. He tried to compensate by being a model child: smart, well behaved, and respectful of elders. After a suicide attempt when he was fourteen, he cut himself off from his feelings and became "driven to make up in outside achievement the inner deficiency I felt" ("The Marriage of Michael and Bill," p. 114).

Unable to talk to anyone, Nava started expressing his feelings through poetry when he was fourteen. "I was a frenetic over-achiever . . . I focused in at an early age that education was going to be my way out of my family and the poverty-stricken community where I grew up" (*Bloomsbury Review*, p. 1). When he graduated from high school he was the class valedictorian, student body president, and captain of the debating team. He earned a full academic scholarship to Colorado College, where he graduated cum laude with a major in history in 1976. Nava was awarded a Thomas J. Watson Fellowship and spent the following year in Buenos Aires, where he studied and translated the poetry of Ruben Dario, which was published by the University of California at Irvine.

After graduating from Stanford Law School in 1981, Nava embarked on a career as a prosecutor for the City of Los Angeles. Intoxicated with the romance of being a trial lawyer, he was excited about doing something that had social utility. But after three years of toiling in grimy courtrooms and run-down prisons, he burned out. "The criminal justice system is a depressing place. It is a system of victims, no matter what side they're on. Terrible things happen to decent people, and there's nothing you can do about it" (*Los Angeles Times*, p. E1). Nava opened a private law practice in Los Angeles and later became a research attorney for the California Court of Appeals.

"When I was in college, I set out to be the great American poet" (*Bloomsbury Review*, p. 1). Even though some of his poetry was published in the early 1980s, Nava soon turned his attention to fiction. He started writing his first mystery, *A Little Death*, during his last year of law school. Rejected by mainstream publishers, it was published in 1986 by Alyson Publications. Sasha Alyson says, "it is rare for an unsolicited first book to be outstanding. . . . In a lot of mysteries, the mystery is good but the writing is so-so. Michael's work is different. He is a poet, and it shows" (*Los Angeles Times*, p. 2). Alyson also published the second book in the series, the award-winning *Goldenboy*. Then in 1990, Nava made the leap from the small press to one of the largest publishers in the United States, a move that has brought his work to a wider audience. The success of *How Town* firmly established Nava as one of the gay community's leading literary figures. Recently Nava completed two more books in the series: *The Death of Friends* and *The Burning Plain*.

Nava's mystery series stars Henry Rios, a gay Latino lawyer who has much in common with his creator. But in a number of interviews, Nava makes it clear that Rios is not Nava: "if you've spent much time with me, you know we're not the same character" (*Gay Community News*, p. 2). Nevertheless, they are similar in a number of ways: both are Latino, lawyers, gay, workaholics, and recovering alcoholics, and they both grew up poor in central California. Also, they both live and work in Los Angeles and the San Francisco Bay Area.

Unlike earlier generations of lesbian and gay writers, Nava never agonized over the sexual identity of the protagonist of his books. He knew that the best writers write from their own experience, and his experience is that of a gay Latino lawyer. Nava notes, "I try to depict the reality in which I live, which in California is multi-ethnic, multicultural, and certainly multi-sexual orientation. I live a very rich life here, and I try to depict it with some veracity. This is one of my goals as a writer, to accurately paint a picture of my world" (*Gay Community News*, p. 1). Nava's worldview stems from his experience growing up as an outsider. "I have spent my life being uncomfortable. As assimilated as I am, I have never for one day forgotten who I am and what I am: a homosexual Latino. Being uncomfortable makes you think, and mindless prejudice sparks anger. My fury has fueled all my accomplishments" (*Los Angeles Times*, p. E13).

In accepting his gayness, Nava remembers saying to himself, "I am a homosexual, and I am still a good human being, notwithstanding what the Catholic Church, or my classmates, or my family members say. That act of compassion toward myself compels me to be compassionate toward others" (*Los Angeles Times*, p. E13). When he was at Stanford he fell in love with Bill, a fellow student. Nava beautifully describes the ways in which love "softened the harshness with which I viewed myself and . . . opened up to me a possibility of happiness that I had never even considered" ("The Marriage of Michael and Bill," p. 112).

In addition to his mystery series, Nava has cowritten a book calling for Americans to defend the Bill of Rights and the Constitution of the United States and give lesbian and gay people what should already be theirs: first-class citizenship. In *Created Equal* the authors explain why anything less denies the guarantee of equality for all American citizens and widens the chasm between what our country promises and what it delivers.

Nava's gay-affirming voice addresses crucial social problems and issues. He unflinchingly tackles tough subjects such as child molestation and abuse, the psychology of addiction, political corruption, and the inequities in the criminal justice system. He has been praised for his insight into character and relationships, his skill with language, and his ability to create a suspenseful book. Although his mysteries are written for adults, some of his other work is appropriate for young adults. Given his interest in social and political issues and the paucity of good books for young readers about gay Latinos, perhaps Nava will choose the field of adolescent literature for some of his future writing projects. He is currently writing a memoir titled *Gardenland*.

MORE INFORMATION ABOUT MICHAEL NAVA

Journals and Newspapers

"Brains and Rage." *Bloomsbury Review* (June 1991), pp. 1–2.
"Gay Latino Lawyer Mystery Writer." *Gay Community News*, July 15–20, pp. 1–4.
"Poetic Justice." *Los Angeles Times*, May 6, 1990, pp. E1, E13.
"The Mysteries of Writer Michael Nava." *San Francisco Sentinel* (June 1990).
"Tough, Smart and Gay." *Los Angeles Times*, April 19, 1990, pp. J1, J13.

Books

"Abuelo: My Grandfather, Raymond Acuña." In *A Member of the Family: Gay Men Write About Their Closest Relations*, edited by John Preston. Dutton, 1992. (See Chapter 5)
Contemporary Authors, Volume 124, p. 323.
Contemporary Gay American Novelists, edited by Emmanuel S. Nelson. Greenwood, 1993.
Gay and Lesbian Characters and Themes in Mystery Novels by Anthony Slide. McFarland, 1993.
The Gay and Lesbian Literary Heritage, edited by Claude J. Summers. Henry Holt, 1995.
"The Marriage of Michael and Bill." In *Friends and Lovers: Gay Men Write About the Families They Create*, edited by John Preston. Dutton, 1994. (See Chapter 5)

Lesléa Newman (1955)

Photo by Mary Vazquez

Writing continues to teach me, surprise me, and inform me in new and exciting ways. I have learned to expect the unexpected, and to push harder just when I am ready to give up. The sources that continue to feed my life and writing are my Jewish heritage and feminist values. They help me to continue to be myself, to take risks, and to explore uncharted territory. I am motivated to learn the truth about my own life, and the learning is in the telling.

Contemporary Authors, Volume 126, p. 322

Much of my writing explores the conflicts and joys of being a lesbian and a Jew. The two identities have much in common: Being a lesbian and a Jew automatically places one inside two vital, active communities that value the group as much as the individual. Both communities have a strong need and desire to put an end to all social oppression; and both communities have a strong sense of history. Sometimes being a Jew and being a lesbian feels like being torn in two, however, especially as one struggles to live in harmony among one's family of origin and one's chosen family.

Am I Blue? p. 173

WORKS BY LESLÉA NEWMAN

For Children

Belinda's Bouquet. Illustrated by Michael Willhoite. Alyson Publications, 1991. Out of print. (See Chapter 1)

Cats, Cats, Cats! Simon & Schuster, forthcoming.

Gloria Goes to Gay Pride. Alyson Publications, 1991. Out of print.

Heather Has Two Mommies. Illustrated by Diane Souza. In Other Words, 1989; Alyson Publications, 1990. (See Chapter 1)

Matzo Ball Moon. Clarion Books, 1998.

Remember That. Clarion Books, 1996.

Runaway Dreydl. Henry Holt & Company, forthcoming.

Saturday Is Pattyday. Illustrated by Annette Hegel. New Victoria, 1993; Women's Press, 1993. (See Chapter 1)

Thea's Throw. Alyson Publications, forthcoming.

Too Far Away to Touch. Illustrated by Catherine Stock. Clarion Books, 1995. (See Chapter 1)

For Young Adults

Fat Chance. Putnam, 1994.

"Supper." In *Am I Blue? Coming Out from the Silence*, edited by Marion Dane Bauer. HarperCollins, 1994. (See Chapter 3)

For Adults

Bubbe Meisehs by Shayneh Maidelehs: An Anthology of Poetry by Jewish Granddaughters About Our Grandmothers (editor). HerBooks, 1989.

Eating Our Hearts Out: Personal Accounts of Women's Relationship to Food (editor). The Crossing Press, 1993.

Every Woman's Dream (Short Stories). New Victoria Publishers, 1994.

The Femme Mystique (editor). Alyson Publications, 1996.

Girls Will Be Girls (Novella and short stories). Alyson Publications, forthcoming.

Good Enough to Eat (Novel). Firebrand Books, 1986; Sheba Feminist Publishers, 1986.

In Every Laugh a Tear (Novel). New Victoria Publishers, 1992, 1998.

Just Looking for My Shoes (Poetry). Back Door Press, 1980.

A Letter to Harvey Milk (Short Stories). Firebrand Books, 1988.

The Little Butch Book (Poetry). New Victoria Publishers, 1998.

Love Me Like You Mean It (Poetry). HerBooks, 1987; Pride and Imprints, 1997.

A Loving Testimony: Remembering Loved Ones Lost to AIDS (editor). Crossing Press, 1995. Out of print.

My Lover Is a Woman: Contemporary Lesbian Love Poems (editor). Ballantine, 1996.

Out of the Closet and Nothing to Wear (Humor). Alyson Publications, 1997.

Pillow Talk (editor). Alyson Publications, 1998.

Pillow Talk II (editor). Alyson Publications, forthcoming.

"Right Off the Bat." In *Speaking for Ourselves: Short Stories by Jewish Lesbians*, edited by Irene Zahava. The Crossing Press, 1990. (See Chapter 3)

Secrets (Short Stories). New Victoria Publishers, 1990.

SomeBody to Love: A Guide to Loving the Body You Have (Non-Fiction). Third Side
    Press, 1991.
Still Life with Buddy (Poetry). Pride and Imprints, 1997.
Sweet Dark Places (Poetry). HerBooks, 1991.
Writing from the Heart: Inspiration and Exercises for Women Who Want to Write (Non-
    Fiction). The Crossing Press, 1993.

Film

A Letter to Harvey Milk. Produced and directed by Yariv Kohn. York University,
    Canada, 1990.

Plays

After All We've Been Through. Women in Performance, Durham, NC, April 1989;
    Portland Women's Theatre Company, Portland, OR, April 1989; Between
    the Acts, Lexington, KY, February 1990.
Rage. Gay Performances Company, New York, 1991.

Lesléa Newman, the author of the groundbreaking book *Heather Has
Two Mommies*, was born on November 5, 1955 in Brooklyn, New York.
She grew up in a traditional Jewish household, where the expectation
was that she would get married and raise a family. After graduating
from the University of Vermont in 1977, she studied poetry at Naropa
Institute as Allen Ginsberg's apprentice. Her first book of poetry, *Just
Looking for My Shoes*, was published in 1980.

After Naropa, Newman (who pronounces her first name "Lez-lee-ah")
entered a master's program at Boston University, but dropped out after
a semester and moved to New York City. But after a year of "counting
cockroaches," she moved to Northampton, Massachusetts at age twenty-
seven.

"Everything broke for me," she says. "I came out, which was 97 percent of the problem all along" (*Contemporary Lesbian Writers of the United
States*, p. 399). She started reading feminist literature and was intrigued
that women were writing about their real lives: what happens in their
kitchens, in their bedrooms, and in their communities. She started writing again, mostly poetry at first. Her first novel, *Good Enough to Eat*, was
published in 1986.

Then one day in 1987, something happened that made children's literature history and started Newman on the path that led her to a parallel
career as a writer of books for young people. She explains, "*Heather Has
Two Mommies* came about because a woman stopped me on the street
and asked me to write a book she could read to her daughter that reflected her family and in which she didn't have to change the pronouns"
(*Poets and Writers Magazine*, p. 56). Newman was dismayed when she
discovered that there were no books for children that portrayed lesbian
families in a positive way. When she was unable to interest either lesbian

or mainstream publishers in the book, she decided to co-publish it with a friend, Tzivia Gover. The two women raised $4,000 in small donations, found an illustrator and a printer, and brought the book into being.

Among the memorable moments along the way was the day in 1989 when forty cartons of 100 books each were delivered to Newman's door. Another was the day that Newman received a letter from Sasha Alyson of Alyson Publications, offering to buy the rights for the new Alyson Wonderland line of children's books. After selling 2,000 copies, Newman gratefully turned over the chore of bookselling to Alyson. "Soon after, the book was on the front page of the *New York Times* and on Phil Donahue. It was something to see this little book, financed by begging for donations, starting a war in Queens" (*Poets and Writers Magazine*, p. 57).

The decision to include *Heather Has Two Mommies* and *Daddy's Roommate* by Michael Willhoite in New York City's Rainbow Curriculum sparked a nationwide controversy. According to figures released by the American Library Association's Office of Intellectual Freedom, *Heather Has Two Mommies* was the third most challenged book in the country in 1993. But in spite of the controversy, or perhaps partly because of it, the book has been very successful and is still in print almost a decade later. The *New York Times* editorial was largely supportive of the challenged books, describing them as portraying lesbian and gay "relationships as loving and strong, much as schoolbooks on heterosexual families portray them at their best. . . . At a time when gay-bashing has become one of the most vicious hate crimes among teen-agers, the need for greater understanding is imperative."

Newman has subsequently written a number of other engaging books for young readers. With courage and integrity, she has not been afraid to tackle some of the painful issues of our times. Her book *Belinda's Bouquet* is one of the few books for children about fat oppression, and *Too Far Away to Touch* is about AIDS and death. Her books for adults are also about significant issues, including bulimia, incest, anti-Semitism, homophobia, AIDS, and the aftermath of rape. She has been widely published in lesbian magazines and anthologies. Her writing plans for the future include a young adult novel entitled *Jailbait* and a collection of poems for children entitled *Billy Goats in Frilly Coats*.

A frequent guest lecturer at colleges, universities, and community centers, Newman has been recognized with numerous awards, including a commendation in the National Poetry Competition in 1988, second place finalist in the Raymond Carver Short Story Competition in 1987, a Massachusetts Artist Fellowship Award in Poetry in 1989, a Poets and Writers Grant in 1991, *Highlights for Children* Fiction Writing Award in 1992, *Parents' Choice* Silver Medal in 1994, and a Poetry Fellowship from the National Endowment for the Arts in 1997. In addition, five of her books have been Lambda Literary Award finalists.

Newman writes with poignant humor about issues of belonging and being an outsider. "I grew up in Brooklyn, where as a Jew I was not the other. But I was a chubby child and a fat adolescent, so my first experience with being the other had to do with that. And then, I didn't come out until I was twenty-seven. Now I'm the size our society considers normal, but I'm oppressed as a lesbian. And then when I left New York and went to New England, I felt that as a Jew I was other. Being all that I am makes me other than the other, because in the lesbian community I'm Jewish; in the Jewish community I'm lesbian" (*Poets and Writers Magazine*, p. 63).

Newman makes her home in Massachusetts, where she and her lifetime companion, Mary Vazquez, held their commitment ceremony in 1989.

MORE INFORMATION ABOUT LESLÉA NEWMAN

Contemporary Authors, Volume 126, pp. 321–322.

Contemporary Lesbian Writers of the United States: A Bio-Bibliographical Critical Sourcebook, edited by Sandra Pollack and Denise D. Knight. Greenwood Press, 1993, pp. 399–404.

Jewish American Women Writers: A Bio-Bibliographical and Critical Sourcebook, edited by Ann R. Shapiro, Sara R. Horowitz, Ellen Schiff, and Miriyam Glazer. Greenwood Press, 1994, pp. 240–247.

Poets and Writers Magazine (May/June 1994), pp. 54–63.

Something About the Author, Volume 71, pp. 138–139.

Cristina Salat

Whether writer, gardener, or business exec, everyone has a muse—
that sassy, inquisitive (hopeful) inner voice. The more I've listened,
the more I've enjoyed the company of mine. She continues to keep
me honest.

Something About the Author, Volume 82, p. 207

It's not fair that people hate other people for being different.

Living in Secret, p. 106

LESBIAN/GAY-THEMED WORKS BY CRISTINA SALAT

"50% Chance of Lightning." In *Am I Blue? Coming Out from the Silence*, edited by
Marion Dane Bauer. HarperCollins, 1994. (See Chapter 3)
Living in Secret. Bantam, 1993; MarcUs Press, 1999. (See Chapter 2)
"Who Will Lead?" In *Sister/Stranger: Lesbians Loving Across the Lines*, edited by
Jan Hardy. Sidewalk Revolution Press, 1993.

Writer, editor, and consultant Cristina Salat was born in New York
and attended Southampton College of Long Island University. After
working in the New York publishing world, she relocated to San Francisco to become a writer in 1987. She moved into a busy household with
three roommates, five dogs, one cat, and a baby, so the rough draft of
her first book, *Living in Secret*, was written in Golden Gate Park and fast
food restaurants. In this engaging book, Salat addresses important social
issues including lesbian custody cases, civil disobedience, children's legal

rights, and racism. *Living in Secret* makes the point that it is personal integrity and not sexual identity that determines whether or not individuals will be good parents. "Being my first book, it holds a special moment of my life." (*Am I Blue?* p. 245).

Many part-time jobs later, Salat moved to a quiet country home where she fulfilled her dream of becoming a full-time writer, editor, and consultant. As part of her Creative Living Workshop Series, Salat offers a number of intriguing workshops and courses. Titles include: "Writing and Selling Your Children's Book," "Young Minds: Writing for Children," "Show Me a Story: Storytelling," "Speak Out: Writing to Perform," and "Preparing for Publication." In addition to these workshops, Salat also does manuscript consultations, provides a monthly salon for emerging writers, and appears as an inspirational speaker at conferences and retreats nationwide.

In the late 1990s Salat launched Shark Productions, an independent film/video company. "My focus is to bring to the screen quality stories of the dangerously unfamiliar (read: underrepresented in media). We'll see through the skin (as sharks are known to do . . .) raw, beautiful, diverse views of our shared universe" (*Creative Living Center Newsletter* [*CLCN*], February 1998). The following spring, Shark Productions shot a dramatic two-camera extravaganza based on a story Salat had written.

In spite of her busy schedule, Salat finds time to send out a newsletter to her students, colleagues, and friends. Her enthusiasm and creativity sparkle through the pages. For example, reflecting on a series of workshops she had just completed, she wrote, "Personally, I discovered the joy of bringing my whole eclectic self to an endeavor (me the writer of work for adults and children, me the editor, me the filmmaking entrepreneur, me the professional, as well as the eccentric, playful, healing, ex-starving artist . . . !)" (*CLCN*, n.d.). Her concern for world events and the environment is apparent in much of her writing. "[Recently] I have taken to making peace ponds to focus good energy towards peace and balance out all the energy I spend battling world ills" (*CLCN*, n.d.).

After over a decade of creative endeavors in northern California, Salat decided to put her dreams for the millennium into action and move to Hawaii, where she plans to launch a new artistic venture. She has written several other books for young readers, and her fiction and nonfiction short pieces appear in *Dyke Review, Writing for Our Lives Literary Journal, Planet Roc, Delta Scene, Pub, Whiskey Island Magazine, Sacred River, Popular Photography*, and *Women's Voices*.

MORE INFORMATION ABOUT CRISTINA SALAT

Contemporary Authors, Volume 149, p. 365.
Something About the Author, Volume 82, pp. 206–207.
Who's Who of American Women 1997–1998.

Sandra Scoppettone (1936)

Photo by Linda Crawford

Homosexuality—and that includes lesbianism—has been part of life as long as there have been people and it always will be.

Trying Hard to Hear You, p. 189

I don't want to spend the rest of my life being what other people want me to be.

Happy Endings Are All Alike, p. 201

LESBIAN/GAY THEMED BOOKS BY SANDRA SCOPPETTONE

For Young Adults

Happy Endings Are All Alike. Harper and Row, 1978; Dell, 1979; Alyson Publications, 1991. (See Chapter 2)

Trying Hard to Hear You. Harper and Row, 1974; Alyson Publications, 1991, 1996. (See Chapter 2)

For Adults: Lauren Laurano Mystery Series

Everything You Have Is Mine. Little, Brown, 1991; Ballantine, 1992.
Gonna Take a Homicidal Journey. Little, Brown, 1998.
I'll Be Leaving You Always. Little, Brown, 1993; Ballantine, 1994.

Let's Face the Music and Die. Little, Brown, 1996; Ballantine, 1997.
My Sweet Untraceable You. Little, Brown, 1994; Ballantine, 1995.

Novelist, playwright, and scriptwriter Sandra Scoppettone was born June 1, 1936 in Morristown, New Jersey and grew up in South Orange, New Jersey. She knew as early as the age of five that she wanted to be a writer. Her parents encouraged her aspirations, telling her that she could accomplish whatever she set out to do. An only child with protective parents, Scoppettone learned to use her imagination to entertain herself. She wasn't allowed to participate in physical activities such as riding a bicycle with the neighborhood children, so she wrote stories. "I remember playing with marbles, not regular marble games, but making a marble a person, giving them a name and moving them around" (*Authors and Artists for Young Adults* [*AAYA*], Volume 11, p. 174). One of her favorite childhood memories is of the times she would hide under the table during family gatherings at her grandparents' house and listen to the grownups' conversation. "I loved to listen and loved to hear adults tell stories and talk" (*AAYA*, p. 174).

Scoppettone enjoyed school until seventh grade, when she experienced what she describes as a personality change. She left school early that year after being diagnosed with chorea, a disease that required a great deal of rest. She returned to school the following fall with a totally different attitude. "I was a good little girl up until then, and then I became sort of a bad little girl. . . . I was no longer quiet, I was no longer a goodie two shoes" (*AAYA*, p. 175).

After graduating from high school, Scoppettone moved to New York City to pursue her dream of becoming a writer. She had no interest in attending college, preferring to put her energies into writing. Her first published works were two picture books—*Suzuki Beane* and *Bang Bang You're Dead*—both illustrated by children's author and illustrator Louise Fitzhugh. Meanwhile, Scoppettone also wrote for television, film, and stage. In 1972 she received a Eugene O'Neill Memorial Theatre Award for *Stuck*, and two years later she received a grant from the Ludwig Vogelstein Foundation.

In 1973, when she was living on the North Fork of Fire Island, Scoppettone volunteered to direct a "Youth on Stage" summer production of the musical "Anything Goes." This experience inspired her to write her first book for young adults, *Trying Hard to Hear You*. "The kids and an incident and the fact that I'm a lesbian led me to write this book that deals with homosexuality" (*Something About the Author* [*SATA*], Volume 9, p. 162). *Happy Endings Are All Alike*, one of the first books for young adults to focus on a lesbian relationship, was published in 1978. Both books were selected as American Library Association Best Books for Young Adults.

After writing these and other books for young adults, Scoppettone turned to detective and mystery writing for adults under the pseudonym Jack Early. Interestingly, these books received more positive reviews and a great deal of attention. *A Creative Kind of Killer* won the Shamus Award given by Private Eye Writers of America and an Edgar Allen Poe Award nomination. "Jack got prizes and all kinds of reviews that Sandra had never gotten, and so I just sort of stuck with the name for a while" (*AAYA*, p. 179). After she completed the third Jack Early book, Scoppettone went through a period of three years when she couldn't write at all. When she did write again it was under her own name and it was the first book in her highly acclaimed mystery series for adults. *Everything You Have Is Mine* introduced Lauren Laurano, a lesbian private investigator. It "is the first book I've written directly about myself" (*AAYA*, p. 180). The series has been praised for its sparkling combination of fast-paced mystery, lesbian comedy, and Greenwich Village flavor.

An out lesbian since the early 1960s, Scoppettone always refers to her partner, Linda Crawford, by name on book jackets and interviews. She opened her interview with *AAYA* with the following statement: "One thing I want to say is that I'm a lesbian. I mean, that should be clear. I also want to say that I've been with the same person for twenty years—I think it's important for people to know that it can be done" (*AAYA*, p. 174). "I live with Linda Crawford who is also a writer. We don't compete" (*SATA*, p. 162). A founding member of Sisters in Crime, Scoppettone's interests include old movies, antiques, yard sales, and suspense novels. Her manuscripts are housed in the Kerlan Collection at the University of Minnesota.

MORE INFORMATION ABOUT SANDRA SCOPPETTONE

Authors and Artists for Young Adults, Volume 11, pp. 173–181.

Contemporary Lesbian Writers of the United States: A Bio-Bibliographical Critical Sourcebook, edited by Sandra Pollack and Denise D. Knight. Greenwood Press, 1993.

Contemporary Literary Criticism, Volume 26, pp. 400–405.

Lion and the Unicorn (Winter 1979–1980), pp. 125–148

Something About the Author, Volume 9, p. 162.

Speaking for Ourselves. National Council of Teachers of English, 1990, pp. 186–187.

Sheila Ortiz Taylor (1939)

I write because at an early age I fell in love with words.... I'm intrigued with the idea that the novelist creates a miniature world with intricate and elusive correspondences between life and fiction. I have always felt that by studying a novel or better yet, by writing one's own, one can come to understand life better.

Personal communication

I believe the writer can both interpret reality and influence reality. That is, by writing with skill and conscience, a writer can change the world. So I write to discover the world and to change the world. I write in humble arrogance.

Personal communication

WORKS BY SHEILA ORTIZ TAYLOR

Coachella. University of New Mexico Press, 1998. (See Chapter 2)

Faultline. Naiad Press, 1982, 1995. (Film rights optioned to Joseph May Productions).

Imaginary Parents: A Family Autobiography. University of New Mexico Press, 1996. (See Chapter 5)

Slow Dancing at Miss Polly's. Naiad Press, 1989. (Out of Print)

Southbound. Naiad Press, 1990. (Out of Print)

Spring Forward, Fall Back. Naiad Press, 1985. (Out of Print)

Sheila Ortiz Taylor, a writer, educator, and scholar, is a professor of English at Florida State University, Tallahassee. She is the author of several novels, a book of poetry, a bibliography on Emily Dickinson, and an autobiography as well as scholarly reviews and articles for journals such as *Studies in the Humanities, College Composition and Communication, Eighteenth Century Studies*, and *Journal of Narrative Technique*.

Born on September 25, 1939 in Los Angeles, California, Taylor has lived in New England, the Midwest, Italy, Spain, and Florida. "The family I knew in Los Angeles was my mother's family, thirteen children presided over by my Mexican-American grandmother, who made flour tortillas so thin you could read a book through them" (*Faultline*, Author's Note). Her mother quit school in the tenth grade and got a job painting yo-yos and her father was a lawyer, musician, and tap dancer.

An active child, Taylor rode her bicycle at breakneck speed, scaled crumbling cliffs of sandstone, explored skeletal new houses, and jumped out of upstairs windows. In kindergarten, she fell in love with Hazel Medina the first day, after Hazel defended her when a classmate criticized her first attempt at painting. She preferred cap guns to dolls and wore T-shirts and slacks instead of the sundresses, pinafores, and velvet jumpers her mother sewed for her. In junior high school Taylor fell in love with Miss Highsmith, her physical education teacher. Years later she would recall how Miss Highsmith's resonant voice curled around her nerve endings and how difficult it was to breathe one time when Miss Highsmith's whistle came to rest on the counter near her hand.

Even though she told one teacher that she would probably be just like her mother and aunt, who dropped out of high school before graduation, Taylor enjoyed reading and checked out fourteen books every two weeks from the public library. She decided to become a novelist when she was eleven. In high school she wrote poetry in a secret notebook and worked on the school paper. "The Mad Scientist," a play she wrote, was performed for her English class. When her friends insisted that she go with them to dances, she secretly preferred to stay home and read.

One year into her coursework at the University of California at Los Angeles, she got married and moved to Iowa City, Iowa. In 1960 she returned to UCLA, where she was awarded the Mabel Wilson Richards Fellowship. After transferring to California State University in Northridge, Taylor was named Outstanding Student of Language and Literature. In 1963 she graduated magna cum laude with a bachelor's degree in English and a minor in Spanish. Her two daughters were born in 1965 and 1966.

While completing her master's degree in English at UCLA in 1964, Taylor began compiling a bibliography on Emily Dickinson, which was published by Kent State University in 1968. She was divorced in 1972 and earned her Ph.D. in English at UCLA the following year. Taylor joined the English Department at Florida State University in Tallahassee in 1973, where she teaches courses on creative writing, the novel, and women's studies. She has taught in Italy, Germany, and Spain, and has given readings in Paris, Bordeaux, Barcelona, Munich, and Taxco.

Taylor's books, *Faultline* and *Southbound*, star Arden Benbow, a lesbian whose household is comprised of her lover, Alice Wicks, her six children, her live-in babysitter, a dog, and 300 rabbits. In her book of poetry, *Slow Dancing at Miss Polly's*, Taylor writes about coming out as a lesbian, family, love, and relationships. *Spring Forward, Fall Back* and the recent book *Coachella* also feature strong lesbian characters who have liberated themselves from the restrictions society tries to impose on women. Taylor's autobiography, *Imaginary Parents*, incorporates artistic installations created by her sister, Sandra Ortiz Taylor, a visual artist from San Francisco. Taylor is currently working on a third Arden Benbow book, titled *Extranjera*, which means "outsider" or "foreigner."

I think of coming out as a process, much like constructing and then emerging from a cocoon. This process, for me, took between three and five years. I have been "out" for about twenty-five years, having begun in my late twenties and early thirties. . . . In 1991 my partner, Joy Lewis, and I celebrated our relationship in a Unitarian ceremony. Our lives are rich and diverse." (Personal communication)

MORE INFORMATION ABOUT SHEILA ORTIZ TAYLOR

Journals and Newspapers

"Interview with Sheila Ortiz Taylor." *The Weekly News* (January 1982), pp. 3, 10.
"Sheila Ortiz Taylor: An Interview." *New Women's Times* (December 1981), p. 13.
"The Sheila Ortiz Taylor Interview: Part I." *Community News* (Tallahassee) (December 1996), p. 19.
"The Sheila Ortiz Taylor Interview: Part II." *Community News* (Tallahassee) (January 1997), pp. 16–17, 26.

Books

Contemporary Lesbian Writers of the United States: A Bio-Bibliographical Critical Sourcebook, edited by Sandra Pollack and Denise D. Knight. Greenwood Press, 1993.
Cyclopedia of World Authors. Salem Press, 1997.
Encyclopedia of Latin American Gay and Lesbian Literature, edited by David William Foster.
Imaginary Parents: A Family Autobiography. University of New Mexico Press, 1996.
Safe Sea of Women by Bonnie Zimmerman. Beacon Press, 1990.
United States Latino Literature: An Essay and Annotated Bibliography. March/Abrazo Press, 1992.

Johnny Valentine

Photo by Mary Ann McQuillan

In the early 1990s I knew more and more lesbians and gay men who were becoming parents, and who were expressing frustration that none of the children's books available to them depicted family situations like theirs. I decided to write a book that tried to capture the flavor of some of my favorite books from when I was young, but in family configurations like those of my friends.

Personal communication

"We cannot give you just one medal," the queen declared. "You have earned two medals. One for saving the kingdom, and another because you did something much harder. You refused to let prejudice stop you from doing what you wanted. We are all indebted to you."

"The Eaglerider," in The Duke Who Outlawed Jelly Beans
and Other Stories, unpaginated

WORKS BY JOHNNY VALENTINE

The Daddy Machine. Illustrated by Lynette Schmidt. Alyson Wonderland, 1992. (See Chapter 1)

The Day They Put a Tax on Rainbows and Other Stories. Illustrated by Lynette Schmidt. Alyson Wonderland, 1992. (See Chapter 1)

The Duke Who Outlawed Jelly Beans and Other Stories. Illustrated by Lynette Schmidt. Alyson Wonderland, 1991. (See Chapter 1)

One Dad, Two Dads, Brown Dad, Blue Dads. Illustrated by Melody Sarecky. Alyson
    Wonderland, 1994. (See Chapter 1)
Two Moms, the Zark, and Me. Illustrated by Angelo Lopez. Alyson Wonderland,
    1993. (See Chapter 1)

Johnny Valentine is a pen name Sasha Alyson used for his writing
while he was publishing the Alyson Wonderland imprint, a line of books
for the children of lesbian and gay parents. Although he never publicly
stated at that time that he was the author of the books, he has now
granted us permission to do so.

Sasha Alyson's first reading books were the Alice and Jerry series, a
series that pre-dated Dick and Jane and Sally. He notes that they were,
if possible, even less interesting. "I wasn't making much progress in
reading until my parents got me a copy of *The Cat in the Hat*. That caught
my imagination, and I soon became an avid reader" (Personal communication).

Alyson began his publishing career in 1968, at the age of 16, by pro-
ducing an underground student newspaper at his high school. He began
publishing gay books under his own imprint in 1980, and three years
later founded *Bay Windows*, Boston's gay newspaper.

From the start, Alyson Publications has been known for addressing
readers who were ignored by other presses. It has long been a leader in
publishing books for lesbian and gay people, and has brought out
groundbreaking works by African-American gay men, bisexuals, and
deaf and hard-of-hearing gay people.

In 1990 Alyson started the Alyson Wonderland imprint, the world's
first line of books about children with lesbian and gay parents. Titles
such as *Heather Has Two Mommies* by Lesléa Newman and *Daddy's Roommate* by Michael Willhoite have provided many children with their
first images of families like their own, yet have come under attack by
fundamentalist groups. Michael Cart, a nationally recognized expert in
children's literature, describes the books as "sweet-spirited." He adds,
"That such a gentle little book [*Daddy's Roommate*] could inspire such
passionate detractors—angry parents kept 230 students out of Juneau,
Alaska public schools on October 25, 1993, to protest its inclusion in
school libraries—is distressing" (*From Romance to Realism*, p. 228). In spite
of the controversy, both books have been very successful and are still in
print.

In addition to publishing these titles, Alyson wrote five books of his
own under the pen name Johnny Valentine. Lesbians and gay men who
were becoming parents had expressed concern about the enormous gap
in literature for children, where families like theirs had been excluded.
Responding to their requests, Valentine wrote his first book, *The Duke
Who Outlawed Jelly Beans and Other Stories*, which won a Lambda Literary

Award for the Best Children's/Young Adult Book and was named one of the outstanding children's books of the season by Robert Hale in *The Horn Book Magazine*. One reviewer wrote, "Finally, an exciting book full of imagination, action, and drama that incorporates lesbian and gay parents without focusing on the 'lesbian/gay issue.' " (*The Purple Crayon*).

Valentine's second book, *The Day They Put a Tax on Rainbows and Other Stories*, includes three original fairy tales that celebrate honesty, generosity, courage, kindness, and resourcefulness. These lively stories are essentially typical fairy tales with one exception: the protagonists all have same-sex parents. Valentine continued tackling issues of gay and lesbian parenthood in *The Daddy Machine*, a playful story about a girl and a boy who have two mothers and no fathers. When they invent a machine that produces fathers, they encounter unexpected results that will have readers of all ages and backgrounds laughing. Valentine's next book, *Two Moms, the Zark, and Me*, is an entertaining book about an assertive little boy who gets lost at the zoo. He is reunited with his two mothers after a series of adventures that demonstrate that families come in all sizes, forms, and colors. *One Dad, Two Dads, Brown Dad, Blue Dads*, Valentine's fifth book, tells the lighthearted story of a girl and a boy who compare notes about their fathers. The rhyming, easy-to-read text and appealing illustrations bring humor to the important message that people are basically the same whatever their skin color or sexual orientation. This funny book will help eliminate stereotypes of gay men.

Using a wry, breezy style, Valentine wrote imaginative books about brave children who solve problems, overcome prejudices, and make a difference. Their lesbian or gay parents are secondary characters who gently support their daughters and sons as they go about their lives. Valentine's books have been described as energetic, delightful, spontaneous, and wholesome. By starting the Alyson Wonderland line and writing these engaging books, he made a significant contribution to the field of literature for young readers.

In addition to publishing these and hundreds of books for adult lesbian and gay people, Alyson also coordinated publication of a free book titled *You CAN Do Something About AIDS*, which served as the publishing community's response to AIDS. Over 1.5 million copies of the book were distributed in bookstores nationwide.

In 1995 Alyson sold Alyson Publications to *The Advocate*, the country's leading gay magazine. He went on to form Alyson's Adventures, Inc., a company that offers active vacations such as biking, hiking, and rock climbing for gay men and lesbians.

Alyson's literary contributions have been recognized with numerous awards, including the Publisher Service Award given at the Lambda

Literary Award ceremony in 1990, the New England Publisher of the Year awarded by the New England Booksellers Association in 1994, the Small Business of the Year Award given by the Greater Boston Business Council in 1994, and the Editor's Choice Award, Adventure Travel category awarded by the *Out and About Newsletter* in 1997.

Michael Willhoite (1946)

Photo by Kippy Goldfarb

My advice to young Lesbian and Gay people is to be true to yourself, and face squarely what your character tells *you* is true. What or who you love is what you are, and you must never make apologies for it. If anyone, even in your own family, tries to make you feel guilty for being who you are, know positively that they are wrong, not you.

Personal communication

My suggestion (to librarians, especially) is to keep doing what you have been doing so splendidly so far, to defend the right of all young people to get the right information about their lives. Alas, the bigoted will always be with us. But with grit and determination, they can be fought; the most positive way to do this is by providing the correct information to the young. The truth shall indeed set you free.

Personal communication

I write and illustrate books for young lesbian and gay people so they can see their own lives, families, and feelings reflected in the literature of their time. I feel that it's important that *all* children feel included in this multicultural society. And the time for Lesbian and Gay youth to take their places in this society is *now*.

Personal communication

WORKS FOR CHILDREN AND YOUNG ADULTS BY MICHAEL WILLHOITE

Written and Illustrated

Daddy's Roommate. Alyson Publications, 1990; translated into German by Jan
  Wandtke as *Papa's Freund*. Magnus, 1994. (See Chapter 1)
Daddy's Wedding. Alyson Publications, 1996. (See Chapter 1)
The Entertainer. Alyson Publications, 1992.
Families: A Coloring Book. Alyson Publications, 1991.
Uncle What-Is-It Is Coming to Visit! Alyson Publications, 1993. Adapted for the
  stage by Bill Jacob and produced at the Speakeasy Theatre in Boston,
  Spring 1997. (See Chapter 1)

Illustrated

The Alyson Almanac. Alyson Publications, 1989, 1990, 1993.
Belinda's Bouquet by Lesléa Newman. Alyson Publications, 1991. (See Chapter 1)
Gay Men and Women Who Enriched the World by Thomas Cowan. Alyson
  Publications, 1996. (See Chapter 5)
Young, Gay, and Proud, edited by Don Romesburg. Alyson Publications, 1995.
  (See Chapter 4)

Michael Willhoite, born on July 3, 1946 in Hobart, Oklahoma, was
raised in part by an aunt who instilled in him a great love of books and
writing.

Books have been vital to my happiness since childhood. Luckily I was reared in
a family where books were readily available. I was blessed with a sister and
three very close cousins who loved books, too; even today we exchange titles
and we all keep tabs on what the others are reading. My first literary impressions
were from illustrated books, the first being Little Golden Books, if memory
serves. (Personal communication)

Willhoite also loved movies and spent many happy hours in front of
the television watching every film he could find. For as long as he can
remember, he was considered the class artist.

Very early in life I showed signs of becoming an artist; indeed, it was always
expected that I should become one. Thus it was probably inevitable that I should
develop an interest in illustrating books for coming generations. My visual imagination was always nourished by illustrations, and even today, I live through my
visual impressions of the world. (Personal communication)

In high school Willhoite became interested in the art of caricature. His
first subject was British Prime Minister Harold Macmillan. After graduating from high school in 1964, Willhoite enrolled at Oklahoma State
University as an art major and graduated in 1968 with a Bachelor of Fine

Arts degree. After joining the United States Navy, he was sent to Medical Illustration School in Bethesda, Maryland, where he enjoyed considerable freedom to develop his artistic talents in design, caricature, and cartooning.

When he left the Navy in 1973, Willhoite's job as a medical illustrator was converted into a civilian position. Eight years later he moved to Massachusetts, where he took a similar position as a civilian attached to the Army. While living in Bethesda he began a parallel career as a freelance illustrator. He also performed in several plays a year until the early 1990s. It was while appearing in a musical revue in the spring of 1979 that Willhoite came out as a gay man.

Willhoite's cartoons about gay life were published on a biweekly basis in the *Washington Blade*, the capitol's gay newspaper, and were later collected and published in a book, *Now for My Next Trick*, in 1986. After moving to Massachusetts, Willhoite created 350 caricatures of noteworthy lesbians and gay men, most of which have been published in two collections by Alyson: *Members of the Tribe* in 1993 and *Willhoite's Hollywood* in 1994.

Then in 1989, Willhoite's career as a writer and illustrator took a dramatic turn when his publisher, Sasha Alyson of Alyson Publications, proposed a series of children's books with lesbian and gay themes. Willhoite's *Daddy's Roommate* was published in the fall of 1989, along with Lesléa Newman's *Heather Has Two Mommies*, as the inaugural titles under the Alyson Wonderland imprint.

The decision to include these two books in New York City's Rainbow Curriculum sparked a nationwide controversy. *Daddy's Roommate* was subsequently withdrawn from many library collections amid charges that exposure to the book might encourage young people to accept or adopt a gay "lifestyle." According to figures released by the American Library Association's Office of Intellectual Freedom, *Daddy's Roommate* was the most challenged book in the country in 1993 and 1994. Indeed, they also estimated that it is the most often banned children's book in U.S. history. *Daddy's Roommate* was the subject of debate on the floor of the U.S. Senate, where conservatives were supporting legislation that would deny federal funding to any school whose books, programs, or teaching materials "encourage or support homosexuality as a positive lifestyle alternative." Opponents of the book often went so far as to remove it from library shelves by checking it out and refusing to return it. Alyson responded by donating free copies of the book to libraries who requested it.

Daddy's Roommate also received a great deal of positive attention. The *New York Times* printed an editorial largely supportive of the two challenged books, describing them as portraying lesbian and gay "relationships as loving and strong, much as schoolbooks on heterosexual families portray them at their best. . . . At a time when gay-bashing has become one of the most vicious hate crimes among teen-agers, the need for greater understanding is imperative." *Daddy's Roommate* was read aloud on a memorable edition of ABCs *Nightline,* and an openly gay New York City school board member took his oath of office with a hand over leather-bound volumes of the controversial books.

In 1990, *Daddy's Wedding* won the Lambda Literary Award for best Gay Men's Small Press book. Subsequently, Willhoite has written and/or illustrated several additional books for children. He feels that lesbian/gay-themed books for young readers are extremely important.

In youth, unfortunately, being just like everyone else seems to be of vital importance. Lesbian and Gay youth are especially vulnerable to the charge of being "different," and therefore seeing their own lives reflected positively is of inestimable value. If I had been told at a tender age that it was perfectly all right to be gay, I might have come out earlier, and therefore come to a fuller realization of my own character much sooner than I did. (Personal communication)

Willhoite adds,

I am an artist in every atom. . . . But an aspect of my art that I've never articulated before is how profoundly my love for literature has informed my artwork. I have an insatiable hunger for art in any form—theatre, architecture, film, music. My art is my lake, and all these are the streams that feed it. (*Gay and Lesbian Literature: Volume 2,* p. 383)

MORE INFORMATION ABOUT MICHAEL WILLHOITE

Gay and Lesbian Literature: Volume 2, edited by Tom Pendergast and Sara Pendergast. St. James Press, 1997, pp. 383–384.
"Teaching About Gays and Tolerance." *New York Times,* September 27, 1992.
Something About the Author, Volume 71, pp. 213–214.

Jacqueline Woodson (1964)

I feel compelled to write against stereotypes, hoping people will see that some issues know no color, class, sexuality. . . . I write from the very depth of who I am, and in this place there are all of my identities.

Contemporary Authors, Volume 159, p. 441

I know what it is like to be hated because of the skin you were born in, because of gender or sexual preference. I know what it is like to be made to feel unworthy, disregarded, to have one's experiences devalued because they are not the experiences of a dominant culture.

The Horn Book Magazine, January/February 1998, p. 37

I write about black girls because this world would like to keep us invisible. I write about all girls because I know what happens to self-esteem when we turn twelve, and I hope to show readers the number of ways we are strong.

Contemporary Authors, Volume 159, p. 441

LESBIAN/GAY THEMED WORKS FOR YOUNG ADULTS BY JACQUELINE WOODSON

The Dear One. Delacorte Press, 1991. (See Chapter 2)
From the Notebooks of Melanin Sun. Scholastic, 1995. (See Chapter 2)
The House You Pass on the Way. Delacorte Press, 1997. (See Chapter 2)

"Slipping Away," In *Am I Blue? Coming Out from the Silence*, edited by Marion Dane Bauer. HarperCollins, 1994. (See Chapter 3)

Jacqueline Woodson is the highly acclaimed author of more than ten books for young readers. She was born on February 12, 1964 in Columbus, Ohio, and spent her early years being shuttled back and forth between South Carolina and New York City. According to an article in *Ms. Magazine*, she "never quite felt a part of either place—a feeling intensified by being raised as a Jehovah's Witness." This feeling of being "outside the world," as she explained in *The Horn Book Magazine*, was heightened when Richard Nixon resigned the presidency in 1974 and Gerald Ford took his place instead of George McGovern. "McGovern was my first 'American Dream.'" Feeling that she and all Black Americans had been abandoned, Woodson became a loner. She turned to writing and spent "hours sitting underneath the porch, writing poetry and anti-American songs" (*Contemporary Authors* [*CA*], Volume 159, p. 441).

Writing became Woodson's passion. In the fifth grade she was the editor of her school's literary magazine. That was also the year that she won a poetry contest with a poem titled "Tribute to Martin Luther King." At first Woodson thought that she could never have a career in writing, even though it was her favorite subject. However, her seventh grade teacher recognized her gift for writing and encouraged her to pursue whatever career would make her happy. Woodson decided then to write about people and communities that were familiar to her. "I wanted to write about communities of color. I wanted to write about girls. I wanted to write about friendship and all of these things that I felt like were missing in a lot of the books I read as a child" (*CA*, p. 441).

Woodson's first crush was on a girl named Alina, who was also a Jehovah's Witness. When she turned fourteen and her girlfriends started dating boys, Woodson revised her intricate love letters by changing the name at the top to that of a boy. She came out in a creative writing class during her sophomore year at Adelphi University in Garden City, New York, where she pledged Alpha Kappa Alpha in spite of its heterosexism. After earning her B.A. in English in 1985, Woodson worked as an editorial assistant at a children's book packaging company. Later she worked in East Harlem doing drama therapy with runaway and homeless youth between the ages of ten and seventeen.

In 1990, Woodson's first book, *Last Summer with Maizon*, was published to wide acclaim. This winner of the ALA Best Book for Young Adults Award was followed by the next two books in the trilogy, *Maizon at Blue Hill* and *Between Madison and Palmetto*. The Maizon trilogy celebrates the close friendship between two eleven-year-old girls. In *The Dear One*, published in 1991, the best friends of the protagonist's mother are a lesbian couple who have a warm, committed relationship. This engaging book addresses a number of important issues and topics including teenage pregnancy and tensions between working-class and middle-class African Americans.

In *From the Notebooks of Melanin Sun*, published in 1995, a thirteen-year-old African-American boy struggles to accept the fact that his mother is a lesbian and has fallen in love with a white woman. Praised for its astute, perceptive insights, brave, thought-provoking story, and sensitive analysis of racism and homophobia, *From the Notebooks of Melanin Sun* is a strong novel that encourages readers to push beyond walls of hatred, secrets, and lies to find the common bonds that connect us all.

The House You Pass on the Way, published in 1997, is one of the most beautifully written books for young adults. It is a book to savor again and again, letting the richly layered words and images gently sink in. Praised for its understated, lyrical writing, complex examination of emerging sexual identity, depth and complexity of characters, and gentle exploration of questions regarding racism and homophobia, this is Woodson's best book to date. The portrayal of Staggerlee, the protagonist, is beautifully wrought. Introspective and sensitive, she possesses the kind of quiet strength that enables her to be true to herself. The same qualities that moved her to think her own thoughts and to take on a proud name like Staggerlee will empower her to embrace her lesbianism as she matures.

In addition to these works for young adults, Woodson has written books for both young children and adults, short stories, articles, essays, and a screenplay. She was awarded a fellowship at the MacDowell Colony in Peterborough, New Hampshire in 1990 and a residency at the Fine Arts Work Center in Provincetown, Massachusetts in 1991–1992. A recipient of the Kenyon Review Award for Literary Excellence and an American Film Institute Award, Woodson has served on the faculties of the Goddard College M.F.A. Writing Program and the Vermont College M.F.A. in Writing for Children Program at Norwich University.

Woodson is one of the most gifted young writers in the field of young adult literature today. With sensitivity and integrity she tackles significant issues including homophobia, racism, classism, child abuse, and alcoholism. "People say you can't put all that material into a book for young people because it'll distress them or they won't be able to absorb it all," she says. "But I believe children's minds compartmentalize—they will put stuff away until they're ready to deal with it" (*Ms. Magazine*, November/December 1994, p. 77). Woodson's future writing plans include a picture book which will be published by Hyperion.

I have chosen to write for young adults with an emphasis on children-of-color to enlighten them to the different issues we as people of color continually struggle with. Issues such as nurturing the gifted black child, racism, classism, and homophobia play major roles in my writing. These are issues that were absent in the literature I read growing up; issues I want my own children to grow up enlightened to. When I go into a classroom to speak about my writing, my objective is to show the children that there isn't a "generation gap" between writers and readers. As a writer, I write remembering the child I was, am still, will always be. That is what, through literature, I hope to bring to the children. (*Black Authors and Illustrators of Children's Books*, p. 200).

MORE INFORMATION ABOUT JACQUELINE WOODSON

Black Authors and Illustrators of Children's Books: A Bibliographical Dictionary by Barbara Rollock. Garland, 1992, p. 200.

"Bold Type: Jacqueline Woodson's 'Girl Stories' " by Diane R. Paylor. *Ms Magazine*, November/December 1994, p. 77.

Completely Queer: The Gay and Lesbian Encyclopedia by Steve Hogan and Lee Hudson. Holt, 1998, pp. 587–588.

Contemporary Authors, Volume 159, pp. 440–444.

Contemporary Lesbian Writers of the United States: A Bio-Bibliographical Critical Sourcebook, edited by Sandra Pollack and Denise D. Knight. Greenwood Press, 1993, pp. 583–586.

The Coretta Scott King Awards Book: 1970–1999, edited by Henrietta M. Smith. American Library Association, 1999.

"Who Can Tell My Story?" by Jacqueline Woodson. *The Horn Book Magazine*, January/February 1998, pp. 34–38.

Appendix A: Calendar

JUNE: LESBIAN/GAY PRIDE MONTH

Annual gay and lesbian pride marches, held in cities around the United States and in other countries around the world, commemorate the June 28, 1969 Stonewall Uprising. The Stonewall Inn was a Greenwich Village, New York City bar whose clientele defied a homophobic attack by police, repelling them with bricks and debris in a courageous act that stirred lesbian and gay people around the nation to action. Although there was already an active movement of more than forty lesbian and gay organizations at that time, the Stonewall Uprising dramatically energized the movement and inspired the formation of numerous groups across the country.

OCTOBER 11: NATIONAL COMING OUT DAY

National Coming Out Day, which has been celebrated every October 11 since 1988, commemorates the October 11, 1987 lesbian and gay rights march on Washington, D.C. The annual celebration is coordinated by an educational nonprofit organization. The executive director of the organization said,

We're a visibility campaign that encourages people to come out of the closet, so we can put to rest the myths that people have used against us. We're dedicated to seeing the lesbian and gay community participate fully, openly, and equally in society. To reach that goal, we encourage groups and individuals across the country and around the world to plan events on and around National Coming Out Day that promote visibility. (*Is It a Choice? Answers to 300 of the Most Frequently Asked Questions About Gays and Lesbians* by Eric Marcus. Harper, 1999, pp. 48–49)

For more information, write to:

National Coming Out Day
P.O. Box 8349
Santa Fe, NM 87504

LAST WEEK OF SEPTEMBER: BANNED BOOKS WEEK

Sponsored by the American Library Association (ALA), Banned Books Week is an annual celebration of the freedom to read. Librarians and teachers across the country use the week to teach about the importance of our First Amendment rights and the power of literature. Resource booklets, posters, bookmarks, and buttons are available from ALA. For more information, contact:

Banned Books Week
American Library Association
Office for Intellectual Freedom
50 E. Huron
Chicago, IL 60611
(800) 545–2433, ext. 4223
oif@ala.org

The following titles provide information about banned books:

Foerstel, Herb. *Banned in the U.S.A.: A Reference Guide to Book Censorship in Schools and Public Libraries*. Greenwood Press, 1994.
Foerstel, Herb. *Banned in the Media: A Reference Guide to Censorship in the Press, Motion Pictures, Broadcasting, and the Internet*. Greenwood Press, 1998.
Foerstel, Herb. *Free Expression and Censorship in America: An Encyclopedia*. Greenwood Press, 1997.
Sova, Dawn B. *Banned Books: Literature Suppressed on Social Grounds*. Facts on File, 1998.
Sova, Dawn B. *Banned Books: Literature Suppressed on Sexual Grounds*. Facts on File, 1998.

Also see:

Annie on My Mind by Nancy Garden (Chapter 2).
Daddy's Roommate by Michael Willhoite (Chapter 1).
Heather Has Two Mommies by Lesléa Newman (Chapter 1).

Appendix B: Resources

HOT LINES

Gay and Lesbian National Hot Line
(888) 843–4564

Linea Nacional de SIDA
(800) 344–7432

Massachusetts Gay and Lesbian Youth Peer Listening Line
(800) 399-PEER

National AIDS Hot Line
(800) 342-AIDS

National AIDS Hot Line for Hearing Impaired People
(800) 243–7889

National Gay Task Force Hot Line
(800) 221–7044

National Runaway Switchboard
(800) 621–4000

Out Youth Austin Help Line
(800) 96–Youth

Samariteens Suicide Prevention Hot Line
(800) 252–TEENS

ON-LINE HELP

!OutProud!
The National Coalition for Gay, Lesbian & Bisexual Youth
glbyouth@aol.com

www.youthweb.com/rainbow/

PUBLICATIONS

Crossroads: Supporting Lesbian, Gay, Bisexual & Transgendered Youth
1638 R Street, NW #300
Washington, DC 20009
(202) 319–7596

Inside/Out Magazine
P.O. Box 460268
San Francisco, CA 94146–0268
(415) 487–6870

In the Life Newsletter
(Includes the national broadcast schedule for the In the Life Television Newsmagazine)
30 West 26th Street, 7th Floor
New York, NY 10010
(212) 255–6012

Lambda Book Report
P.O. Box 73910
Washington, DC 20056
(202) 462–7924

Lesbian Review of Books
P.O. Box 515
Hilo, HI 96721–0515
(808) 969–9600

OutYouth Newsmagazine
208 West 13th Street
New York, NY 10011

Teaching Tolerance
400 Washington Avenue
Montgomery, AL 36104
FAX (334) 264–7310

Y.O.U.T.H.
P.O. Box 34215
Washington, DC 20043
(202) 234–3562

Zine for Teens
Square Pegs c/o Equinox

903 Pacific Avenue #207 A
Santa Cruz, CA 95060

POSTERS

Available through GLSEN: (800) 247–6553

"Bigotry in Our Schools Is Wrong." Black and white photograph with graffiti. "Make a Difference" is printed at the bottom.

"Unfortunately, History Has Set the Record a Little Too Straight." Striking photographs of ten famous lesbian and gay figures from literature, music, politics, and art, such as James Baldwin, Eleanor Roosevelt, and Michaelangelo.

VIDEOS

All available through GLSEN (800) 247–6553

"Both of My Moms' Names are Judy: Children of Lesbians and Gays Speak Out." Features children ages 7–11 candidly discussing their families, classroom silence, and playground teasing.

"Gay Youth." A milestone video that details the lives of two remarkable young people, showing that information, acceptance, and support can make an enormous difference.

"I Just Want to Say." A panel of parents, students, and teachers talk about anti-gay bias in our schools. Hosted by Martina Navratilova.

"I Know Who I Am . . . Do You?" Documentary featuring Black and Latino/a Gay and Lesbian youth successfully reaching their goals despite discrimination.

"In the Life: Back to School." From the award-winning public television newsmagazine series. This episode includes segments on Gay/Straight Alliances, supportive Mormon families, youth suicide, the ex-Gay movement, and gay youth support services around the country. Ideal for presentations in meetings, trainings, and the classroom.

"It's Elementary: Talking About Gay Issues in School." Inspiring footage taken in schools across the United States show examples of school activities, faculty meetings, and classroom discussions.

"Lesbian Teenagers in High School." A documentary about young women's experiences in high school. Touches on racism and homophobia.

"On Being Gay." A comfortable conversation with Brian McNaught, ideally suited for introducing questions and issues and opening up dialogue.

"Out of the Past: The Struggle for Gay and Lesbian Rights in America." Traces the emergence of Lesbian and Gay people in American history through the perspective of a young woman coming to terms with her sexual identity.

"Reaching Out." Contemporary stories of lesbian, gay, bisexual, and transgender youth are told by the young people themselves and the educators who help them.

"Straight from the Heart." A video containing stories of parents' journeys to a new understanding of their lesbian, gay, and bisexual children.

"Teaching Respect for All." Kevin Jennings, Executive Director of GLSEN, presents a comprehensive training video dealing with anti-gay/lesbian bias in schools.

ORGANIZATIONS AND CENTERS

American Federation of Teachers National Gay and Lesbian Caucus
P.O. Box 19856
Cincinnati, OH 45219
(513) 242–2491

American Indian Gays and Lesbians
P.O. Box 10229
Minneapolis, MN 55458–3229

American Library Association Gay, Lesbian, Bisexual, and Transgendered Round Table
50 East Huron Street
Chicago, IL 60611
(800) 545–2433

Asian Pacific Islander Lesbians and Gays
P.O. Box 826
Portland, OR 97207
(503) 232–6408

Children of Lesbians and Gays Everywhere (COLAGE)
2300 Market Street, #165
San Francisco, CA 94114
(415) 861–5437

Department of Gay, Lesbian and Bisexual Studies
City College of San Francisco
Cloud Hall, Room 203 B
50 Phelan Avenue
San Francisco, CA 94112
(415) 239–3876

Family Diversity Project
P.O. Box 1209
Amherst, MA 01004–1209
(413) 256–0502

Family Pride Coalition
P.O. Box 34337
San Diego, CA 92163
(619) 296–0199

Feminist Bookstore News
P.O. Box 882554
San Francisco, CA 94188
(415) 626–8970

Friends of Project 10
Virginia Uribe, Director
7850 Melrose Avenue
Los Angeles, CA 90046
(213) 651–5200

Gay and Lesbian Alliance Against Defamation (GLAAD)
8455 Beverly Boulevard, #305
Los Angeles, CA 90048–9886
(323) 658–6775

Gay and Lesbian Arabic Society
P.O. Box 4971
Washington, DC 20008

Gay, Lesbian and Straight Education Network (GLSEN)
121 West 27 Street, #804
New York, NY 10001
(212) 727–0135

Gay Vietnamese Alliance
P.O. Box H48
9353 Bolsa Avenue #J-K
Westminster, CA 92683

Hetrick-Martin Institute
401 West Street
New York, NY 10014
(212) 633–8920
(212) 633–8926 for hearing impaired people

Human Rights Campaign (HRC)
1012 14th Street NW
Washington, DC 20005
(202) 628–4160

The International Lesbian and Gay Youth Organization
P.O. Box 42463
Washington, DC 20015

Lambda Legal Defense and Education Fund
120 Wall Street STE, 1500
New York, NY 10269–0703
(212) 809–8585

Lambda Youth Network
P.O. Box 7911
Culver City, CA 90233

Lesbian Teachers Network (LTN)
P.O. Box 301
East Lansing, MI 48826–0301

National Advocacy Coalition on Youth and Sexual Orientation (NACYSO)
(202) 783–4165, ext. 49

National AIDS Information Clearinghouse
P.O. Box 6003
Rockville, MD 20849–60003
(800) 458–5231

National Center for Lesbian Rights—Youth Project
870 Market Street, #570
San Francisco, CA 94102
(800) 528–6257

National Coalition for Black Lesbians and Gays
P.O. Box 19248
Washington, DC 20036

National Coming Out Day
(October 11)
P.O. Box 8349
Santa Fe, NM 87504

National Council of Teachers of English
Advisory Committee on Lesbian, Gay, and Bisexual Issues in Academic Studies
1810 E. Court St.
Flint, MI 48503
(800) 369–NCTE

National Education Association Gay and Lesbian Caucus
P.O. Box 3559
York, PA 17402
(717) 848–3354

National Gay and Lesbian Task Force (NGLTF)
1734 14th Street NW
Washington, DC 20009–4309
(202) 332–6483

National Latina/o Lesbian and Gay Organization (LLEGO)
P.O. Box 44483
Washington, DC 20026
(202) 544–0092

National Youth Advocacy Coalition
1638 R Street NW, #300
Washington, DC 20009
(202) 319–7596

Parents, Families, and Friends of Lesbians and Gays (PFLAG)
1726 M Street NW, #400
Washington, DC 20036
(202) 638–4200

Rainbow Alliance of the Deaf
P.O. Box 14182
Washington, DC 20044–4128

The Shared Heart
P.O. Box 562
Brookline, MA 02146

Trikone: Gay and Lesbian South Asians
P.O. Box 21354
San Jose, CA 95151
(408) 270–8776

Selected Bibliography

Allen, Paula Gunn. "*Hwame, Koshkalaka*, and the Rest: Lesbians in American Indian Cultures." In *The Sacred Hoop: Recovering the Feminine in American Indian Traditions*. Beacon, 1992.

Allison, Dorothy. "Believing in Literature." In *Skin: Talking About Sex, Class and Literature*. Firebrand Books, 1993.

Blinick, Barbara. "Out in the Curriculum, Out in the Classroom: Teaching History and Organizing for Change." In *Tilting the Tower*, edited by Linda Garber. Routledge, 1994.

Bloom, Harold, editor. *Lesbian and Bisexual Fiction Writers*. Chelsea House, 1997.

Boutilier, Nancy. "Reading, Writing, and Rita Mae Brown: Lesbian Literature in High School." In *Tilting the Tower*, edited by Linda Garber. Routledge, 1994.

Brogan, Jim. "Gay Teens in Literature." In *The Gay Teen: Educational Practice and Theory for Lesbian, Gay, and Bisexual Adolescents*, edited by Gerald Unks. Routledge, 1995.

Brunner, Diane DuBose. "Challenging Representations of Sexuality Through Story and Performance." *Overcoming Heterosexism and Homophobia: Strategies That Work*. Columbia University Press, 1997.

Cart, Michael. *From Romance to Realism: 50 Years of Growth and Change in Young Adult Literature*. HarperCollins, 1996.

Cart, Michael. "Saying No to Stereotypes." *Booklist*, June 1 and 15, 1999, pp. 1810–1811.

Clyde, Laurel A. and Marjorie Lobban. *Out of the Closet and into the Classroom: Homosexuality in Books for Young People*. ALIA Thorpe, 1992.

Crow, S. R. "The Reviewing of Controversial Juvenile Books: A Study." *School Library Media Quarterly* 14 (1986), pp. 83–86.

Cuseo, Allan A. *Homosexual Characters in YA Novels: A Literary Analysis, 1969–1982*. Scarecrow Press, 1992.

Davidson, Cathy N. and Linda Wagner-Martin, editors. *The Oxford Companion to Women's Writing in the United States*. Oxford University Press, 1995.

Faderman, Lillian, editor. *Chloe Plus Olivia: An Anthology of Lesbian Literature from the Seventeenth Century to the Present*. Viking, 1994.

Ford, Michael Thomas. "Gay Books for Young Readers: When Caution Calls the Shots." *Publishers Weekly* 241 (February 21, 1994), pp. 24–27.

Foster, David William. *Gay and Lesbian Themes in Latin American Writing*. University of Texas Press, 1991.

Foster, Jeannette H. *Sex Variant Women in Literature*. Naiad Press, 1985.

Furtado, Ken and Nancy Hellner. *Gay and Lesbian American Plays: An Annotated Bibliography*. Scarecrow Press, 1993.

Garden, Nancy. "Annie on Trial: How It Feels to Be the Author of a Challenged Book." *Voice of Youth Advocates* 19 (June 1996), pp. 79–82, 84.

Garden, Nancy. "Banned: Lesbian and Gay Kids' Books Under Fire." *Lambda Book Report* 4 (November/December 1994), pp. 11–13.

Gillon, Margaret. *Lesbians in Print: A Bibliography of 1500 Books with Synopses*. Odd Girls Press, 1995.

Goodman, Jan. "Out of the Closet, But Paying the Price: Lesbian and Gay Characters in Children's Literature." *Interracial Books for Children Bulletin* 4 (1983), pp. 13–15.

Gordon, Lenore. "What Do We Say When We Hear 'Faggot'?" In *Rethinking Schools: An Agenda for Change*, edited by David Levine, Robert Lowe, Bob Peterson, and Tita Tenorio. New Press, 1995.

Gough, Cal and Ellen Greenblatt, editors. *Gay and Lesbian Library Service*. McFarland, 1990.

Greenbaum, Vicky. "Literature Out of the Closet: Bringing Gay and Lesbian Texts and Subtexts Out in High School English." *English Journal* (September 1994), pp. 71–74. A later expanded version of this essay was published as "Bringing Gay and Lesbian Literature Out of the Closet" in *Open Lives, Safe Schools*, edited by Donovan R. Walling. Phi Delta Kappa Educational Foundations, 1996.

H., Pamela. "Asian American Lesbians: An Emerging Voice in the Asian American Community." In *Making Waves: An Anthology of Writings by and About Asian American Women*, edited by Asian Women United of California. Beacon, 1989.

Hanckel, Frances and John Cunningham. "Can Young Gays Find Happiness in YA Books?" *Wilson Library Bulletin* (March 1976), pp. 528–534.

Harris, Simon, editor. *Lesbian and Gay Issues in the English Classroom: The Importance of Being Honest*. Taylor & Francis, 1990.

Henkin, Roxanne. *Who's Invited to Share? Using Literacy to Teach for Equity and Social Justice*. Heinemann, 1998.

Jenkins, Christine. "Being Gay: Gay/Lesbian Characters and Concerns in Young Adult Books." *Booklist* 1 (September 1990), pp. 39–41.

Jenkins, Christine. "Young Adult Novels with Gay/Lesbian Characters and Themes 1969–1992: A Historical Reading of Content, Gender, and Narrative Distance." *Journal of Youth Services in Libraries* 7 (Fall 1993), pp. 43–55.

Katz, Jonathan. *Gay American History: Lesbians and Gay Men in the U.S.A.* NAL/Dutton, 1992.

Keating, AnnLouise. "Heterosexual Teacher, Lesbian/Gay/Bisexual Text: Teaching the Sexual Others(s)." In *Tilting the Tower,* edited by Linda Garber. Routledge, 1994.

Kehoe, Monika. *Lesbians in Literature and History.* Harrington Park Press, 1986.

Kitch, Sally L. "Straight But Not Narrow: A Gynetic Approach to the Teaching of Lesbian Literature." In *Tilting the Tower,* edited by Linda Garber. Routledge, 1994.

Koponan, Wilfrid R. *Embracing a Gay Identity: Gay Novels as Guides.* Greenwood Press, 1993.

Lilly, Mark, editor. *Lesbian and Gay Writing: An Anthology of Critical Essays.* Temple University Press, 1990.

Maggiore, Delores J. *Lesbianism: An Annotated Bibliography and Guide to the Literature, 1976–1986.* Scarecrow Press, 1988.

Malinowitz, Harriet. *Textual Orientations: Lesbian and Gay Students and the Making of Discourse Communities.* Heinemann, 1995.

Malinowski, Sharon and Christa Brelin. *The Gay and Lesbian Literary Companion.* Visible Ink Press, 1994.

McLean, Mari M. "Out of the Closet and onto the Bookshelves: Images of Gays and Lesbians in Young Adult Literature." In *Reading Across Cultures: Teaching Literature in a Diverse Society,* edited by Theresa Rogers and Anna O. Soter. Teachers College Press, 1997.

Nelson, Emmanuel S. *Contemporary Gay American Novelists: A Bio-Bibliographical Critical Sourcebook.* Greenwood Press, 1993.

Pendergast, Tom and Sara Pendergast. *Gay and Lesbian Literature: Volumes 1 and 2.* St. James Press, 1997.

Pollack, Sandra and Denise D. Knight, editors. *Contemporary Lesbian Writers of the United States: A Bio-Bibliographical Critical Sourcebook.* Greenwood Press, 1993.

Roy, Paula Alida. "Language in the Classroom: Opening Conversations About Lesbian and Gay Issues in Senior High English." In *Overcoming Heterosexism and Homophobia: Strategies That Work,* edited by James T. Sears and Walter L. Williams. Columbia University Press, 1997.

Scoppettone, Sandra. "Some Thoughts on Censorship: An Author Symposium." In *Writers on Writing for Young Adults,* edited by Patricia E. Feehan and Pamela Petrick Barron. Omnigraphics, 1991.

Shockley, A. "The Black Lesbian in American Literature." In *Women-Identified Women,* edited by T. Darty and S. Potter. Mayfield, 1984.

Steweig, John. "Self-Censorship of Picture Books About Gay and Lesbian Families." *The New Advocate* 7 (Summer 1994), pp. 184–192. This article is also available in *Open Lives, Safe Schools,* edited by Donovan R. Walling. Phi Delta Kappa Educational Foundations, 1996 and *The United States Board on Books for Young People Newsletter* 22 (Fall 1997), pp. 16–18.

Summers, Claude J., editor. *Gay and Lesbian Literary Heritage: The Readers' Companion to the Writers and Their Works, from Antiquity to the Present.* Holt, 1995.

Takagi, Dana Y. "Maiden Voyage: Excursion into Sexuality and Identity Politics in Asian American." In *Making More Waves: New Writing by Asian American Women*, edited by Elaine H. Kim, Lilia V. Villanueva, and Asian Women United of California. Beacon, 1997.

Tyrkus, Michael. *Gay and Lesbian Biography*, Gale Research, 1997.

Wilson, David E. "The Open Library: YA Books for Gay Teens." *English Journal* (November 1984), pp. 60–63.

Wolf, V. "The Gay Family in Literature for Young People." *Children's Literature in Education* 20, no. 1 (1989), pp. 51–58.

Woog, Dan. *Friends and Family: True Stories of Gay America's Straight Allies*. Alyson Publications, 1999.

Woog, Dan. "Library Shelves Are Opening Up." In *School's Out: The Impact of Gay and Lesbian Issues on America's Schools*. Alyson Publications, 1995.

Title Index

Author Index

Topic Index

About the Author

Frances Ann Day is the author of *Multicultural Voices in Contemporary Literature* (Heinemann, 1994; 1999) and *Latina and Latino Voices in Literature for Children and Teenagers* (Heinemann, 1997). *Multicultural Voices in Contemporary Literature* won the 2000 Skipping Stones Award, which honors resources that encourage social justice, peace, understanding, and communication. Her second book won the Denali Press Award given by ALA to recognize outstanding ethnic and minority reference works. Day retired in 1993 after thirty years of teaching in Colorado, Nebraska, and California. She conducts workshops nationwide, writes reviews and articles for numerous publications, and teaches classes at Sonoma State University in California. She also serves on the Advisory Board of the Center for Multicultural Literature for Children and Young Adults at The University of San Francisco and is included in *Who's Who of American Women, 2000–2001*.